John Ellerton, Henri Housman

John Ellerton - Being a Collection of his Writings on Hymnology

together with a sketch of his life and works

John Ellerton, Henri Housman

John Ellerton - Being a Collection of his Writings on Hymnology
together with a sketch of his life and works

ISBN/EAN: 9783337014049

Printed in Europe, USA, Canada, Australia, Japan

Cover: Foto ©ninafisch / pixelio.de

More available books at **www.hansebooks.com**

JOHN ELLERTON

Being a Collection of his Writings on Hymnology

TOGETHER WITH

A SKETCH OF HIS LIFE AND WORKS

BY

HENRY HOUSMAN, B.D.

LATE DIVINITY AND HEBREW LECTURER, CHICHESTER THEOLOGICAL
COLLEGE; SOMETIME CURATE OF BARNES

Portraits of Canon Ellerton and other leading Hymn Writers

PUBLISHED UNDER THE DIRECTION OF THE TRACT COMMITTEE

SOCIETY FOR PROMOTING CHRISTIAN KNOWLEDGE
LONDON: NORTHUMBERLAND AVENUE, W.C.;
43, QUEEN VICTORIA STREET, E.C.
BRIGHTON: 129, NORTH STREET.
NEW YORK: E. & J. B. YOUNG & CO.
1896.

Richard Clay & Sons, Limited,
London & Bungay.

TO

The Reverend Francis George Ellerton, M.A.

RECTOR OF WARMINGHAM, CHESHIRE,

AND HIS BROTHERS AND SISTERS,

THESE BRIEF MEMORIALS OF ONE DEAR TO MANY,

DEAREST OF ALL TO THEM,

ARE AFFECTIONATELY DEDICATED.

PREFACE

THIS book is the development of a very limited design. The original intention was merely to reprint (at the desire of many who were interested in Hymnody) the papers on "Favourite Hymns and their Authors," which Canon Ellerton had written for the *Parish Magazine*, and which subsequently re-appeared in the *Church Monthly*, prefixing to them a Sketch of the Author's Life and Works. But it was soon perceived that his most important contributions to Hymnology, apart from his own hymns, were those articles which he had composed for the *Churchman's Family Magazine*, Church Congresses, or for special occasions, and that the work would be a far more valuable contribution to the literature of the subject if these were included. Then among the Canon's papers were found drafts of several original hymns, translations, and poems which could not be omitted.

The Sketch of the Author's Life, while it still remains but a sketch, could not have attained to any degree of completeness had it not included much interesting matter connected with the compilation of the chief Hymnals now in use, and thus the work grew to its present size.

It is obvious that these pages could never have

been written but for the kind co-operation of many with whom the Canon had been associated, both in friendship and in work. By far the greater share of the labour has fallen upon his eldest son, the Reverend Francis George Ellerton, who undertook the heavy task of examining his father's papers, and selecting from among them such as threw light upon his hymnological work. Had the idea of constructing a complete biography been entertained there would have been no lack of material. To him, therefore, both for his zeal in collecting matter for this tribute to his father's memory, as well as for much valuable counsel in the construction of the work, my gratitude must, in the first place, be gratefully expressed.

To Canon Erskine Clarke, late proprietor of the *Parish Magazine*, and to Frederick Sherlock, Esq., proprietor of the *Church Monthly*, my best thanks are due for generously giving me permission to republish anything from Canon Ellerton's pen which had appeared in their periodicals, as well as to use the original blocks for the portraits of the hymn writers.

To the Right Reverend Edward Henry Bickersteth, Lord Bishop of Exeter, I am greatly indebted for the loan of a correspondence between his lordship and the Canon on the subject of the *Hymnal Companion to the Book of Common Prayer;* and also to the Reverend Prebendary Godfrey Thring for a similar favour with regard to the Church of England Hymn-Book.

Very cordially, too, must I thank Mrs. Carey Brock, not only for allowing me to see and make use of the letters which passed between her and Canon Ellerton while the *Children's Hymn-Book* was in preparation, but also for allowing me to submit to her revision the chapter describing that work.

To W. M. Moorsom, Esq., one of the Canon's staff of lay workers at Crewe, I owe the graphic picture of Mr. Ellerton's work in that place as a parish priest, and for permission to print the useful paper on the "Bondage of Creeds."

I have also much pleasure in acknowledging the assistance I have received from the Venerable Archdeacon Thornton, the Reverend Gerald Blunt, and the Reverend John Julian, D.D., whose monumental work, the *Dictionary of Hymnology*, has been of infinite use in correcting dates and verifying references.

Nor can I sufficiently express my obligations to the Reverend James Mearns, curate of Whitchurch, Reading, and assistant editor of the *Dictionary of Hymnology*, for his kindness in correcting the proofs of the first part of the book, and offering many valuable suggestions.

My last, but by no means least, acknowledgment of kindly co-operation must be offered to Professor Henry Attwell, K.O.C.,[1] one of the late Canon's most intimate and most valued friends. To him I am indebted not only for the loan of some of the Canon's charming letters, but also for kindly revising the whole of the book while passing through the press.

The plan I have adopted in gathering into one

[1] Knight of the Oaken Crown of Holland.

view each of the Hymnals treated of entailed of necessity some repetition, but it is hoped the arrangement will be found sufficiently clear and satisfactory. If the work should be instrumental in preserving some records of the life-work of one of the Church's sweetest poets, if it should be the means of making known many of his hymns which else might have lain unpublished and unknown, it will not have been written in vain.

H. HOUSMAN.

St. Wilfriths, Chichester,
  May 17, 1896.

CONTENTS

CHAPTER I
1826—1850

	PAGE
BOYHOOD—CAMBRIDGE	15
THE DEATH OF BALDUR	25

CHAPTER II
1850—1872

EASEBOURNE—BRIGHTON—CREWE GREEN	32
THE BONDAGE OF CREEDS	40

CHAPTER III
1872—1876

HINSTOCK	61

CHAPTER IV
1876—1884

BARNES	66
CHURCH HYMNS	72
THE CHILDREN'S HYMN-BOOK	87
THE CHURCH OF ENGLAND HYMN-BOOK	92

CHAPTER V
1884, 1885

SWITZERLAND AND ITALY:

	PAGE
VEYTAUX	99
PEGLI	102
AN ITALIAN POOR-HOUSE	109

CHAPTER VI
1885—1893

WHITE RODING	116
HYMNS ANCIENT AND MODERN	130
THE LAST HYMNS	138
THE CLOSE	156

CHAPTER VII

CRITICAL ESTIMATE OF CANON ELLERTON'S HYMNS 161

CHAPTER VIII

CONCLUSION ... 178

PAPERS ON HYMNS AND HYMN-BOOKS

I.—ON SOME PECULIARITIES IN THE PAST HISTORY OF ENGLISH HYMNODY	185
II.—ON THE POSSIBILITY AND DIFFICULTIES OF AN AUTHORIZED HYMNAL	206
III.—ON THE PRINCIPLES ON WHICH A HYMN-BOOK SHOULD BE CONSTRUCTED	223
IV.—PRACTICAL HINTS TO THOSE WHO USE HYMN-BOOKS AT PRESENT	245
SPEECH UNSPOKEN AT THE NOTTINGHAM CHURCH CONGRESS, 1871	260

CONTENTS xiii

	PAGE
HYMNS AND HYMN-SINGING	266
HYMNS AND HYMN-BOOKS	276
AN AUTHORIZED HYMNAL	284
MODERN THEOLOGY AS SHOWN BY MODERN HYMNODY	288

FAVOURITE HYMNS AND THEIR AUTHORS

JOHN COSIN AND THOMAS KEN	301
ISAAC WATTS AND PHILIP DODDRIDGE	309
THE WESLEYS AND TOPLADY	316
WILLIAM COWPER AND JOHN NEWTON	323
REGINALD HEBER AND HENRY HART MILMAN	329
JAMES MONTGOMERY	337
HENRY FRANCIS LYTE	344
HYMNS OF THE OXFORD MOVEMENT. THE TRANSLATORS	350
JOHN KEBLE AND JOHN HENRY NEWMAN	359
EDWARD CASWALL AND FREDERICK WILLIAM FABER	366
CHRISTOPHER WORDSWORTH AND HORATIUS BONAR	374
CHARLOTTE ELLIOTT AND FRANCES RIDLEY HAVERGAL	381
HORATIUS BONAR AND HIS HYMNS	387

SOME FAMOUS HYMNS

SOME FAMOUS EASTER HYMNS	391
SOME FAMOUS ADVENT HYMNS	397
CHILDREN'S HYMNS BY MRS. ALEXANDER	405
INDEX	415

JOHN ELLERTON

CHAPTER I

1826—1850

BOYHOOD—CAMBRIDGE

THERE are some men the records of whose lives have an interest for the many, and there are others whose memory will only be treasured by the few. Every particular illustrating the career of one who has been a ruling power in Church or State, or a shining light in literature, science, or art, is justly regarded as among the most precious things which the present can inherit from the past or bequeath to the future. But although of less common interest, the memorials of many a life passed in comparative obscurity may be very precious; and, within the orbit in which they are designed to move, be as highly prized as those of earth's great ones. Quiet lives may make but quiet reading, lacking the excitement of stirring scenes and startling actions; still, there are times when it is a relief to turn from the study of those who lived in the full glare of the world's observation to the simple narrative of some favourite poet who sang, so to speak, in the shade. In fact, the one is as necessary as the other if we are to form an adequate conception of all the minds which mould an age. A work on birds, to be complete, must include the nightingale as well as the eagle, or one on flowers must not, while it describes the rose, despise the violet.

The present sketch—and the reader is begged to remember that it is only a sketch, not designed to be a finished portrait—is an attempt to record for the lovers of sacred song the outlines of a very sweet singer, one whose life was quite uneventful, who was heard rather than seen, but some of whose hymns are as immortal as those of St. Ambrose, St. Bernard of Clairvaux, or of Venantius Fortunatus. The present generation is rapidly giving place to a younger; its facts and personalities are fast fading into memories. If the records of those who have adorned it by their lives or writings are to be preserved for those who shall come after us, they must be harvested at once before they become dimmed by distance or altogether lost; and we believe that in every succeeding age there will be some who will be glad to possess a few particulars of the life of John Ellerton, pronounced by Matthew Arnold—no mean authority—to be the "greatest of living hymnologists."

John, the elder son of George and Jemima Frances Ellerton, was born in London on Saturday, December 16, 1826, and baptized in the parish church of St. James, Clerkenwell, on the sixteenth of the following month. He came of a Yorkshire family, and Ellerton Priory, a small house in Swaledale, near Richmond, now in ruins, indicates the locality from whence it derived its name. Having but one brother, eleven years younger than himself, and no sisters, he was practically an only child, a fact which must have materially tended to foster the peculiar shyness and sensitiveness of his temperament. The memory of his parents was throughout his life a most precious and sacred thing. "I used to feel," such are his own words, "how happy my father and mother were, even more than how good they were; and yet I knew even then, and know still better now, that they had many sorrows and anxieties. They had no personal religious doubts or fears; their delight in prayer, in hymns, in the Bible, and occasionally in spiritual converse with one or two friends, was most true and deep and real; there was no mistake about it. It never occurred to me to connect their religion, even in its severest denunciations and gloomiest forebodings for the world, with the faintest shadow of cant or unreality; and in their family and with intimate friends there was plenty of merriment and fun. My father especially overflowed with humour, with quaint sayings and stories, all perfectly good-humoured and kindly. Often do I laugh to myself, even now all alone, at some of his overflowings of mirth at which there are now none left to laugh."

To his mother especially the shy and sensitive boy was indebted for the guiding of his opening mind into those channels of thought which it never afterwards forsook. She was a woman of considerable literary ability, and among the many short stories which proceeded from her pen, *How Little Fanny Learned to be Useful* still holds its own as a delightful tale for children. She was left a widow in 1844, and she and her son lived on in the old house at Ulverston until he went to Cambridge. She then left the house for a time and went to live in a smaller one at Norham-on-Tweed, which also belonged to the family. It was here that John Ellerton passed all his college vacations, and from here one memorable summer he went with his mother to the Lakes, and he often used to speak of his delight in spending whole days in a boat on Windermere, devouring Wordsworth and Tennyson. His mother was so devoted to him that she could never bear to be away from him for long, and on his leaving Cambridge she followed him to his first curacy at Easebourne, and afterwards to Brighton. In both places she helped him much, in the schools at Easebourne, and in district visiting at Brighton. On his appointment to Crewe Green she accompanied him, and shared his home there till her death in March 1866.

It was in London that the early boyhood of the future poet was passed, and where his earliest religious impressions were received. How deep and lasting these impressions were may be gathered from his own "Recollections of Fifty Years Ago."[1] "On the whole," he writes, "the religious world at that time was rather gloomy. The great fight against slavery had been won, so completely won that some of the most earnest abolitionists began

[1] A paper contributed to the All-Saints Scarborough Parish Magazine.

to think that the great Emancipation of August 1834 had been rather an extreme and hasty measure. There was no great social or theological battle to fight; religious people talked about Edward Irving and his followers, but they too had dropped out of notice a good deal by 1837. I thought of him chiefly as an open-air preacher, for more than once on Sunday mornings, on my way to St. John's, Bedford Row, with my father, had I had a vision of that marvellous face and form, in his little movable wooden pulpit, sometimes in pouring rain, holding an umbrella over his head with one hand, as he poured forth his fervid oratory to a scanty group of hearers outside the walls of the great prison. But the favourite, the inexhaustible subject of talk among serious people was unfulfilled prophecy. The Irvingite movement (as people would call it) had popularized Millenarian speculations among many who resisted steadily all belief in the new 'Miracles' and 'Tongues.' Names now utterly forgotten of writers on prophecy formed the staple reading, I am afraid, for a good many of the religious folk among whom I lived; and their speculations turned chiefly on the chronology of the future—in what year the Jews were to be restored, Popery to be destroyed, and the Millennium to begin. Some great event— I believe the final overthrow of the 'ten kingdoms' of Europe, including England, and accompanied by troubles hitherto unheard of—was predicted for 1844. Boy as I was, I entirely believed in this calculation, which was pictorially set forth in a great coloured chart; so much so, that when

1841 came I remember being quite shocked at my father for letting some ground to a tenant on a seven years' lease."

"In those days," he continues, "I was taken several times to Exeter Hall to some of the great religious meetings, often to those of the Church Missionary Society, and always rejoiced when a 'real missionary' got up, instead of the usual London clergyman with his usual platform address. There were of course exceptions among them, conspicuously Hugh Stowell and Hugh McNeile.

"The impression generally made on the mind of a rather precocious and sensitive boy by this religious atmosphere was that the world was very wicked, the country going from bad to worse, and no hope for anything but the great Revolution which, among untold miseries, was to usher in the 'Day of the Lord.' And yet within the charmed circle of those who used to meet at my father's house there was much, very much of peace, brightness, and happiness such as I seldom see now."

His parents used to take their two children, John and George Francis, to spend every summer with an uncle, Dr. John Ellerton, who owned a small property at Ulverston in Lancashire, which, upon his death in 1838, passed to his brother George, and the family in that year left London and settled in Ulverston. John, twelve years old, now began his school-life, for what instruction he had hitherto received, in addition to the inestimable training he had been daily experiencing at the hands of his Godly parents, had been in private academies. Now he was sent to King William's

College, Isle of Man, where he remained till the death of his father in 1844. He afterwards spent a year at Brathay Vicarage, Ambleside, reading with the Rev. C. Hodgson; from thence to Cambridge, where he matriculated at Trinity College in 1845. The close of his boy-life was marked by two events: the death of his father and of his young brother, both in the same year, could not fail to have a lasting impression on the mind of one so sensitive as the youthful poet, and may have tended to give that sub-melancholy colouring to his character which continued through life.

At Cambridge he came into contact with men of very different calibre from those of St. John's, Bedford Row. The conversation to which he now listened, or in which he bore a part, was not so much upon "the little horn," or "the mark of the beast," as upon those great questions concerning the Church and Society which were then engrossing the minds of the leaders of thought in both Universities. Now it was that he made the acquaintance, amongst others, of Henry Bradshaw and Dr. Hort, and his lifelong friendship with these eminent scholars dates from this period. Now also it was that he came under the influence of Frederick Denison Maurice. In a letter written many years afterwards he writes, looking back on his College days, "I was first attracted by one or two of his pamphlets; then I fagged on at *The Kingdom of Christ*, but did not get as much out of it as I ought at the first time, probably because I was miserably ignorant of theology, and only had got up stock formulæ of evangelicalism, which I had to produce in themes for a private tutor. But I think the books that helped me most at first were Maurice's *Lord's Prayer, Prayer Book*, and *The Church a Family.*" He goes on to say, "after three or four of his books you will be accustomed to his peculiarities, the strange *flashes* of deep insight, the reverent hesitation and fear of misstatements which makes people call him hazy; and his worst fault in the eyes of the common herd of readers is, that he refuses to tell you what your opinion is to be, but will have you think about a question, and generally leaves you with the impression that you have been talking nonsense very positively in all you have hitherto said about it." And here let me state once for all what I believe to have been the tone and colour of his Churchmanship. No one of the three great schools of religious conviction could claim John Ellerton as its partisan. He always seemed to me to combine in himself the distinguishing excellency of each—the subjective piety of the Evangelical, the objective adoration of the High, the intellectual freedom of the Broad. He has told me he had celebrated with the Revised Liturgy of the Church of Scotland with no less, perhaps greater, satisfaction than with the humbler and less primitive ritual of the Anglican Communion. Absolute reality, utter sincerity, always struck me as the governing spirit of his devotion. No ritual was too ornate, provided it was real, founded on the traditions of Catholic antiquity, and embodied the purest principles of worship; but anything approaching unreality, sham, show, or mediæval sentimentalism his soul abhorred. It seemed as though his feelings on this matter were founded on such passages as "The Lord is Great, and cannot worthily be praised;" "O worship the Lord in the beauty of holiness;" "Glory and honour are in His presence:" "A son honoureth his father, and a servant his master: if then I be a Father where is mine honour? and if I be a Master, where is my fear?"

The records of his college days are, at this distance of time, necessarily scanty and fragmentary. One, however, who was his contemporary, and continued his firm friend through life,[1] in kindly answering my request for some information relating to this period, writes thus:—

"I wish I could give you any help in writing a sketch of our dear friend John Ellerton; but nearly half a century is a long time to look back, and it is all that since I first knew him at Cambridge. What I most distinctly remember of him is the impression he made on us all at a small literary society got together chiefly by Hort and himself, which we called, somewhat ambitiously, *The Attic Society*. We met at each other's rooms, and read original papers, I think on any subject we chose individually. Ellerton charmed us all by his poetic taste, and his contributions (sometimes original, and sometimes translations from classic authors) were rendered still more striking by the fine, deep, emotional tone in which he read them to us. I think he delayed taking his degree through delicate health, which obliged him to go down for a year, so that his intercourse with us was somewhat broken. I do not think he took much interest in

[1] The Rev. Gerald Blunt, Rector of Chelsea.

the ordinary out-door life of the University, but in all subjects of the highest kind he had a wide and extensive knowledge, and felt the keenest attraction. He was then, as ever afterwards, one of the best and noblest specimens of what a fine and pure Evangelical training can produce when it widened out into the more excellent way of Maurician High Churchism."

While an Undergraduate at Trinity he made his first public essay as a poet in competing for the Chancellor's Medal for an English poem on *The Death of Baldur*. His effort gained the honourable distinction of *proxime accessit;* and it displays, besides a considerable acquaintance with northern mythology, unmistakable indications of a high poetic gift. Unfortunately an attack of small-pox prevented his going in for the Honour Examination, and he was obliged to pass with an *aegrotat* degree ; after taking this in 1849 he spent a year in Scotland engaged in tutoring and reading for Holy Orders. Doubtless he would gladly have passed this time at one of the Theological Colleges which had already begun to spring up in some dioceses. At Chichester, for example, which had been founded by Bishop Otter in 1839, and at this time was presided over by Philip Freeman, he might have received much useful guidance and assistance preparatory to his entering the diocese as a curate. For it was in Sussex that he received the title for his first curacy, and in the Cathedral Church of Chichester that he was ordained Deacon by Bishop Gilbert on St. Matthias' Day, February 24, 1850.

THE DEATH OF BALDUR,

WRITTEN FOR THE CHANCELLOR'S MEDAL,

1848.

> Καὶ σ' ἐν ἀφύκτοισι χερῶν
> εἷλε θεὰ δεσμοῖς·
> τόλμα δ', οὐ γὰρ ἀνάξεις ποτ' ἔνερθεν
> κλαίων τοὺς φθιμένους ἄνω.
>
> Eurip. *Alcest.* 983.

Thee too in her hands irrefugable
Bonds the Power hath clutcht :
Yet endure ; for not ever shalt thou draw thee from Below
Upward, by weeping, the perished.

THE PERSONS.

Odin.
Frigga, his Queen.
Thor.
Baldur. ⎫
Loki, the evil principle. ⎬ Children of Odin.
The Æsir, or Gods, generally spoken of as sons of Odin.
Bragi, the Bard.
Freya, the Queen of Love.
Niord, the Sea God.
Hel, or Hela, the Sovereign of Niflheim the Death Kingdom, daughter of Loki.
Nanna, wife of Baldur.
Forseti, the Principle of Justice, his Son and Successor.
Berserks, retainers of Odin.

Asgard, the dwelling of the Gods, centre of Earth.
Idavöll, the central spot of Asgard.

THE DEATH OF BALDUR.

List to a Norland lay, which many a time
To some bluff sea-king by his Yuletide fire
The Skalds have sung ; which liveth yet for us
In the fair dreamland of that elder faith.

There came a woman to the shining gates
Of Asgard, and to golden Fensalir
The hall of Frigga. Frigga sate alone,
A wan sad smile upon her face, like that
A sungleam from a clouding sky lights up
On some dark water ; for her thoughts were far
In deeps of time to come. But she was ware
Of a low footfall, and downlooking then
Slowly the pale light died from off her brow.
She saw her kneeling at her feet—a crone
Wrinkled and cripple, and bowed down with years.
Then asked of her the Queen of Gods and men
"Whence comest thou? A messenger from where
The mighty Gods are met ? Say, knowest thou
Their pastime there?" Answered that beldame gray,
"Mother and Queen of Æsir, I am come
From thence, in sooth, much marveling ; for all
The Gods are gathered there, and Baldur stands
Over against them ;—stones and spears at him
They cast, and o'er him glancing broadswords flash,
And arrows hurtle round about his hair—
Yet lo, he standeth scatheless. I am come
To rede thee of this marvel ; for both here
In Asgard, and in all the girdling worlds
Great sorrow were it, bale for evermore,
If ill should chance to Baldur." "Fear it not,"
Quoth Frigga, "all for love and gladsome sport
They smite him as thou seest : fear it not ;
I tell thee nought there is in earth or heaven
Can work him hurt ; for I have bound them all
With a great oath." "And have then all things sworn?"
She askt, and Frigga answered, "Even so,
For evil dreams had come to him, and fear

Of some strange chance ; whereat I took an oath
Of all that is in earth, and sea, and sky,
And every world ;—of water and of fire,
Of stones, and ores in the deep hill-caves hid,
Of tree, and beast, and bird, and creeping thing,
Yea of all deaths—all sickness, poison-drink,
Sword-edge and spear-point ; and they sware to me
To harm him not. One living thing alone—
Men call it mistletoe—it groweth east
Of Valhall—I past by, too young methought
To do him hurt ; I laid thereon no ban."
She ceased ; and slowly crawled the muttering crone
Forth from the hall ; she reached the outmost gate,
And lo ! a change came over her ; at once
Snake-like, she rose from out her loathly self
And cast her weazen slough, and lifted up
Her lean face to the sun :—no woman now,
In fulness of his wicked might he stood
Loki the evil one, falsehearted Loki ;
And lengthening out his thin lips to a smile,
Past forth from Fensalir toward the East.

Fair-faced, black-hearted, forth among the trees
The shadow of whose tops at sunrise falls
On Valhall gate, he passed ; thence, in his hand
Swaying the fresh-pluckt mistletoe, he came
O'er the broad meadow where in stormy sport
Were gathered gleeful all the mighty Gods.
Without the border of that ring there stood
One with broad chest and stout limbs iron-thewed ;
But dark and sorrowful the face he turned
To the sweet sunlight. Gently Loki came
Unto his side, and spake him underbreath,
"Hödur! alone, and still ? Thy shaft belike,
Flies not so true ; or is it that thy love
Runs shallower than theirs ? " He answered sad :
" I see not him they shoot at ; I am blind,
Nor wot I whence to take a shaft." " Take this,"
The false one cried—" come, let me lay my hand
On thine, and thou shalt bend the bow ; that all

May see thou lovest Baldur." Hödur bent
The bow, for Loki's hand was laid on his ;
Hurtled the shaft,—and Baldur with a groan
Upleaping fell heartstricken, and the life
Welled red from his fair breast, and on his eyes
The dusk of death came down.
         Tearless and dumb
The Æsir stood ; none stirred to touch the dead,
For a great fear had fallen on them, and each
Lookt on the other ; till when one essayed
To speak, a wild and mingled wail from all,
Of anguish and of wrath together, pealed
To the clear sky. And Odin in the midst,
Odin the Father both of Gods and men
Lookt on his son, and lifted up his voice
And wept aloud. Through worlds on worlds it sped
That bitter cry ; and all their dwellers heard,
And every heart beat thick, and every face
Grew pale, and all men shouted, " Woe to us,
For some great scathe hath chanced ! " But evil things
Were glad ; away along the broad sea rolled
The noise of weeping, and with stormy joy
Writhed the Great Worldsnake in its green depths coiled;
The fettered wolf leapt up ; and down afar
Wan Hela laught, and knew a nobler guest
Hied him to wassail in her dreary hall.

A voice of wail in Asgard ! And it came
Into the ears of Frigga, where she sat,
And woke her, as the stormburst waketh up
A sleeper by the shore. She knew the time,
The evil time, was come ; uprising slow
She came where Odin yet and all the Gods
Were gathered weeping round about the dead.
Tearful she stood, and spake, " Who is there here
Among the Æsir that would win himself
Goodwill and love from Frigga ? Let him go
Down to the gates of Hel, and speak for us,
And bid a ransom, that we may have back
The Bright One home to Asgard." Then stept forth

THE DEATH OF BALDUR

Hermodur, Odin's page, the fleet of foot,
And kneeling took her errand on himself.
So led they thither Sleipnir, the great horse
Whom Odin rideth—mortal hoof is none
May tramp like that gray steed's—and to the selle
Clomb brisk Hermodur, and fared down the dale
Where Hel's road lieth.

                    Then beside the shore
Bare they the dead, to where his long black ship
Lay, keel in sand. And sorrowful there came
The dwellers in all worlds : came Odin first,
With his twin Ravens, and those Maidens stern—
The Choosers of the Slain—whose stormy joy
Is from the stun of foughten fields to fetch
Brave souls to Valhall ; Frigga by his side
Came, and the Queen of Love, whose fire-eyed cats
Bare her fleet car ; came the grim War-god Tyr,
And mighty Freyr in his boar-chariot ; came
Bragi the Wise, and holy Forseti,
Gerda, and Fulla with the long fair locks,
And Niord, the stout old Sea-king ; and the bright
Heimdall, Heaven's warder, who all noise of life
Hears, and his keen eyes look into all worlds.
From their drear kingdom Giants of the Rime
And dark Hill-ogres came ; came sunny Elves
Of light, and blear-eyed Dwarves, that with lean limbs
Crouch night and day among red heaps of ore
In the deep bosom of the trackless fells ;
And doughty Berserks, biters of the shield
In their strong madness, when the fight is high.
The pile was builded now ; and with the rest
Wan-faced and nigh to swooning, Nanna stood,
Nanna, dead Baldur's wife ; and round her all
Her sisters thronged with broken words of cheer,
And eyes of pity. Dumbly she the while
Beheld until they bore him to the place
Of burning ; then her full heart burst, and with
A shriek that shivered in their blood, she fell
Dead on dead Baldur.

                    Side by side they laid
Those two upon the wood, and Baldur's horse
With all his gear they bound unto the pile.
Then Thor stood up, and lifted his strong hand,—
And that Great Hammer with its lightning stroke
Crashed on the wood.

                    A pillar of tall smoke !
And redder now—and now a blaze, whose gleam
Flashed fitful on their sleeping foreheads calm !
Seaward the slow tide ebbing drifted now
The bark, and freshly blew the sunset breeze
From off the shore, as each broad-bosomed wave
Lifted the black hull toward the harbour mouth
And caught the flush of fire. And darkness crept
Over the great deep like a shroud, till all
The host of faces on the peopled shore
Shone in the firelight, and its ruddier glow
Blurred the white stars from out the glooming heaven.

And bravely sped gray Sleipnir ; for he leapt
Over the gates of Hel, and in her hall
Hermodur stood, and all unflinching there
Looked on her deathly face, and bade her ask
A ransom. " Do the Æsir wail their dead ? "
Quoth Loki's daughter ;—" Nay, let all things weep
In every world, and I will send him back."
" Let all things weep for Baldur " :—Odin gave
The word, and all around, from Idavöll
To the drear Icefells, pealed the bitter cry.
" Let all things weep for Baldur " :—and behold
From all the corners of the peopled earth
Tears and great wailing like a cloud uprose.
Onward from land to land the Berserks sped
With Odin's bidding, and from land to land
The noise of weeping followed after them ;
But lo ! they found within a black hill-cleft
With tearless eyes, unmerciful, a crone
Wrinkled and cripple, and bowed down with years.

Fiercely she laughed and gave them back the word,
"Dry are the tears I weep for Frigga's son ;
Hel hold her own !" Ah, well, I ween, they **wist**
Falsehearted Loki so had answered them !
Slowly, their bootless errand sped, they came
Back once again to Asgard ; wrathful words
And stormy cries their meed. But Frigga shewed
Her wan face in the midst, and bidding "Peace,"
Slowly with calm lips spake the hidden weird

"Weep on, for we have lost him ; nevermore
The sunshine of his smile shall lighten up
Asgard for us. But unto us, not him,
The hurt is. Not for ever must we dwell
In this our kingdom, but the Sons of Fire
Must quell us, and the Evil Ones be strong,
Till we and they have fallen. Then once again,
Scathless and bright, shall Baldur fare from Hel,
And here for ever under a clear sky
Talk of old tales, and all these baleful times,
As of a troublous dream long past away."

"*As then he that was born after the flesh persecuted him that was born after the Spirit, even so it is now.*"

CHAPTER II

1850—1872

EASEBOURNE—BRIGHTON—CREWE GREEN

MR. ELLERTON'S ministerial life began in the little village of Easebourne, now a suburb of Midhurst in Sussex, best known from the stately wreck of Cowdray House which stands in the parish, and from the oaks of immeasurable age, the wonder of visitors from all parts of the world, which still survive in the park. In this quiet and beautiful spot he spent three happy years with his mother, combining faithful parochial work with diligent study. Here he surrounded himself with his favourite authors, Plato, Clough, Kingsley, and above all, Maurice. Maurice's influence was, as we have already seen, a powerful factor in the education and development of his mind; and if, on the one hand, it convinced him of the unsatisfactory character of the "Evangelical" school, on the other it acted as a caution against the extremes of the opposite party. Perhaps at this period, and in the fervour of his admiration of Maurice, he may have felt strong inclination towards the school so ably championed by Arnold, Stanley, Kingsley, and Maurice; but later on, as we have seen, he was content to take the middle current of Churchmanship of which Samuel Wilberforce, Richard Chenevix Trench, and Edward Meyrick Goulburn were among the great leaders. At this time, too, the condition of the poor and the education of the labouring classes greatly occupied his thoughts, and though with the co-operation of his mother he started a night-school at Easebourne, it was not until he became a vicar, and could work with unfettered hands, that he was able to put his long cherished ideas into execution.

On Trinity Sunday, 1851, John Ellerton was ordained priest in Chichester Cathedral by Bishop Gilbert, and two years afterwards was promoted, upon the recommendation of his bishop and Archdeacon Julius Hare, to the senior curacy of St. Nicholas, then the parish church of Brighton, receiving at the same time the appointment of Evening Lecturer at St. Peter's, now the parish church. For St. Nicholas he always retained a strong affection, and left his mark upon it, for it was at his suggestion, made at a later time, that the scheme of the windows all round the church, with their couplets from Latin hymns, was carried out. For the children of this parish his earliest hymns were composed; while so lately as 1882 he wrote the fine hymn, "Praise our God for all the wonders," for the Dedication Festival of the church. When a Mission in which he took part was held in Brighton in 1890, it was touching to see how the poor old people flocked to see and hear him once more: they had not forgotten him, though it must have been nearly thirty years since he had left the parish; a striking proof of how he had won their hearts when ministering among them. His vicar, the Rev. H. M. Wagner, was a notable man in his way, but is remembered not so much for his unceasing labours for the good of the vast population of Brighton, as for his unhappy controversy with Frederick Robertson, incumbent of Trinity Chapel. As was natural, and in accordance with the loyalty of his nature, the young curate of St. Nicholas tried to regard his vicar's conduct in the matter in as favourable a light as possible, and in after years maintained that Mr. Wagner's line of action was not unkind, but misunderstood by Robertson, owing to the over-excitement of his brain.

It was while curate of Brighton that John Ellerton began to try his wings as an author. His first flights, though short, were successful. In conjunction with the Rev. George Wagner, nephew of the vicar, and incumbent of St. Stephen's Church, he drew up a little manual of *Prayers for Schoolmasters and Teachers*. Now too it was that he made his first essay as a writer of hymns. For the Brighton National School he compiled a small hymnal entitled, *Hymns for Schools and Bible Classes*, which, besides containing four translations by Dr. Hort, introduced four original compositions of his own. These were—

1. "Day by day we magnify Thee." 1855. A morning hymn for school children.

2. "The hours of school are over."[1] 1858. Companion to the foregoing; for evening.

[1] *Children's Hymn-book*, 580, "The hours of day are over."

3. "Now returns the awful morning."[1] Re-written 1858. For Good Friday. Founded on a hymn by Joseph Anstice. Largely altered for *Church Hymns*, 1870.

4. "God of the living, in Whose eyes." 1859. Re-written and considerably enlarged and improved in *Hymns Original and Translated*, where it is dated July 6, 1867. This is one of the hymns sung at his funeral.

Although these early hymns can hardly be expected to attain to the high standard of those of later years, they are not deficient in those characteristics which distinguish the author's noblest compositions. They are not, what so many of our mis-called hymns are, merely prayers put into metrical form; they breathe the same devout spirit of thanksgiving, hope, and love, are conspicuous for the same absence of self-consciousness which we observe in his best; and especially is it to be noted that, with exception of the one for Good Friday, they are addressed not to the Second Person of the Holy Trinity, but to the First. Bishop Christopher Wordsworth's canon that "the songs of the Church ought to be addressed *to the Lord*," enforced, strangely enough, by a text which tells strongly against his own dictum, he always dissented from emphatically—" Whatsoever ye do, in word or deed, do all in the Name of the Lord Jesus, giving thanks to GOD AND THE FATHER by Him."—*Miscellanies*, ii. 236.

Mr. Ellerton held the senior curacy of Brighton, together with his Evening Lectureship at St.

---

[1] *Church Hymns*, 120.

Peter's, till 1860, when he was presented by Lord Crewe to the Vicarage of Crewe Green, Cheshire; and on May 19th in the same year he was married at St. Nicholas to Charlotte Alicia, daughter of William Hart, Esq., of Brighton.[1]

About a mile from the busy station of Crewe, famous for its extensive iron and steel works in connection with the London and North-Western Railway, is the village of Crewe Green. Its population of between four and five hundred consists partly of mechanics employed in the Company's works, and partly of farmers and labourers working for the most part on the estate of Lord Crewe, whose fine mansion, Crewe Hall, stands in the parish.

In 1859 his lordship erected on the Green a church and school-house for the benefit of his numerous tenants and fellow parishioners. The church, dedicated to St. Michael and All Angels, is remarkable in its way as being one of the very few brick churches, if not the only one, built by Sir Gilbert Scott. Externally red brick is used, and internally that of a lightish yellow; and the building, which is adorned with a small spire, consists of nave, chancel, and apse. Over against the church, on the opposite side of the Green, stands the parsonage, at that time a low, rambling house of whitewashed brick, since replaced by a structure more in accordance with modern ideas.

The parish, combining many attractions, together with difficulties peculiar to itself, difficulties arising from the necessity of ministering at once to a population of rustics and intelligent mechanics,

[1] She died March 18, 1896.

offered a congenial field of work to the new vicar, who, on accepting the charge, had also been appointed domestic chaplain to Lord Crewe. The charm of his preaching soon began to attract, and many, including University men, and pupils in the Railway works, came to spend their Sundays at Crewe Green, frequently being the guests for the day at the hospitable vicarage.

In addition to the usual routine of Church work, Mr. Ellerton threw himself with all his accustomed earnestness into every scheme calculated to raise the moral and social tone of the artisans of the Railway works. The following communication, for which I am indebted to W. M. Moorsom, Esq., at that time one of the chief officials in the Crewe works, gives some idea of his great activity, an activity all the more remarkable, because naturally his was rather the meditative, poetic temperament, than that of the energetic man of business.

Mr. Moorsom writes as follows—" In 1864 Mr. Ellerton, then Vicar of Crewe Green, and chaplain to Lord Crewe, was nominated by the Directors of the London and North-Western Railway Company for election upon the council of the Company's Mechanics' Institution at Crewe. His election followed, and within a short time he became Chairman of the Educational Committee.

"During his connection with the Institution, which lasted until 1872, when he became rector of Hinstock, the Educational Department was entirely re-organized under his auspices, the library re-arranged, and a new catalogue prepared. Into this work he threw a large amount of zeal and energy, and it was in great measure due to his tact and power of winning the confidence of those with whom he worked that during this period the Institution became, with one exception, the largest in the northern counties, and probably the most successful, educationally, in England.

"But his labours were not confined to administration. During several years he conducted the class in English History, and for a short time the Scripture History class also, with a widening of the interest of the members of these classes which was very marked and most encouraging to those (thirty years ago a mere handful) who regarded the 'education of our masters' as a requirement vital to the nation.

"The unwearied patience with which night after night he would trudge into dirty, black, smoky Crewe, bringing with him an air of wide-reaching interests and warm sympathy for the toiling masses, made a deep impression; and he gradually won his way into the hearts of large numbers of the artisans, to whom such a character was somewhat novel. The writer has frequently heard expressions of wonder from onlookers, themselves artisans—'What it could be that led Mr. Ellerton to take so much trouble to teach the lads from whom he had nothing to expect in return, and who were not worth the expenditure of time so valuable in other directions as his was known to be.' Among those mechanics who were themselves inspired by the same zeal, this self-devotion caused him to be greatly loved and honoured with a love and honour which deepened and extended as the years went on. There were but few capable of appropriating the ideas he set before them on history, poetry, or Scripture exegesis, but all could see that he was working without thought of reward, and many were fascinated by the beauty of such an example of self-devotion.

"During these years numerous were the disagreements which arose among the Council, leading to disputes, to compose which needed a weighty and judicious leader, in which capacity Mr. Ellerton was pre-eminent. He possessed the faculty of never perceiving a rudeness directed against himself; and after an acrimonious wrangle, in which nearly every one present had been either insulted or the insulter, or both, a few quiet words from him would calm the tempest, and lead the Council back to business."

But if it is the duty of the parish priest to take the lead in all matters concerning the welfare spiritual, intellectual, and temporal of his flock, it is no less his duty to "banish and drive away all erroneous and strange doctrines contrary to God's word." How ably Mr. Ellerton kept this portion of his ordination vow, and defended the faith against the teaching of a strange preacher who came to Crewe to exhort his hearers to free themselves from "the bondage of creeds," the following paper will show. It is as remarkable for the courtesy with which he treats his opponent as for the firmness and dignity with which he holds his own position, or rather that of the Church he represented.

THE BONDAGE OF CREEDS

THOUGHTS ON MR. G――'S ADDRESS TO THE INHABITANTS OF CREWE.

"I HAVE been asked by a friend to say what I think about an address recently printed by the Rev. Mr. G――, explanatory of his own religious position, and offering its advantages to others. Mr. G―― does not profess to address himself to those belonging to other Churches; and therefore it may seem unfair, or at least needless, for the minister of another Church to notice his address. My plea for doing so is that it has been widely circulated and much talked about in this neighbourhood, and that it touches upon certain important questions which it is quite possible to discuss, apart from those which definitely denote his religious position. I have neither the right nor the wish to criticize his specific teaching. I trust that he may be privileged to open to the love of God many a heart now closed against its influences; and to witness to the Divine Fatherhood in the consciences of many who have never yet realized that first and deepest of all truths. With regard to other, and, as I hold, co-ordinate truths, we must be content to part company until the time when all shall be made clear.

"I am only concerned with the language which Mr. G―― holds on the subject of Creeds. 'We are not bound together by a Creed;' 'Christianity does not depend on a Creed;' 'The followers of

Jesus are not to be known by their belief in a Creed.' Now this word Creed is a hard, ugly-sounding word, and carries with it a kind of savour of 'damnatory clauses' and trials for heresy. It is very easy by thus reiterating it to make it appear important and terrible. Yet after all it is a very simple matter. A Creed means nothing more than a form of words in which people express their religious belief. It is odd that Mr. G—— does not see that he himself cannot advance one step in explaining himself to the world without a Creed. In his very first sentence he says, 'I desire for myself, and for the congregation I represent, to place before you a *statement of the views we hold.*' Exactly so; this statement of the views he and his congregation hold is precisely what we mean by a Creed. We could not have desired a better definition of the word. In my congregation the Apostles' Creed and the Nicene Creed are 'statements of the views we hold.' But Mr. G—— goes on to give us his Creed—'We are, in religious belief, Unitarians.' Observe, he does not say, '*I am*,' but '*We are*,' that is, himself and his congregation. 'We accept Christ as our Divine Teacher, the sent of God.' These are the two articles of their Creed.

"But Mr. G—— continues, 'We are not bound together by a creed.' Now this must mean one of two things; either that the pastor is not bound to keep to the views in this 'statement,' or that the members of his congregation are not bound to hold them. As to the first, it seems strange to put forth a statement of views with one breath, and with the next to say, I don't pledge myself to these. However, as a believer in the Catholic faith, I should rejoice to think Mr. G—— did not feel himself bound by this statement. Only I cannot be blind to the fact that the Unitarian community is an organized body, with recognized leaders, and a central congress or conference; and I question whether our friend would be able to retain his present position were he to see reason to modify the views he here states to us. In fact, I doubt whether he is in reality less bound by his creed than I am by mine. Were he to cease to be an Unitarian, he would have to seek some other sphere of labour; so should I, were I to cease to be 'Catholic,' in the sense in which the Athanasian Creed uses the word.

"But what Mr. G—— doubtless means is, that his Creed does not bind his congregation; that a man may attend his church regularly without believing as he does; and since of course this is no more than any one of us may say, he intends, I suppose, to intimate that the full privileges of Church membership, and sacramental communion, are open in his Church to all, whatever their belief. Although, if this be the case, it is not easy to specify what that body is of which Mr. G—— says '*We are* in religious belief Unitarians;' yet the general tenor of Mr. G——'s address makes it clear that this is his great point. This then is the real question between us, the only question which has induced me to take up my pen: is it unfair to require the assent of a religious society to a Creed? Are Creeds contrary to the spirit of Christ's teaching? Are they an unreasonable bondage, a hindrance to free thought? I say—speaking for myself and for my own Church—distinctly No to all these questions.

"1. Creeds, *i.e.* public confessions of belief, or 'statements of views,' are not in themselves an unreasonable bondage, or a hindrance to free thought. Of course they may be made so. Many religious communities are over-burdened with tests of membership. Of course, too, it is possible to conceive of 'statements of views' to which none but a few fanatics could assent. But supposing the views to be not unreasonable in themselves, and supposing them to be entertained by the Church or community at its first constitution, the custom of reciting the statement of them in public implies no unfairness towards new members. Each one who joins the Church hears his neighbours say, 'I believe' so and so. If he feels he can unite in this, surely it is well for him to be invited to *say* what he has been brought to *believe*. But if he cannot, what then? He is not obliged to retire, he is not constrained to remain. He may listen to the public ministry, he is at full liberty to think and say what he pleases about it, to speak his mind freely, so long as he does not interrupt the common worship. Take the Church of England and its Creeds. The shortest and simplest of them is put in the form of questions to candidates for baptism, and to the Church members who bring their infants for that purpose. But as baptism can scarcely have any meaning at all for persons who do not believe in the alleged facts contained in the Apostles' Creed, its use at such a time is designed as an indication that baptism is sought in an intelligent and reasonable spirit. Beyond this no further test is imposed upon lay members of the Church of England. The only grounds upon which our Prayer-book allows a priest to refuse the other sacrament to members of the Church are 'open and notorious' immorality, and open, wilful enmity towards a neighbour. The ministry themselves, it is true, are bound by other tests of belief; but so are the ministers of every community, including, I suspect, Mr. G——'s own. And as to freedom of thought, if that does not exist in the Church of England, the world must be greatly mistaken. Why, it is the constant reproach of all the bigots around us, Romanist and Protestant alike, that we are so provokingly lax, that we will persist in tolerating, with shameless impartiality, Ritualist, Rationalist, Calvinist, thinkers who in no other Church on earth could find a common home.

"2. Again, a Creed is not contrary to the spirit of Christianity. Mr. G—— prints in capital letters the assertion that Christianity does not depend on a Creed. If by Christianity he means, what is usually meant by the term, the body of thoughts which Christ and His followers introduced among mankind, all I can reply is that a Creed is the expression—more or less imperfect, of course—of that body of thought. The Christianity of each man, in this sense, depends upon how much of this thought he has really and practically taken in, and made his own. The Creed he adopts is simply an idea of this—of his level of Christian thought. It is surely absurd to maintain that it is contrary to Christianity for a man to say what Christianity appears to him to be; or for a body of men to agree, so to say.

"But if Christianity means a life 'made beautiful by Christian virtues,' then while it is plain that there is no necessary connection between the practice of virtue and the expression of belief, yet, on the other hand, there is no opposition between the two. The Sermon on the Mount contains, it is true, no Creed; but does it imply none? And why stop at the beginning of Christ's ministry? Did He not compel the Apostles to confess what they thought of Him? And when His life on earth was at an end, and those events which are enumerated in what is called the Apostles' Creed had taken place, did any of them ever preach a sermon without making a statement of what they believed respecting these events?

"Most cordially do I join Mr. G—— in proclaiming 'the *right* of every man to think for himself;' only I would rather call it the *duty*. God forbid that I should dictate to any man what he is to believe, if that dictating implies that he is to believe it because I tell him so. The first Christian teachers declared that by manifestation of the truth they commended themselves to every man's conscience. I desire no more. But if it be truth indeed that a man receives in his conscience, that truth will make him free. To acknowledge it may be a bond of unity, it can never be a bondage to him. Even Mr. G——'s two articles of religion separate him from some of his fellowmen. But would he love his neighbour the better if he did not in any way define his belief? I think not. Even to say, 'God is your Father, Christ is sent from God,' is better than to say, My friends, I am sure of nothing; I have nothing to tell you from God.

"JOHN ELLERTON."

It is not, however, with John Ellerton as a parish priest but as a poet that we have mainly to do in this short sketch of his life. It was at Crewe Green that the foundation of his fame as a writer of hymns was laid; not that he had not exercised his wonderful poetical talent prior to his removal into Cheshire, for, as we have seen, he had already published a few while curate of Brighton. The first in order of time belonging to this period seems to be, " Sing Alleluia forth in duteous praise," 1865, or "The Endless Alleluia," first published in the *Churchman's Family Magazine* for April 1865, and revised for the Appendix to *Hymns Ancient and Modern* in 1868. The original Latin is in the Mozarabic Breviary, and was used also in the Church of England before the Norman Conquest. The epithet *endless* is thus explained by the translator—" Alleluia was discontinued from Septuagesima (or from Lent) to Easter, hence the contrast here between the interrupted Alleluias of earth and the endless (*perenne*= continuous) Alleluia of heaven."[1] As it appeared in the Appendix, the first verse ran—

> "Sing Alleluia forth in duteous praise,
> O citizens of heaven; and sweetly raise
>   An endless Alleluia."

---

[1] *Notes and Illustrations to Church Hymns*, No. 497.

This was altered by the Appendix Committee to—

"Sing Alleluia forth in duteous praise,
Ye citizens of heaven ; O sweetly raise
An endless Alleluia.'

In his letter suggesting the alterations Sir Henry Baker writes, " I have little doubt of our idea of the hymn being right. It ought to be sung just before Lent (Septuagesima), as the Church on earth leaves off for a time Alleluia. Ye citizens of *heaven* (she exclaims), sing the unceasing Alleluia ; ye who stand near the Eternal Light, go on singing *still— henceforth—hinc*—onwards from this time, though *we* on earth cease awhile the endless, never-ceasing Alleluia. The 'Holy City' below will take up your strain again (*i.e.* at Easter), and sing the endless Alleluia again with you. The rest of the hymn is the Church delighting (as so many hymns at that season do) in the praise of and thought of the Alleluia which never ceases above."

" Saviour, again to Thy dear Name we raise." This, one of the author's sweetest and most favourite hymns, was originally written in 1866 for a Festival of Parochial Choirs at Nantwich ; he revised and abridged it for the Appendix to *Hymns Ancient and Modern* in 1868. Both forms are given in *Hymns Original and Translated.* By its condensation into four verses its spirit and power are wonderfully increased, and now it ranks with Bishop Ken's " Glory to Thee, my God, this night," Keble's " Sun of my soul, Thou Saviour dear," and Lyte's " Abide with me ; fast falls the eventide," as one of the great evening hymns of the English Church.

Beautiful as is Dr. Dyke's melody "Pax Dei" in *Hymns Ancient and Modern*, Mr. Ellerton once told me he himself preferred the less known tune in A flat for unison singing, with its varied harmonies, by Dr. Edward J. Hopkins, Organist of the Temple Church. The last verse formed the third hymn at his funeral.

Three very beautiful hymns were written in 1867—

1. "Father, in Thy glorious dwelling," not included, strange to say, either in *Church Hymns* or *Hymns Ancient and Modern*.

2. "This is the day of light," which first appeared in the *Selection of Hymns Compiled for use in Chester Cathedral*, 1868.

3. "Our day of praise is done," written for a Choral Festival at Nantwich, and recast in 1869 for the *Supplemental Hymn and Tune-Book*, by the Rev. R. Brown-Borthwick.[1]

It was a saying of John Wesley's, that the appearance of a new first-class hymn was as rare as that of a comet; but now the production one after another of hymns of the highest excellence began to attract the attention of lovers of sacred song; the reproach implied in Wesley's words was taken away, and the Vicar of Crewe Green was soon recognized as standing in the very front rank of Church poets, not only as an original writer but also as a translator. In 1868 four translations were made—

1. "On this the day when days began," from *Primo dierum omnium*, one of the eight hymns

[1] *Notes and Illustrations*, No. 42.

which the Benedictine editors assign to St. Gregory the Great[1] (540—604). It had been translated by Dr. Neale, Sir Henry W. Baker (*Hymns Ancient and Modern*), J. Keble, and several others.

2. "Jesu most pitiful." *Jesu dulcissime;* a very beautiful, albeit late Latin hymn, probably not earlier than 1650. This translation first appears together with so many of the following in the Rev. R. Brown-Borthwick's *Sixteen Hymns*, 1870.

3. "Welcome, happy morning! age to age shall say." 1868. Writing to his friend, the Rev. Godfrey Thring, about *Salve Festa Dies*, the original of this hymn, Mr. Ellerton says, "I am rather proud of my little translation of it, because it has a swing about it, I think, and goes well to Brown-Borthwick's tune,[2] not so stiffly as many translations; and yet I hope it is fairly accurate.

"There *is* an Ascension-day *Salve Festa*, as also one for Corpus Christi, one for Pentecost, and one for the Dedication of a Church; but these are all imitations of the original hymn, and all from the York Processional. The hymn itself is an extract from the seventh poem of the Third Book of Venantius Fortunatus; its title is 'De Resurrectione Domini. Ad Felicem Episcopum.' It contains one hundred and twelve lines of elegiac verse. Different centos were used in different books, *i.e.* some verses were in the York book which were not in the Sarum, etc. The verses I have translated are the chief part of those given in Daniel, from two or three books put together. Fortunatus was born about 530, and

---

[1] Julian's *Dictionary of Hymnology*.
[2] The second to which it is set in *Church Hymns*.

died Bishop of Poictiers about 609. There is considerable interest connected with this hymn from its widespread use. It was early translated into German by an English monk of Sarum,[1] and was sung by Jerome of Prague at the stake. In Latimer's sixth Sermon before Edward VI. he says, 'They (the Puritans) must sing *Salve festa dies* about the Church, that no man was the better for it, but to shew their gay coats and garments.' But most interesting of all is a letter from Cranmer to Henry VIII. from Beakesbourne, October 7, 1544, about publishing an English Processional, some translated, some original, by Royal authority. In this letter he speaks of *Salve festa dies* as one to be included, and says, 'As concerning the *Salve festa dies*, the Latin note, as I think, is sober and distinct enough; wherefore I have travailed to make the verses in English, and have put the Latin note unto the same. Nevertheless, they that be cunning in singing can make a much more solemn note thereto. I made them only for a proof, to see how English would do in song.' I wish we had Cranmer's version, as a curiosity, for it would probably be unsingable; but it would appear from this letter that this was the first Church hymn ever translated from Latin directly into English. Coverdale had previously translated from the German several of Luther's spiritual songs, some of which were free versions of Latin hymns." In a

---

[1] Mr. Mearns tells me this is an error. The monk was a Benedictine called Johannes of Salzburg. His translation was made in 1366 at the request of the Archbishop of Salzburg.

postscript he adds, "The 'Latin note' to which Cranmer refers has been reprinted by Neale and Helmore in *Accompanying Harmonies to the Hymnal Noted*, 1852, No. 79, p. 249. The music is from the Sarum and York processionals."

4. "Jesu, Who alone defendest." *Jesu Defensor omnium*, a midnight hymn in the Mozarabic Breviary.[1]

The fine Processional for the Restoration of a Church—

5. "Lift the strain of high thanksgiving," was written in 1869 at the request of the late Canon Cooper for the re-opening of St. Helen's Church, Tarporley, Cheshire.

It seems to be in the very nature of the poetic faculty, whatever particular form that faculty may assume, to have, like an intermittent spring, its seasons of comparative rest varied by bursts of irresistible activity. Such must have been the experience of Handel when, after composing the *Messiah* in three weeks, he at once followed it up with *Samson*, and if we knew more than we do of Shakespeare, no doubt we should find that he too had his seasons of special inspiration. The years 1870 and 1871 were a period of marvellous poetic activity with Mr. Ellerton, for in these two years he produced no fewer than twenty-six hymns

[1] The Mozarabic (or Muzarabic) is the old national Liturgy of Spain, and though now almost wholly supplanted by the Roman, which was forced upon the Spanish Church in the tenth and eleventh centuries, is said to be still used in two or three Churches in Toledo, and one in Salamanca. See Hammond's *Liturgies Eastern and Western*.

and translations, all good, many of the very highest excellence. In 1870 we find the following ten to have been composed—

1. "O shining city of our God," founded on 1 John iii. 2, "It doth not yet appear what we shall be." It first appears in Rev. R. Brown-Borthwick's *Sixteen Hymns*, and was the fifth of the six hymns sung at the author's funeral.

2. The above hymn was written January 21st; on the 25th, only four days after, and published at the same time, it was followed by a hymn of the tenderest beauty for Burial of the Dead, scarcely if at all inferior to "Now the labourer's task is o'er,"—

> "When the day of toil is done,
> When the race of life is run,
> Father, grant Thy wearied one
>   Rest for evermore!"

This hymn was first sung at the funeral of Mr. Thomas Stubbs, chief manager of the Crewe Railway Works, September 25, 1870. The sermon which the Vicar preached on the Sunday following the funeral, and afterwards published, is a touching tribute to the memory of a good and faithful servant. Among many memorable words which it contains the following may well be repeated. Alluding to the early age [1] at which the deceased was called away, he says—"The true measure of the length of a life is not its years but its usefulness." Again, with reference to the comparatively obscure sphere of labour to which many are called—"We honour

---

[1] Thirty-five years.

the soldier who gives his life upon the field, in obedience to the call of duty; or the sailor who goes down in his sinking ship in giving or in carrying out his orders. And surely it is just as heroic, just as honourable, to be found faithful to death in any other service to which a man has been called; to care more for doing our daily work well, than for doing it easily; to treat it not merely as a means of getting bread, but as a task which it is a duty to God to do thoroughly, and a sin against God to do carelessly."

This was the second of the six hymns by the poet sung at his funeral.

3. "Come forth, O Christian brothers," composed for a Festival of Parochial Choirs at Chester, May 1870.

4. "God the Almighty, in wisdom ordaining," written for a country congregation during the French and German war, 1870, in imitation of "God the all-terrible! King Who ordainest," attributed to Henry Fothergill Chorley. It is dated August 28, 1870.

5. "O Thou in Whom Thy saints repose," for the consecration of a burial ground. Written upon the occasion of an addition to the parish churchyard of Tarporley, Cheshire, Nov. 19.

6. "The Lord be with us as we bend." "Written at the request of a friend, for use at the close of service on Sunday afternoons, when (as in summer) strictly *Evening* hymns would be unsuitable." [1]

7. "The day Thou gavest, Lord, is ended." Contributed to a "Liturgy for Missionary Meetings,"

---

[1] *Notes and Illustrations*, Hymn 52.

revised for *Church Hymns*, the first line borrowed from an anonymous hymn in *Church Poetry* (1855).

8. "Behold us, Lord, a little space," for a mid-day service in a city church.

9. "God, Creator, and Preserver," for times of scarcity and bad harvest; written for *The Hymnary* (470).

10. "Sing, ye faithful, sing with gladness." The full and authorized form of this noble hymn on the Incarnation is found in *Hymns Original and Translated*, and consists of eight stanzas, with the refrain "Evermore and evermore." In *Church Hymns* (499) it is cut down to five stanzas and the refrain omitted, by which it is considerably shorn of its beauty and spirit. It deserves a fine tune to itself. It is partly an imitation of *Da puer plectrum* of Prudentius [1] (b. 348).

To compose these ten hymns, and at the same time to comply with the incessant demand for sermons, lectures, and addresses of all sorts, made by so busy a place as Crewe, to say nothing of the time spent in visiting and other parochial work, shows a wonderful activity, intellectual and bodily, on the part of the Vicar. He had no curate to take some of the duties off his hands and leave him time for quiet study; everything had to be done by himself, and the united voice of the parish, expressed on his resignation two years after, pronounced that it was done well, thoroughly, and faithfully.

Still more prolific was the following year (1871),

---

[1] Poëta eximius—eruditissimus et sanctissimus scriptor—nemo divinius de rebus Christianis unquam scripsit. Such is Barth's praise of Prudentius, quoted by Archbishop Trench. —*Sacred Latin Poetry*, p. 119.

producing twelve original hymns and four translations from the Latin, not of course all of equal excellence, but among them some of the very best. The first one, bearing date January 14, is—

1. "King Messiah, long expected." A much-needed hymn for the Circumcision, written for *Church Hymns*. *Hymns Ancient and Modern* has only two, and *The Hymnary* only one for this festival. Bishop Christopher Wordsworth, to supply the want, wrote "Giver of law is God's dear Son," by no means his happiest inspiration. Among these "King Messiah, long expected" shines out as a star of the first magnitude.

This was followed February 13 by—

2. "Another day begun," for a week-day morning service.

3. "We sing the glorious conquest," for the Conversion of St. Paul; written Feb. 28, 1871, for *Church Hymns*, and passed into *Hymns Ancient and Modern*.

4. "Father! Name of love and fear." A Confirmation hymn, dated March 18.

5. "O Son of God, our Captain of salvation." St. Barnabas. Also written for *Church Hymns*, and incorporated into *Hymns Ancient and Modern*. Dated April 5, 1871.

6. "O Lord of life and death, we come." A hymn for time of pestilence; remarkable for its common-sense and courage in attributing pestilence to what is frequently its true source—bad drainage—

"Forgive the foul neglect that brought
   Thy chastening to our door:
   The homes uncleansed," etc., dated October 20.

7. " Thou in Whose Name the two or three." For Wednesday.

8. " King of Saints, to Whom the number." A fine hymn for St. Bartholomew, in the tetrameter trochaic metre of fifteen syllables broken into two parts, a break which Bishop Christopher Wordsworth calls "a serious evil to Hymnology," though why we cannot see. The very probable conjecture that this saint is to be identified with the Nathaniel of the fourth Gospel[1] is neatly expressed in the third verse—

> " Was it he, beneath the fig-tree
>   Seen of Thee, and guileless found ;
> He who saw the Good he long'd for
>   Rise from Nazareth's barren ground :
> He who met his risen Master
>   On the shore of Galilee ;
> He to whom the word was spoken,
>   ' Greater things thou yet shalt see ' ? "

" None can tell us."

This favourite hymn, written for *Church Hymns*, is also to be found in *Hymns Ancient and Modern* (419).

9. " Mary at the Master's feet." For Catechizing ; written for *Church Hymns*.

We now come to the loveliest and most loved of all Mr. Ellerton's hymns—

10. " Now the labourer's task is o'er." It has been sung, and will continue to be sung, at the grave-side of princes, divines, statesmen, poets, artists, authors, as well as of many a Christian

---

[1] St. John i. 45 ; xxi. 2.

labourer in humble life. No hymnal is now deemed complete without it.

Like the Te Deum, Bishop Ken's Evening Hymn, and many another composition of highest excellence, this hymn contains evidences of pre-existing material. This the author himself points out in his *Notes and Illustrations to Church Hymns*. "The whole hymn," he says, "especially the third, fifth, and sixth verses, owes many thoughts and some expressions to a beautiful poem of the Rev. Gerard Moultrie's, beginning 'Brother, now thy toils are o'er,'" which will be found in the *People's Hymnal*, 380.

There can be no doubt that the popularity of the hymn has been largely increased by the lovely and sympathetic melody "Requiescat," by Dr. Dykes, in *Hymns Ancient and Modern*, to which it is now exclusively and inseparably united.

11. "In the Name which earth and heaven." Processional for the foundation of a Church. The author observes, "A cento from this and 'Lift the strain of high thanksgiving,' was compiled and sung for the first time at the re-opening of the nave of Chester Cathedral, January 25, 1872."

12. "Praise to our God, whose bounteous hand
    Prepared of old our glorious land."

A hymn of national thanksgiving, first printed in Rev. R. Brown-Borthwick's *Select Hymns*.

The four translations made this year (1871) are—

1. "Oh come, all ye faithful, joyful and triumphant." Translated from a cento of four stanzas from the favourite *Adeste fideles, laeti triumphantes*.

The original poem, the full text of which is given in Julian's *Dictionary of Hymnology*, contains eight stanzas, but the shortened form is the English use. The author of the article on this hymn in Julian's *Dictionary* mentions no fewer than thirty-eight renderings—a striking proof of its popularity as a Christmas hymn. One aim of Mr. Ellerton's translation appears to be to give as far as possible a syllable to each note of the traditional melody, and its chief peculiarity is his version of the first line of the fourth stanza—"Thou, Who didst deign to be born for us this morning," instead of "Yea, Lord, we greet Thee, born this happy morning,"[1] as it stands in Canon Oakeley's arrangement (*Hymns Ancient and Modern*).

With regard to the authorship and date of this hymn all is uncertainty. Mr. Ellerton's note is—"Doubtless not older than the fifteenth century, and not originally written for liturgical use;" while the writer in Julian's *Dictionary* says, "Probably it is a hymn of the seventeenth or eighteenth century, and of French or German authorship." If, however, the late Vincent Novello erred not in attributing the traditional melody to John Reading, organist of Winchester Cathedral, 1675—1681,[2] the hymn may not be later than the seventeenth century. But whensoever or by whomsoever composed the hymn has taken an assured place as emphatically *the* Christmas Hymn of the Western Church.

2. "Giver of the perfect gift," *Summi largitor praemii*, an anonymous Lenten hymn of the ninth

[1] In *The Hymnary* this last line reads—"Born of Virgin Mother."   [2] Julian's *Dictionary*, p. 20.

or tenth (?) century. The *Hymns Ancient and Modern* rendering, by J. W. Hewett, "O Thou Who dost to man accord," is perhaps better known.

3. "We sing of Christ's eternal gifts," *Aeterna Christi munera, Apostolorum gloriam*, an adaptation for apostles as distinct from martyrs, of the celebrated Ambrosian hymn, *Aeterna Christi munera, Et martyrum victorias*. Whether this hymn be St. Ambrose's, to whom the Benedictine editors ascribe it, or not, it is certainly not later than the fifth century.[1] The rendering in *Church Hymns* is partly that of Dr. Neale,[2] and partly Mr. Ellerton's. The *Hymns Ancient and Modern* translation is by Dr. Neale.

4. "To the Name that speaks salvation." Translated from *Gloriosi Salvatoris*, an anonymous Latin hymn of German origin, possibly of the fifteenth century. There are several translations; that in *Hymns Ancient and Modern* is an altered version of Dr. Neale's; Mr. Ellerton's is adopted in *Church Hymns*.

The amazing fertility of Mr. Ellerton's poetic genius during these two years has seldom if ever been surpassed by any sacred writer. Of all species of composition the hymn is one which cannot be hurried, cannot be produced to order like a catalogue or a sermon; it is the sudden and often unpremeditated inspiration which sweeps

---

[1] Trench, *Sacred Latin Poetry*, p. 210. St. Ambrose was Bishop of Milan, 374—397.

[2] Not of J. D. Chambers, as stated by Mr. Ellerton in his *Notes and Illustrations*.—Julian's *Dictionary of Hymnology*.

down upon the singer, it may be at some unexpected moment, never more accurately expressed than by the Psalmist—

> "My heart was hot within me;
> And while I was thus musing a fire kindled:
> And at the last I spake with my tongue."[1]

---

[1] Ps. xxxix. 4.

CHAPTER III

1872—1876

HINSTOCK

ON the main road between the two Shropshire towns of Market Drayton and Newport, the latter on the borders of Staffordshire, lies the village of Hinstock. It nestles among the low smooth hills of the new red sandstone, a fact at once betrayed by the little church as it raises its square tower among the surrounding trees. The building itself, which stands hard by the rectory, on a little raised mound entirely surrounded by the road, possesses no architectural pretensions.[1] Like many churches in Shropshire, it is dedicated to St. Oswald, "that most Christian King of the Northumbrians," as Bede calls him, who was slain by Penda, king of the Mercians, in the battle of Maserfeld,[2] on August 5, 642. The church has to some extent been beautified by a later rector, but in 1872 it was a very plain modern structure with absolutely no chancel. The rectory was a modern red-brick

---

[1] It was always a matter of regret with Mr. Ellerton that none of his churches, until he came to White Roding, had any architectural interest.

[2] Considered by some to be the former name of Oswestry, before it was re-named after Oswald.

house, with a lawn extending to the churchyard, a grand old yew-tree standing in the boundary line, as if to guard against any encroachment of the one upon the other.

A parish so utterly secluded and cut off from the ordinary channels of intercourse with the great centres of life and intellectual activity might afford a fitting sphere of work for a clergyman who would find congenial occupation and relaxation in rural intercourses and pursuits ; but for a man who had achieved renown as a sacred poet, for a preacher and scholar of no ordinary calibre, for one who loved and adorned the society of thinkers and workers—to put such a man, in the very prime of life and power, into a parish like this was to consign him to a living grave.

Yet notwithstanding the many drawbacks and disadvantages arising from the difficulty of access to public libraries, it was here that the greater part of his *Magnum opus*, the *Notes and Illustrations to Church Hymns*, published in the folio edition of that work, was written. It was here too that he composed the article " Hymns " in the *Dictionary of Christian Antiquities*, a piece of writing which, as he told me, cost him many a journey to Cambridge. In fact, his work at Hinstock was not so much the composition of hymns as assisting in the compilation of hymnals, and the improving of congregational singing.

The first of these was, however, by no means dropped. Between the years 1872 and 1876 several original hymns and one translation appeared—

1. " Thou Who once for us uplifted." Written

for Canon Cooper, then rector of Tarporley, a small town between Crewe and Chester, as a dedication hymn for the Chapel of Ease of St. John and the Holy Cross, Cote Brook, a hamlet in the parish. It was sung at the laying of the corner-stone, September 13, 1873.

The hymn as it now appears in *Hymns Original and Translated*, p. 43, differs somewhat from its early form. The second verse, beginning " In Thy Name, O Lord, we lay it," does not appear, and the third, which owed its special significance to the occasion, is omitted—

> " By Thy Cross, that day of sorrow,
> Stood Thy loved Apostle John,
> Till he heard the Cry that witnessed
> All Thy mighty labours done ;
> Till he saw the cruel spear-point
> Pierce the Breast he leaned upon."

This is the only hymn bearing the date of 1873.

2. " Thou Who sentest Thine Apostles." 1874.

3. " Throned upon the awful Tree." 1875. The grandest of his original compositions.

4. " Once more Thy Cross before our view." 1875. For the evening of Good Friday.

5. " O Father, all creating." January 29, 1876. A wedding hymn, written at the request of the Duke of Westminster, for the marriage of his daughter, the Lady Elizabeth Harriet Grosvenor, to the Marquis of Ormonde, Feb. 2, 1876.

6. " Speak Thou to me, O Lord." Entitled " The Voice of God." 1876.

Two years after his coming to Hinstock, Mr. Ellerton accepted, at the request of Bishop Selwyn, the post of Diocesan Inspector for Salop-in-Lichfield. The duties of such an appointment were in every way congenial to his love for children. It was for them that at Brighton his earliest hymns were composed, and his first book was published.

It was about this time too that, in conjunction with his friend Canon Walsham How, Mr. Ellerton compiled *Children's Hymns and School Prayers*,[1] the forerunner of the more important *Children's Hymn-Book*. This very useful little work consists of School Prayers, Occasional Prayers, and a form for Children's Service, the last being drawn up by Canon How. The hymns (including four appropriate Litanies) are one hundred and fifty-three in number, of which eight are by Mr. Ellerton. Seven had appeared before, but one was now published for the first time, namely, the very spirited and melodious—

> "Again the morn of gladness,
> The morn of light, is here."

With the beautiful refrain—

> "Glory be to Jesus,
> Let all His children say;
> He rose again, He rose again
> On this glad day!"

though it deserves a tune to itself instead of borrowing *Wir Pflügen* from "We plough the fields and scatter," to which it is set in the *Children's Hymn-Book*.[2] It was written in 1874, at the request of his

[1] Published by S. P. C. K.
[2] A hymn and the tune composed for it, provided that each be worthy of the other, so unite them that to separate them and make the tune do double duty is a species of di-

friend, the Rev. D. Trinder, Vicar of Teddington, as a processional for Sunday School children on their way to church.

The translation referred to is "All my heart to Thee I give" (June 3, 1874), from the anonymous Latin hymn *Cor meum Tibi dedo*. This, however, is for private and devotional use rather than for public worship, a distinction which Mr. Ellerton was always careful to observe.[1] It has been set to music as a sacred song by Dr. John Naylor, organist of York Minster.

Happily Mr. Ellerton's residence at Hinstock did not last long, only five years, for in 1876, owing, I understand, to the thoughtful kindness of his friend Canon (afterwards Bishop) Lightfoot, he was presented by the Dean and Chapter of St. Paul's to the suburban rectory of Barnes, Surrey.

---

vorce which we instinctively resent. We feel that the substituted hymn is clad in a garment not made for it, which fits it badly, and which can only be worn gracefully by its rightful owner.

[1] It is interesting, however, to observe how some hymns, written solely for personal and devotional use, have found their way into public worship, *e.g.* "Abide with me; fast falls the eventide." "This hymn, written by Mr. Lyte in his last illness, was not intended for use by a congregation, or as an Evening Hymn. The references throughout are to the close, not of the day, but of life." (MS. note by J. E.)

CHAPTER IV

1876—1884

BARNES

Church Hymns—Children's Hymn-Book—Church of England Hymn-Book—London Mission Hymn-Book

THE parish of Barnes, large, populous, and important, offered a noble field for ministerial work, and into this the new rector threw himself with unreserved devotion, giving all his powers of mind and body to the welfare of those whom he had been called to serve. A very different congregation now listened to him from what he had been accustomed to address in Cheshire, a congregation which had been taught to look for teaching of the highest order from a pulpit long occupied by the eloquent Henry Melvill, and after him by the scholarly Medd. As these pages are designed to be but a sketch of Mr. Ellerton's life, and by no means a full biography, I say but little of his ministerial work at Barnes, where I had the privilege of being associated with him as his curate, and dwell rather upon the literary side of his industry. Suffice it to say, that every detail of parochial work was thoroughly mastered. In one part of the parish a room was opened for special services for the poor; in another an iron church, since replaced by a permanent and handsome structure, was erected. Whether it was the choir, the schools, district visitors, or confirmation classes, upon each in its turn he concentrated his whole mind, spending and being spent in his Master's service, until his strength broke down under the burden, and he was compelled to resign it to another. Perhaps it was only the few who could appreciate his rare gifts of oratory, his elegant scholarship; but all loved him, all, that is, whose hearts were capable of responding to the reality of his sympathy, and the warmth of his loving heart. One [1] who knew him well wrote, on the occasion of his death—"that he was a man of deep learning and of varied and extended reading, no educated listener could fail to discover, although his sermons were remarkably free from parade of erudition or excess of ornament. But it was not his mastery of English, his many-sided culture, and his transparent sincerity that gave to his sermons the attractiveness to which we refer. It was rather that rare and indefinable *something* which radiates from poetic natures, and makes other hearts burn within them."

One of the results of Mr. Ellerton's coming to the neighbourhood of London, was a more intimate and personal share in the affairs of the Society for Promoting Christian Knowledge, for which he had already done such good work. He was a member of the Tract Committee from 1878 until the time of his death. One of his colleagues, the present Archdeacon of Middlesex, writes, "On the Tract

---

[1] Professor Henry Attwell, K.O.C.

Committee he was our authority in matters of poetry and music; and was looked up to by all as a sound theologian." His great work for the Committee was his editing the *Manual of Parochial Work*, and subsequently revising it for the second edition. "A great deal of the Manual (as you are well aware) is from his pen. All who had the pleasure of working with him remember with affection his gentle and quiet manner, and the touches of humour which he not unfrequently threw into his observations."[1]

In connection with this Society Mr. Ellerton also wrote a series of Tracts; two for Ash-Wednesday, one for Lent, Good Friday, Easter, Ascension Day, and Whit Sunday.

In addition to the vast amount of hymnological work accomplished at Barnes in connection with *Church Hymns with Notes and Illustrations*, the *Children's Hymn-Book*, and the *London Mission Hymn-Book*, Mr. Ellerton composed the following hymns:—

1. "Thy Voice it is that calls us, bounteous Lord." August 21, 1877. Written for Early Communion at a meeting of Clergy; the idea taken from St. John xxi. 12, "Jesus saith unto them, Come and break your fast."[2]

2. "This day the Lord's disciples met." For Whit-Sunday, written for the *Children's Hymn-Book*.

3. "In the Name which holy angels." September 1878. A hymn which he very kindly wrote at my

---

[1] Letter to the Author.

[2] R.V. giving the true translation of ἀριστήσατε, which the A.V. "come and dine" obscures.

request for the opening of the temporary iron church of St. Michael and All Angels, in the district of Westfields, Barnes.

4. "Oh how fair that morning broke." March 13, 1880. Septuagesima; written for the *Children's Hymn-Book*.

5. "Before the day draws near its ending." April 22, 1880. After service, Sundays or Festivals.

6. "O Thou Whose bounty fills the earth." For a Children's Flower Service. As it is dated Chelsea, June 6, 1880, it was no doubt written at Chelsea Rectory when on a visit to his friend, the Rev. Gerald Blunt, the author of the favourite Flower Service hymn, " Here, Lord, we offer Thee all that is fairest," *Hymns Ancient and Modern*, 598. These hymns of the two old friends stand together in the *Children's Hymn-Book*.

7. " Hail to the Lord Who comes." October 6, 1880. Presentation of Christ in the Temple; written for the Rev. Godfrey Thring.

8. "Praise our God, Whose open Hand." Written for a bad harvest, and printed in the *Guardian*, August 1881.

The Rev. F. G. Ellerton writes to me, " Numerous letters and telegrams at once showered on my father asking permission to use it, or announcing the fact of having done so, requesting copies, or bidding him order some for them, etc., etc. I have no less than twenty-seven of them."

9. " Break Thou to us, O Lord,
  The Bread of Life to-day;
  And through Thy written Word
  Thy very self display." 1881.

10. "O Thou Who givest food to all." August 30, 1882. Harvest Thanksgiving. Stated in *Hymns Original and Translated* to have been written for the Church of England Temperance Society, but it is not in their hymn-book; perhaps the boldness which did not fear to assert that both Corn and *Wine* are God's "high gifts," in accordance with the whole teaching and tenor of Holy Scripture, condemned it in the eyes of the Society.

11. "Thou Who wearied by the well." September 23, 1882. For the opening of a Workman's Coffee Tavern.

12. "Within Thy Temple, Lord, of old." Written for the Fiftieth Anniversary of the Dedication of Christ Church, Coventry. This Jubilee was held in August 1882.

13. "Praise our God for all the wonders." December 1882. Composed for the Dedication Festival of St. Nicholas Church, Brighton. A fine historical Processional similar in conception to the St. Martin's hymn.[1]

Among the minor hymnological works, but nevertheless a very important one, which Mr. Ellerton completed at Barnes must be included the *London Mission Hymn-Book*. In 1884 the General London Mission was held, and it was thought desirable to prepare a hymn-book for it. Mr. Ellerton, being selected as one of the editors, consulted with other hymnologists of eminence, especially Canon Walsham How, and Bishop E. H. Bickersteth; but the weight of the burden

[1] p. 143.

was mainly borne by himself. The book was published by the Society for Promoting Christian Knowledge in July, and contained, inclusive of the Appendix, 211 hymns, to which were added the Venite, Te Deum laudamus, Magnificat, Nunc dimittis, and Psalms li. and cxxx. It was for this book that Mr. Ellerton wrote his spirited Processional—" Onward, brothers, onward ! march with one accord."

CHURCH HYMNS

SINCE it was at Barnes that *Church Hymns with Notes and Illustrations*, and the *Children's Hymn-Book*, two out of the three[1] of Mr. Ellerton's most important hymnological labours, were completed and published, this seems the most fitting place to introduce some account of these works.

Even before leaving Crewe Green the foundations of his fame as a sacred poet were laid, but by the time he was promoted to Barnes his influence had impressed itself indelibly on the hymnody of the Church. His hymns were now known far and wide, their catholicity and comprehensiveness gaining for many of them acceptance in other Christian congregations both at home and abroad.

When or under what circumstances he first began to make hymns his special study it is impossible to say. In 1879 he speaks of his "more than twenty years devotion to hymnology," and it was in 1859, when curate of the parish church of Brighton, that he compiled *Hymns for Schools and Bible Classes*. In 1863 we find Dr. Kennedy,

[1] The third, the complete edition of *Hymns Ancient and Modern*, was published in 1889, when Mr. Ellerton was Rector of White Roding.

Head-master of Shrewsbury School, then preparing his *Hymnologia Christiana*, appealing to him as an authority on the subject. With him the first object in life was ever to make full proof of his ministry; to feed the flock of God over which he had been appointed; to preach the Word; to be instant in season, out of season; to reprove, rebuke, exhort with all long-suffering and doctrine. He was priest first, and only after that a poet. His first thought and aim was absolute self-dedication to his Master's service, and next to devote what spare time he found to hymnology, to promote God's honour by perfecting, so far as in him lay, the service of song in the house of the Lord.

To estimate at its true value the part which Mr. Ellerton took in that great awakening of Church music which accompanied the revival of Churchmanship, begun by the Wesleys, carried on by the leaders of the old Evangelical School, and strengthened by the Oxford movement, we must compare what it was some forty or thirty years ago with what it is at the present day. With regard to hymn-books, their number was well nigh countless. They had sprung up like mushrooms in an autumn meadow. Between 1820 and 1850 Dr. Julian enumerates at least seventy-eight as having appeared, differing vastly in their degrees of merit. In fact, as to the clergy in this matter every man did that which was right in his own eyes. Many who could afford it compiled collections for their own congregations, so that it was difficult to find two churches in a town using the same book. The singing too was equally deplorable. The hymns, given out by the clerk, were generally restricted to four verses, and it was considered the correct thing for the organist to play an interlude between each verse. Such Churches as did not adopt or compile a book of hymns for their own use commonly used Tate and Brady's metrical version, or rather perversion, of the Psalms.[1]

Among the many attempts to put forth a book which should more or less tend to put a stop to the general confusion, the S. P. C. K. published a small collection in 1852. Three years afterwards (1855) it was issued in an enlarged form as *Psalms and Hymns*, to which, in 1863, an Appendix was added. But a new star had already risen, not particularly brilliant at its first appearance, still bright enough to attract the gaze of many, and draw forth the question—Is this the long-expected Hymnal for which we have been waiting, and which is destined to become the accepted hymn-book of the Anglican Church? This was *Hymns Ancient and Modern*, published in 1861, followed by an Appendix in 1868.

It would seem that Mr. Ellerton was by no means satisfied with either of these collections, for in 1869 he had thoughts of issuing, in conjunction with a few friends, a Hymnal independent of both, and a prospectus was drawn up and sent to London friends. But the energy displayed by the S. P. C. K. led him to reconsider his project. That Society, perceiving there was room for improvement in their Hymnal of 1863, proposed to add a

---

[1] As St. Jerome calls the numerous and unauthorized Latin translations of the New Testament in his day not *versiones* but *eversiones*.

comprehensive Appendix, but the proposal eventually resulted in the compilation of a new book under the title of *Church Hymns*. In reference to the proposed Appendix, Mr. Berdmore Compton, then on the Tract Committee, and editor of the Appendix of 1863, wrote as follows to Mr. Ellerton:—
"The Tract Committee have now completed their selection from those hymns which I have brought before them. They decided not to revise the existing book for the present, but to add a Supplement containing indeed a few *restorations* of hymns, which I thought absolutely necessary, they having been miserably curtailed in the present work. But the Supplement will mainly consist of new hymns, and will be large, probably about 220 in number." He then asks permission to include "Sing Alleluia forth in duteous praise," and "Saviour, again to Thy dear Name we raise," and for help with regard to discovering the authorship of other hymns.

In consequence of this move on the part of the Society, Mr. Ellerton abandoned his design of a separate work, and wrote to Mr. Berdmore Compton the following letter, valuable as setting forth the principles upon which, in the writer's opinion, a Hymnal should be compiled, principles which he himself applied to the various hymnals for which his advice or co-operation was sought :—

"*Crewe Green Parsonage, Crewe,*
"*July* 3, 1868.

"DEAR SIR,
"If I can be of any use to you in your task of improving the present S. P. C. K. Hymnal, I

shall have much pleasure in assisting so good a work.

"The system upon which you propose to act appears to me to be a very sound one; my only fear is lest alterations, which ought to be extensive ones in order to make the book as good as it is possible to make it, may be productive of serious inconvenience to the congregations which already use the Hymnal. I am strongly of opinion that, notwithstanding this, the effort you propose to make ought to be made; but still I fear that this objection may weigh very strongly with some members of the Tract Committee, and may hinder the free development of your plan.

"The existing Hymnal has the advantage of representing more than one school of English devotional theology, and the hymns which it contains are (in the later edition) presented in a less corrupt text than usual. It contains of course also many hymns of sterling worth and beauty; still a very careful examination of it last winter led me to the conclusion that it has some great defects.

"1. The area from which its sources are drawn is, I think, far too narrow. In its first form there were, I believe, no ancient hymns except the *Veni Creator;* now there are a certain number of Gallican ones, but very few representing the richest period of Latin hymnody, and no Greek ones at all. I feel sure that an examination of the best mediæval hymns will convince you that there is no real reason for their exclusion, any more than for that of the contemporary collects which fill so large a space in our Prayer-book. That which is unsuitable for the use of a Reformed Church ought of course, however fine the hymn, to be most rigidly excluded. I would not wish to see *Vexilla Regis* or *Pange lingua* admitted;[1] but there are many of our older hymns full of true congregational spirit, of simplicity, devotion, and depth, which would adorn any collection, and ought not to be left as the heritage of one particular school in the Church. This can, I think, be easily shown by a reference to such a book as Daniel's *Thesaurus Hymnologicus*, which I mention chiefly because Dr. Daniel is a most sincere Protestant. It would be worth the while of the Tract Committee to consider whether they might not secure good translations of some of these, and purchase the copyright of existing translations of others.

"This leads me to refer to another case, the absence of many popular hymns by living authors. Surely these would not refuse permission to the Society to print hymns of theirs, but I should most respectfully suggest to the Committee whether it would not be worth while, even as a money specu-

---

[1] This seems rather hard upon two of the very finest hymns of the Latin Church. Only certain parts are unsuitable for Anglican use. *Vexilla Regis* is represented in *Church Hymns* by Bishop Walsham How's "free imitation," "The Royal Banner is unfurled," and in *Hymns Ancient and Modern* by Dr. Neale's "The Royal Banners forward go." *Pange lingua* is also admitted into the former book as "Sing, my tongue, the Saviour's glory," by Rev. F. Pott, and into the latter as "Sing, my tongue, the glorious battle," by Dr. Neale, the eighth verse of which might well have been omitted, savouring as it does too strongly of mediæval sentimentalism.—H. H.

lation, to lay out a certain sum in the purchase of the copyright of others.

"Again, the great position of the S. P. C. K. gives it a matchless opportunity for investigating and using foreign hymnody. Germany is of course a very wide field, and the value for congregational use of German hymns is just now rather over-rated than under-rated, but still many, little known, might I think be found of service to us among especially the older German books. And the hymns of Denmark[1] and the *Chants Chrétiens* of Protestant France are almost or quite unknown to us here. Could not the Committee further communicate with the American Committee of Convention, who are at this moment engaged in preparing a new Hymnal for the Protestant Episcopal Church in the United States? I believe much matter worth examining might be obtained from that quarter.

"2. The character of too many of the hymns in the Society's present book is certainly a rather dull and colourless mediocrity. And as I am writing to you freely and confidentially, I hope you will forgive my making one remark. Of course I feel that the position of the S. P. C. K. in relation to existing divisions within the Church is a very difficult one, and requires the utmost wisdom and firmness in those who conduct it. But for a Society which seeks to be a Church and not a sectarian Society, there is always the danger of ignoring

---

[1] "Through the night of doubt and sorrow." Mr. Ellerton revised the Rev. S. Baring-Gould's translation of this favourite hymn from the Danish, and it was first sung in Crewe Green Church.—H. H.

truths out of the very fear of overstating them. It is easy to try to steer a safe course by omitting what will offend one or other school in the Church, but often the result is to leave a mere dull residuum of that which is certainly common to both, but which satisfies the faith of neither. Surely if each side (within due limits) were *represented* in a Hymnal, as it is in our Prayer-book, the object of wide and common use would be attained in a nobler and more effectual way, *e.g.* in the section on Holy Communion I would retain the old evangelical hymns of Watts and Doddridge which are justly dear to thousands; I would insert such hymns as "Thee we adore, O blessed Saviour, Thee," and one or two more which give that side of the doctrine which the Catechism and Communion Service express; and I would exclude such hymns as 119 and 122, which really satisfy neither school, and are simply vague. Forgive me if I have gone beyond the range to which I ought to have restricted myself.

"3. The number of hymns which ought to be excluded because too *private* for *public* worship is much less, I think, in the S. P. C. K. collection than in many others. The rule I would suggest is this: where a hymn expresses faith or feeling such as is, or ought to be, common to the whole or the greater part of the congregation, the mere occurrence of the singular number is no reason for excluding it. No one would banish 'Rock of Ages,' or 'Sun of my Soul'; on the other hand, such a hymn as Cowper's 'Oh for a closer walk with God' belongs to a particular state of mind, and ought not to be put into the lips of a whole congregation. It is therefore out of place in a Hymnal for congregational use.

"4. Another point of some importance seems to me to be the preponderance, at least, of hymns which are acts of worship—direct utterances of praise to God. I would not exclude all others; but there are in most Hymnals far too many sets of verses which are nothing more than religious meditations or paraphrases of texts, etc. In the Middle Ages this sort of verse was only allowed at one particular part of the service, viz. at the Prose or Sequence before the Gospel. Now if, without attempting to fix an arbitrary rule of this kind, the hymns under each head could be so grouped as to put first those of direct worship, and next such of a freer type as might be admitted (and that sparingly) into a general collection, I think the effect would be to guide the clergy better in selecting hymns, and to improve thereby the devotional character of our singing.

"I will close this long letter with a few suggestions as they occur to me:—

"*a.* Metrical Psalms are now so generally acknowledged to be a mistake, and the chanting Psalms so common, that I should like to abolish the title *Psalms and Hymns,* and to throw the selection from the Psalter into the general body of Hymns, which contains already a large number of paraphrases of Psalms, as indeed every good English hymnal must necessarily do. But probably this is scarcely practicable.[1]

---

[1] It is interesting thus to see a new thought feeling its way towards the light. What J. E. deemed scarcely practicable not thirty years ago is now generally adopted.—H. H.

"β. The section of 'General Hymns' ought to be much enlarged. It should also be furnished with a very copious and complete Index of Subjects. I should like to see that on 'Holy Communion' enlarged also, something on the plan of Mr. Jellicoe's *Songs of the Church* (you will not understand me as recommending the hymns he has selected) by a selection of Eucharistic hymns varying according to the seasons and greater Festivals.

"Something of this too would be good for morning and evening hymns; and we want a few for noon and afternoon to meet the increased division and multiplication of services.

"γ. May I say something about your Tune-Book? This of course would have to be revised simultaneously with the Hymnal. I have never yet met with a congregation that uses it freely, and with pleasure. It is grievously dull, the tunes often sadly unfitted to the hymns (*e.g.* how can 97 and 268 go to the same tune? and that a Sunday School song, originally written, as the composer's son himself told me, for 'Twinkle, twinkle, little star'!), and the whole book quite unworthy of the hymnal. I think a little effort might give the Society a Tune-Book of a far higher character. But again I fear I am travelling out of my province.

"I will only add one suggestion. Many clergymen (and laymen) would like to see an annotated edition of the Hymnal, with something of the history of the hymns and the names of the authors. I think this would sell well. Will you suggest it?

"Believe me, dear sir, yours faithfully,

"JOHN ELLERTON."

Apparently, however, plans widened as the work went on, and eventually Mr. Ellerton, Canon (now Bishop) Walsham How, and Mr. Berdmore Compton became the editors of a new work which was published in 1871, under the title of *Church Hymns*. The musical editorship was first undertaken by Mr. (now Sir Arthur) Sullivan, and afterwards by Mr. J. W. Elliott, then organist to Rev. R. Brown-Borthwick, Vicar of All Saints, Scarborough.

The labour, however, great as it was, in sifting and examining the existing stores of hymnody for this book, was accompanied by the far more arduous task of carrying out the scheme suggested in the foregoing letter, and preparing an Introduction which should contain an account of every hymn in the collection, its authorship and history, a work which Mr. Ellerton tells us in his Preface, " occupied pleasantly such leisure time as could be given to it during nine years of a busy life."

At all to realize the enormous labour which the work must have entailed, let the reader take the notes on one or two of the hymns, and he will at once see the wide acquaintance with the subject and the patient research among the stores, in many languages, of ancient and modern Hymnology, and the labour of verifying of authorities which it reveals. Take as a specimen the very first—Bishop Ken's morning hymn, " Awake, my soul, and with the sun." First comes a sketch of the career of the saintly Bishop, his birth, fellowship, consecration, deprivation, death, with places and dates. Then the first appearance of the hymn, its textual variations, and its claim to originality discussed. Or take one of the Latin hymns, *Pange lingua gloriosi proelium certaminis*, for instance. Here we have first the translation by the Rev. Francis Pott, and subsequent variations; then as it appears in the Roman Missal; next, its authorship and the correction of Bingham's error in ascribing it to Claudianus Mamertus; and lastly, a very interesting sketch of the life of its true author, Venantius Fortunatus.

Think of labour such as this spread over nearly six hundred hymns, the later portion of it written amid the falling shadows of advancing life, at a time when the over-work of a large suburban parish was pressing heavily upon him and undermining his health, at a time too of acute domestic bereavement, and we shall gain some idea of what it must have cost him to produce this standard work of hymnological research which, as *Notes and Illustrations to the Hymns*,[1] forms the introductory portion of the magnificent folio edition of *Church Hymns* issued in 1881.

For this Hymnal eleven original hymns were composed, and nine translations.

1. "Another day begun." Feb. 13, 1871.
2. "Behold us, Lord, a little space." p. 54.
3. "In the Name which earth and heaven." p. 57.
4. "King Messiah, long expected." p. 55.
5. "King of Saints, to Whom the number." p. 56.
6. "Mary at the Master's feet." p. 56.
7. "Now returns the awful morning." For Good

---

[1] It was afterwards proposed to publish these *Notes* in a small volume separate from the Hymnal, which would largely have increased its usefulness.

Friday. Stated in *Notes and Illustrations* to have been re-written in 1858 for a class of school-children from a hymn by Joseph Anstice,[1] and largely altered for *Church Hymns*. Verses 3 and 4, representing respectively Professor Anstice's third and second verses, are all that is left of the original, and these are much varied, so the hymn may be placed among Mr. Ellerton's original compositions.

8. "O Lord of life and death, we come." p. 55.

9. "O Son of God, our Captain of salvation." p. 55.

10. "Thou in Whose Name the two or three." p. 56.

11. "We sing the glorious conquest." p. 55.

TRANSLATIONS.

12. "Bride of Christ, whose glorious warfare." *Sponsa Christi quae per orbem.* Considered by Mr. Mearns "one of the finest of the more recent French Sequences."[2] The author is Jean Baptiste de Contes, who became Dean of Paris in 1647.

This fine All Saints' Day hymn appears in a shorter form in *Church Hymns*. It was re-cast in 1887 with considerable variations and improvements for the complete edition of *Hymns Ancient and Modern*, 1889, where the original title "Bride of Christ," etc., is restored.

---

[1] He became Professor of Classical Literature at King's College, London, at the age of 22, and died at Torquay in 1836, aged 28. (Julian, *Dictionary of Hymnology*.)

[2] *Dictionary of Hymnology*, p. 1081. See p. 134.

13. "From east to west, from shore to shore." *A solis ortûs cardine.* By Coelius Sedulius (*cir.* 450), a poet of whom next to nothing is known, save what can be gathered from two letters. This translation is made from a fragment of a long alphabetical poem, another cento from which begins "How vain the cruel Herod's fear" (*Hymns Ancient and Modern*, 75).

14. "Giver of the perfect gift." *Summi largitor praemii.* Attributed, but without sufficient evidence, to St. Gregory the Great.

15. "Joy! because the circling year." *Beata nobis gaudia.* Ascribed, but like the last upon insufficient evidence, to St. Hilary of Poitiers. In the Mozarabic Breviary it is a Whit-Sunday hymn. Dr. Hort was associated with Mr. Ellerton in this translation. 1870.

16. "Morn of morns, the best and first." *Die dierum omnium.* Based partly on the translation by the Rev. Isaac Williams. The original Latin is by Charles Coffin, Rector of the University of Paris (1718). Most of his hymns appeared in the Paris Breviary of 1736; this one is for Lauds on Sundays from Candlemas to Septuagesima (Julian, and *Notes and Illustrations*).

17. "O Strength and Stay, upholding all creation." *Rerum Deus tenax vigor.* The original has been attributed to St. Ambrose, but it is not one of the twelve accounted his by the Benedictine editors. Among the translators of this hymn are found the names of many of our greatest hymnologists, but this version soars high above them all, the second stanza being inexpressibly lovely—

> " Grant to life's day a calm unclouded ending,
> An eve untouch'd by shadows of decay,
> The brightness of a holy death-bed blending
> With dawning glories of the eternal day."

The third verse is original. This was the closing hymn sung at Mr. Ellerton's funeral. 1870.

18. "Oh come, all ye faithful." 1871. *Adeste fideles, laeti triumphantes;* the famous Christmas hymn of the Western Church, p. 57. Like *Veni Creator Spiritus* and many another great hymn, the authorship is lost.

There is little to choose between this version and what might almost be called the *authorized* one by Canon Oakley in *Hymns Ancient and Modern*. The metre is more regular, and consequently there are fewer slurs in the singing.

19. "On this the day when days began." 1868. *Primo dierum omnium.* For early morning, on Sunday. p. 48.

20. "To the Name that speaks salvation." 1871. " The Name of Jesus" (Aug. 17). This Commemoration was removed at the Reformation from the Second Sunday after the Epiphany to Aug. 7.[1] p. 59.

In addition to these twenty hymns and translations written for this Hymnal, it contains six previously composed, but published now for the first time in a collection, and thirteen previously published—thirty-nine in all, no small contribution from one individual pen.

---

[1] Blunt's *Annotated Prayer-book.*

THE CHILDREN'S HYMN-BOOK

In 1877 an intimation reached Mr. Ellerton, through a friend, that Mrs. Carey Brock, to whom the acting editorship of the new *Children's Hymn-Book* had been entrusted, was anxious to consult him with regard to its compilation. He immediately wrote to that lady, not only placing at her service any of his own hymns, but also offering any help he could give in the preparation of this important work.

This branch of hymnody was by no means new to him. Even when curate of Brighton he had compiled his *Hymns for Schools and Bible Classes*, and while at Hinstock had joined Canon Walsham How in editing for the Society for Promoting Christian Knowledge their *Children's Hymns*, contributing to it seven hymns of his own.

It need hardly be said that this offer of assistance was as gratefully accepted as it was generously made. He had offered to take the subordinate part of examining such hymns as might be submitted to him and offering suggestions, but the proprietors knew his value too well not to covet for the book his co-operation, as one of the revisers in conjunction with Bishops Walsham How and

Oxenden. In reply to this request he writes—
"When you did me the favour to write to me about your very important and interesting work, and I expressed my willingness to help, I did not think of your naming me as one of the publicly avowed revisers, and I should perhaps have shrunk both from the honour and the responsibility of the task. All I thought was, that as I happen to have a pretty large collection of children's hymns, and some little experience, I might have been able to add to your materials, and to suggest *gaps* for filling up. However, I will not draw back now, as you are pleased to wish me to occupy so difficult a post."

One of the first things to decide in the compilation of the work was what age of childhood was to be provided for by it, and on this point Mr. Ellerton's opinion was quite clear. "I am quite of your mind," he writes to Mrs. Carey Brock, "that we do not want it to be a book of baby hymns, still less of hymns written down for 'infant minds' by people who are well-meaning, but do not understand children. By all means have a large infusion of strong and vigorous hymns such as are generally used in church; *so long as the sentiments they convey are such as children can be expected to appreciate.* If you do not make that limitation what is the *raison d'être* of a *children's* book as distinguished on the one hand from an *infant* book, and on the other from an adult book?" In another letter he says—"I think that you will be obliged to fix a limit, say, the usual age for Confirmation, and determine not to have a hymn that is above the comprehension or beyond the spiritual experience (which is *far* more important) of the average Confirmation candidate. I know, of course, that many young people, especially well-educated girls, enjoy at thirteen or fourteen such hymns as 'Lead, kindly Light,' or 'Abide with me,' or 'Lord of our life, and God of our salvation,' but the question is rather, Are these hymns good to be put before the *average* child, even at fourteen? Well-educated (I mean *spiritually* well-educated) girls can get the books in which these hymns are to be found. But to me it is simple *misery* to hear a noisy Sunday School singing 'Abide with me'—I don't mean a class of upper girls; I know there are many exceptions. So there are with adults. I knew a costermonger's wife who was sustained through a terrible operation by repeating to herself over and over again Novalis'[1] wondrous hymn, 'What had I been if Thou wert not;' but it does not follow that I should put the hymn in a book for the poor."

As the report of the forthcoming book spread many persons volunteered their effusions, which Mr. Ellerton characterized as "some of them valuable in themselves, but *unreal* for children; others, and these the worst, written for children by people who desire that children should undergo certain religious experiences, easily simulated, but most perilous to the simplicity and honesty of their relations with God." "I think," he writes, "many

---

[1] This was the *nom de plume* of G. F. Philipp von Hardenberg, d. 1801. The translation is by Miss Winkworth (James Mearns, *Dict. of Hymnology*).

a hymn not meant for children would not be at all out of place in your book. The only difficulty about these is that you must suppose children will use the hymn-book ordinarily and in the church they attend, and so become familiar with many hymns they will love all their lives; and you want the space for hymns which deal especially with the thoughts and ways of young people, and give them the spiritual help to realize and to love Divine things, which at their time of life, and with the temptations of opening life, they really need."

At last, in 1881, after years of thought and labour and prayer, the book was published. The Preface, written by Mr. Ellerton himself, embodies many expressions we have already met with in his letters. In it he writes as follows:—" The object of this collection is to provide a hymnal for the young, in which, whilst a high standard of excellence and a healthy religious tone are preserved, every hymn shall be, as regards the sentiments conveyed and the expressions used, within their possible experience, and, as far as may be, within their comprehension. In adhering to this rule, the compilers have necessarily been obliged to exclude from their pages many hymns which, however valuable and beautiful in themselves, it would be impossible for children to use without a simulation of religious experience dangerous to the simplicity and truthfulness of their relations with God. At the same time, they have not forgotten the necessity of making children familiar in childhood with such hymns as they can love and value all their lives."

Such labour, such learning, such research, so

much prayerful thought bestowed by Mr. Ellerton and his fellow revisers upon *The Children's Hymn-Book* have been abundantly rewarded. **The** work was immediately recognized as supplying **a want** long felt in the Church. The latest and **highest** authority on the subject, Julian's *Dictionary of Hymnology*, says it " has at once taken **the leading** place among Church books, and contains **not only** the best hymns hitherto published, but new **hymns,** some of which are of equal value."

THE CHURCH OF ENGLAND HYMN-BOOK

IN addition to the laborious and difficult task of acting as reviser, we might almost say editor, of the foregoing important hymnals, *Church Hymns*, and the *Children's Hymn-Book*, Mr. Ellerton's opinion and advice were much sought by the compilers of other books. At this time the Rev. Prebendary Godfrey Thring was preparing for publication his *Church of England Hymn-Book*, and many were the letters which passed between the two poets with regard to it. It is true that Mr. Ellerton had no hand in the construction of the work, for, as Mr. Thring tells me, the whole book was entirely thought out and finished before he saw it, he seeing only the proof copy just before it was published, and too late to make any alteration in it. As specimens of the correspondence between the two friends, the two subjoined letters are interesting, the one showing the high value which Mr. Thring placed upon his friend's criticisms, the other containing the writer's estimate of some well-known hymns, and of one of his own.

> "*Hornblotton Rectory,*
> "*Castle Cary, Somerset.*
> "*Oct.* 17, 1879.

"MY DEAR MR. ELLERTON,

"Oh dear! I am inclined to say. I wish I could have shown you the proof-sheets before the work had gone so far, for some of your remarks are very valuable, and you cannot think how I appreciate your kindness in taking all the trouble you have done, and even now I shall be able to do something towards repairing some of the omissions. But unfortunately Skeffington sent out his circular stating 'This day,' etc., so that, as he says, he is receiving daily orders for specimen copies and cannot supply them, and is urging me on to publish at once, and this is impossible, for even now, with all the revisions that it has been through, there are heaps of blunders, and in my state of health I am overburdened. This morning I have difficulty in gathering my thoughts. The book, however, is gone so far that I cannot put in or omit hymns now without incurring too great an expense, unless I can manage to get them into the same space. I will go through some of your chief criticisms as well as I can.

"First—morning hymns. I see I have marked some of the hymns you mention, and am very sorry that I did not put in 6 (Wesley's), 'Forth in Thy Name.' I hardly know how I came to omit this; only for the last three or four years I have had to move about in search of health, and at one time I found that I had mislaid or lost several selected hymns, and I always feared lest I might have lost some of importance, and I rather think this must have been one of them. The other two (3 and 5) I might have had, but I have a large selection, and I do not think have lost much here. 815, Kennedy's *Hymnologia*, I have referred to, and find that I have cut out some hymn, and with it all but the first verse of the above; but that I do not think much of, if the rest of the hymn is not of a higher standard.

"24. It is too late now to revert to 'Towards the eve.' You are right, though, the other reads better. I fear I did not compare this with Chandler; I could only get a copy lent me for a time.

"26. You are quite right about 'wishing' being the consequence, not the cause. Perhaps you are rather hard in some of your other remarks on the poetic mind! Still I had perhaps better have omitted the hymn altogether; but again, too late.

"42. I cannot recollect having shortened this hymn. I fancy you must have sent me this in MS., otherwise I do not know how I got it; but how came it to be altered in *Church Hymns?* I hope I have the proper text, for it is better than that in *Church Hymns*. I have made a note of your alterations; it is a beautiful hymn, one of if not your best.

"'Alleluia! fairest morning,' *Ch. Hymns* 38. A good hymn, but I fear it is too late, and I have, I think, a very good and sufficient selection for Sundays. I should, however, have inserted it had I known it sooner. You do not state who it is by.[1]

---

[1] It is a translation from *Hymns from the Land of Luther*. The original is by Jonathan Krause (*Dict. of Hymnology*, p. 633).

It is not, however, of sufficient consequence to pay a large sum to admit it now.

"85. 'Gird thee at the martyr's shrine.' You are rather hard upon this. I don't think that we need be quite as realistic as your sarcastic remarks would imply.

"88. Litanies are difficult matters. I thought myself fortunate in getting one on each of the most desirable subjects that were not rubbish. If people require more there are plenty of penny books, such as Pollock's (his is the best), and none others that I have seen come up to the literary standard which I fixed in my own mind . . . .[1] Only those who, like myself, have tried, can have any idea of the labour of such an undertaking. I hope you will appreciate the Indexes, for those are a work of themselves.

"Ever very truly yours,
"GODFREY THRING."

"*The Rectory, Barnes,*
"*Feb.* 10, 1881.

"MY DEAR THRING,

"My conduct to you has been perfectly disgraceful, and no apology can cover it. But I have been very busy with my two bantlings, *Church Hymns* and the *Children's Hymn-Book*, which are both just ripe for publication, and will be out, I suspect, simultaneously.

"Well, now to your letters. You were quite right to abuse my Purification Hymn; I know it is very bad. Don't be angry with me for not doing

---

[1] Part of this letter is lost.

an Easter Eucharistic Hymn; I always use (and rejoice in) 'At the Lamb's high feast we sing;' but even without that I *could* not add a mediocre one to the stock of really fine Easter hymns we possess. Don't you like the rough force too of Luther's 'Christ Jesus lay in Death's strong bands'? I do think *that* is so full of Easter life and joy and strength!

"I don't know anything about F. S. Pierpont[1] (so spelt, I think) except as a contributor to Orby Shipley's *Lyra Eucharistica*, and a layman. If you have *Lyra Eucharistica*, and intend to use 'For the beauty of the earth,' look at it as it is there. The text in *Church Hymns* is very corrupt. But I added nothing; Compton, I think, sent us the hymn. Unluckily I have not got the enlarged edition of *Lyra Eucharistica*, and it is not in the first.

"I don't think C. Wesley's hymn you enclose is one of the very best, it seems to me rather heavy, and lacking in vitality—an unusual fault with his earlier hymns. But very likely I may be prejudiced by my liking for some of his other Eucharistic hymns.

"The doxology to 'Angels from the realms of glory' we took from Chope's *Book of Carols;* I thought it was a good finish to the hymn.

"I like rather the 'Alleluia dulce carmen' coming before Septuagesima. For though, of course, the change does not really come till Lent, there always has been a *subordinate* change at Septuagesima.

---

[1] F. S. Pierpoint, author of the favourite hymn, "For the beauty of the earth," *Children's Hymn-Book*, 256.

The Christmas cycle of festivals comes to an end with Purification, and of Sundays with the last after Epiphany. Then the days are reckoned backwards from Easter. Septuagesima is a new start, and in places where they change altar-cloths I suppose the Lenten colours always begin at Septuagesima; and it seems to me the hymns ought to be arranged on a similar cycle. Historically, too, the hymn is a memorial of the fact that 'Alleluia' was discontinued when Septuagesima began; the substitute being 'Praise ye,' etc. A curious thing, by the way, that the Hebrew words should have to our fathers a festal *ring* about them which the vernacular translation did not have. But I suppose it was the association with the triumphal songs of Revelation.

"I am so very sorry to hear of your watery calamities. We have been comparatively unscathed, not quite, but nearly so. Kind remembrances to all.

"Ever yours sincerely,
"JOHN ELLERTON."

The Church of England Hymn-Book, adapted to the Daily Services of the Church throughout the Year, was published in 1882. Dr. Julian speaks of it in terms of the highest commendation, higher indeed than of any of its competitors; and had not *Hymns Ancient and Modern* been before it in the field, and already taken deep root, it is more than possible that Mr. Thring's book would have become the leading Hymnal in the Church of England.

It has been seen, then, that between 1876 and

1884, that is, the eight years of his residence at Barnes, Mr. Ellerton completed *Church Hymns*, with its *Notes and Illustrations;* the *Children's Hymn-Book;* to say nothing of the assistance he rendered to other hymnals, especially the *Hymnal Companion* and *Hymns Ancient and Modern*. When it is remembered that all this, and much more, was done, not in the quiet leisure of some cathedral close, or even of a country living, but amid the incessant calls and interruptions of a populous suburban parish, where the writer of these lines was his only curate, entailing long night vigils, for the day gave him but scant time for literary work, it is no marvel that at last he broke down under the burden. A severe attack of pleurisy in the cold spring of 1884 completely prostrated him, and for a time the issue was very doubtful. By God's mercy, however, he rose from his bed of danger, but he knew that he could no longer work as he had worked. He resigned the Rectory of Barnes, and leaving England in the autumn, sought rest and health first at Veytaux, near Chillon, overlooking the lake of Geneva, finally accepting the winter chaplaincy of Pegli.

CHAPTER V

1884, 1885

SWITZERLAND AND ITALY

Veytaux—Pegli—An Italian Poor-House

IN the autumn of 1884 Mr. Ellerton left England to seek rest and recreation in Switzerland. His first stay was at Veytaux at the extreme eastern end of the Lake of Geneva, near Montreux, to the winter chaplaincy of which he had been appointed by the S. P. G. There, amid lovely scenery, and health-restoring breezes from mountain and lake, he soon recovered much of his former strength and cheerfulness. With the burden of Barnes off his shoulders, and feeling that his many years of unremitting labours in hymnology were bearing good fruit in *Church Hymns* and the *Children's Hymn-Book*, both of which had been successfully launched, he felt that he had earned his holiday, and was determined to enjoy it thoroughly.

His first impressions of Veytaux may be gathered from the following extract from a letter to one of his sons at home :—" As for the walks, they are endless, and ever fresh in deliciousness. Each day reveals some new vision of mountain glory, and the very road into Montreux is never twice alike. Moreover, there are charming groups of picturesque châlets, fountains, wood, and rock at every turn; but to say that is only to say that this is Switzerland. There is, too, a novelty about all manners and customs that is always amusing. The people are neither bureau-ridden nor priest-ridden, nor drilled into obedience; there is a curious '*Fais-ce-que-vouldras*' way of doing among them, and yet a great deal of accuracy and regularity in all business matters, which I suppose finds its parallel in America, but which is new to me: *e.g.* Chillon is the 'Wandsworth Gaol' of the canton; but being also a 'Tower of London,' and a great show place, people walk in and out from morning till night, and especially on Sundays, when all nationalities lounge into the prison chapel when service is going on. One of the 'prisoners of Chillon,' probably a Swiss Mr. Sykes, objected to attending church in consequence of not liking his 'uniform' to be noticed by strangers; whereupon the Governor considerately lent him a Sunday suit!"

The following charming letter will also be read with interest; it is Veytaux seen through a poet's eyes :—

"*Veytaux, Oct.* 28, 1884.

"MY DEAR ——

". . . . As to the place itself, it is indescribable. How can I give you an impression of these hills of the Chablais, St. Francis de Sales' old diocese—the 'Alps of Savoy' as they have been called, which confront me every time I lift my eyes from the paper; and which, whether glowing in the morning sun, or veiled and wreathed with folds of soft white cloud, or gleaming in the moonlight, or dark and stern with their tempest-scarred precipices and streaks and sheets of snow, are ever changing, ever beautiful, ever fresh to us? How can I tell you of the view up the lake, with colours indescribable—the grey old castle rising sheer out of the bluest of water, with little white waves washing its walls—the wooded hills, in such hues of scarlet, purple, crimson, and gold as no paint-brush could draw—the stern pine-clad ridge behind—the Rhone valley opening up at the head of the lake, with the central distance filled with the most beautiful of all the mountains, the seven-topped 'mystery,' wonderful 'Dent du Midi'? How can I draw to you the strange contrast as we turn to the right, and look westward down the lake, of vineyard and white villas, and spires, and châlets hanging on the green hill-side, sunny smiling land edging the great lake far into the dim distance, where we just catch the long grey ridge of the Jura—the barrier that parts us from the north, and home, and all familiar things? Or how can I tell you of the hundreds of bits of beauty which every walk opens out, quaint villages with their châlets hanging one above another, women nursing their babies in the carved wooden balconies, or carrying them strapped to a pillow in the glory of their Sunday best—the roadside fountains with their tiny troughs of ever-running and deliciously clear water, with two or three old cronies gossiping and washing their linen around them; the old church on a magnificent rock, which goes sheer down from the churchyard wall; its churchyard planted beautifully, and with seats commanding—oh! *such* a view; the roses and fuchsias and scarlet salvias still in full bloom, in the many gardens which hang on the hill-side. No, it is only heaping words together that mean nothing. I don't think I can make any one fancy it.

"I send you the French hymn[1] which I have copied out from the hymn-book used in the Swiss National Church of this canton. It is by Vinet, the greatest man by far of modern French and Swiss Protestantism, whose words, you may remember, are the striking motto of Maurice's *Theological Essays*. It was a great comfort to me when I found it on my arrival here, very depressed and weary, hardly able to find comfort even from Nature, in the glory which she wears here. K—— has heard from C——, who seems to be full of the influence of that wonderful Rome. Shall I ever see it? I don't know. Even St. Paul wanted to 'see Rome.'"

From Veytaux he was summoned, evidently much against his will, to take the winter chaplaincy at Pegli, near Genoa. The following characteristic letter to his friend, Professor Henry Attwell of Barnes, shows that although he would rather have stayed at Veytaux, he was quite disposed to make the best of and enjoy to the utmost his new surroundings. To be on Italian ground was a new experience to him, and with his mind so full as it was of power to appreciate everything that was

[1] Beginning, "Pourquoi reprendre, O Père tendre,
　　Les biens dont Tu m'as couronné?"

beautiful in nature and art, and every historical association, it is no wonder that when once settled, he enjoyed the change thoroughly.

> "*Casa Puppo, Pegli, Genova, Italia,*
> "*Jan.* 21, 1885.

"MY DEAR PROFESSOR,

"The snowstorm which has blocked Mont Cenis has not only kept our children from joining us, but has kept us for some days separate from all English letters and papers. Last night, however, a telegram reached us from Veytaux, and I hope that this letter will make its way to you in a day or two without unusual delay. Let it bring you not only all good wishes for 1885, but most cordial thanks to you for your most welcome New Year's letter, and for the valued MS. from Max Müller, which has caused you so much kind trouble; and of which more anon.

"You will be glad to hear that we are safely lodged on a 'piano' in a respectable Italian house, not exactly in sight of the Mediterranean, at least not on its shore, but in full southern sunshine, and with many elements of interest and enjoyment. We have pretty views both of the sea and the Apennines from the Piano above. The S. P. G. Secretary summoned me hither in rather a headlong way from Veytaux, and at first there was everything to make the contrast emphatically disagreeable. We came from those ever-delightful mountains to the suburbs of a busy Italian city,[1] from châlets picturesque in spite of themselves,

[1] *i.e.* Genoa.

where every shed and every fountain was a picture, to rows of hideously-painted and colour-washed tall houses; from a very happy and congenial group of English exiles, whom Christmas had drawn together into a very pleasant intimacy, to a huge barrack of a German hotel, built for some hundred and twenty, and holding only the odd twenty, among whom we were literally the only English—I had almost said the only English-*speaking* people, but for some pleasant Dutch folk who took to us rather than the Germans, and talked English to us; from a large congregation in church and cheerful services to a little empty church of our own. But all that is over; and the gloomy weather, which made us feel as if the Sea of all history met us with a scowl, has given place to sunshine, which, despite the 'tramontana,' makes us feel that we are south of the Alps. And as all our strange surroundings become by degrees familiar, we feel that it is quite possible we may grow so to like them as to be quite sorry when we have to leave. Genoa itself is irresistible in its attractions; the talk about its dazzling beauty may be rather 'tall,' and its palazzi may represent a good deal of tasteless luxury; but still there they are, these streets of marble buildings, all teeming to this hour with busy life; for the great names of past Genoese history are still to-day the names of men who build factories, launch ships, speculate on companies, and amass wealth to an extent which rivals what one hears of American millionaires. And really if Jay Gould lived in a house built for his family in Queen Elizabeth's days, hung with portraits by Van Dyck of seventeenth century Goulds, one might—inconsistently perhaps, but excusably—think his money-making a little more respectable. But anyhow Italy—at least this Northern Italy—is all alive. People who have known it for thirty years say the change is simply marvellous. The beggary, the rags, the bare feet, the lazy lounging, the filth of which one has heard—I rub my eyes and ask where they are? On an average one meets two beggars a day; everybody has good boots and stockings; there are handsome State schools close to this, filled with children—schools where at stated hours the clergy are allowed to teach. Our lodgings are delightfully clean—'heating' quite superfluous! the cookery better than at Veytaux, and I don't think that six francs per head a day, which includes two bottles of excellent wine, is extortionate. Of course there are drawbacks; the villas of the rich, and the big barracks of houses in which the working people live are more hideous than can be conceived; the universal practice of hanging out of window all day every shred of clothing not on the person is wholesome, but not even picturesque; and of course one's nose is occasionally as much annoyed as one's eyes. And Pegli is not exactly a Paradise, though my church is overshadowed by a palm instead of a yew-tree, and oranges hang from the trees in every cottage garden in golden glory. I hope we shall be very happy when we are all together again, till we are released from duty here, and perhaps enabled to take one peep at Florence before coming north again.

"I was saddened and shocked at the instant of

leaving Veytaux by the news of Bishop Jackson's sudden death, for all my personal recollections of him are most happy. Inconspicuous as a public man, he yet won the deep respect of men like Tait and Lightfoot, indeed something like enthusiastic affection from the latter, and in his home circle, and among his neighbours, he always seemed a most perfect Christian gentleman. I wish the Premier well over his hard task of selecting his successor; perhaps by this time it is all over.

"I have very much enjoyed the extracts from Max Müller which you have been good enough to copy for me. The tribute to Stanley is touching and interesting, and I am sure describes what he was from Max Müller's point of view. The earlier letter is also most interesting. All such papers help one to understand and to love many who are far off from us now in thought, but who will doubtless one day come from East and West and sit down at the Eternal Feast of the Kingdom of God, while some of us children of the Kingdom find ourselves in darkness after all. If I fail to see that Max Müller realizes the absolute uniqueness of our Lord, a uniqueness which I think myself nothing but the Catholic hypothesis accounts for, yet I feel he has grasped some of the leading ideas of Christ's teaching as to the Father and Himself, with a force all the more striking because he approaches the question from his own special point of view, that of the historian of religious ideas. And he is right about the perpetual danger of orthodox people lapsing into Tritheism, as well as about the unreality and baseness of much orthodox devotional language addressed to Christ, language which paves the way for parallel addresses to Mary, such as *In te salus nostra est*, which is under a crowned Madonna not many yards from this house. This comes of forgetting the teaching of Christ's own prayer.

"With love to Mrs. Attwell and all your circle,
"Believe me ever, my dear Professor,
"Affectionately yours,
"JOHN ELLERTON.

"Scraps from London papers always most welcome—above all in this land."

The following beautiful poem—not a hymn in the strict sense of the word—included in his *Hymns Original and Translated*, is inserted here as showing how his heart overflowed with love and gratitude to his Heavenly Master for the rest and peace he was enjoying.

HYMN OF THE WORKER ON A HOLIDAY.

Here in this peaceful time and place of rest,
I lift my thoughts, dear Master, unto Thee;
Seeking in calm repose upon Thy breast
Some gracious pledge that Thou art come with me.

Thou too hast known the thronging of the crowd,
The 'many coming' as the hours went by,
The weary head in deep exhaustion bowed,
The broken sleep, the sudden midnight cry.

All these were Thine, O Bearer of our woes;
No rest for Thee our suffering manhood gave;
Through Thy three years no leisure for repose,
Till that last Sabbath in Thy garden-grave!

Yet Thy compassion knows my feebler frame,
Mine is the rest my Master would not take;
And if my work indeed be in Thy Name,
These quiet hours are hallowed for Thy sake.

Thou art with me; as when Thy Twelve returned
And poured their tale of labours at Thy Feet,
Thy pitying Eye their weariness discerned,
Thy Love provided them some still retreat.

With Thee they climbed the gorge whence Jordan falls,
Saw Hermon's snowpeaks glow with dawn's red fire,
And watched, beneath the heathen's broken walls,
The blue sea whitening on the shores of Tyre.

Thou lovedst Thy fair land; the solitudes
Of her grey hills, fit home for musings high;
Spring with her glowing flowers and nestling broods,
The moonlit garden and the sunset sky.

Nor these alone; for Thou didst condescend
The joys of human fellowship to share,
The simple welcome of some village friend,
Mary's deep gladness, Martha's loving care.

In toil, in leisure, I may learn of Thee;
Keep Thee beside me in my mountain walk,
Set to Thy Name the music of the sea,
And open all my heart in voiceless talk.

So when Thy call shall bid me to return
With strength renewed, to labour in my place,
My lips shall overflow, my heart shall burn
With new revealings of Thy boundless grace.

Pegli, Feb. 1885.

While in the neighbourhood of Genoa Mr. Ellerton often paid visits to that city. He knew that in the Poor-house there was to be seen Michael Angelo's incomparable *Pietà*, and thus he describes it :—

"AN ITALIAN POOR-HOUSE

"High on the hillside above the city of Genoa, surrounded by broad roads and wealthy private houses, stands a stately building, which might be a Royal Palace. Its stairs, its pavements, its long pillared corridors, are of white marble; from the broad terrace in front you look down upon the great harbour crowded with vessels of all countries, upon the lighthouses, the churches, and busy streets of the famous 'City of Palaces,' and then the encircling arms of blue mountains clasping the bluer sea. Over the door is a shield with that cross of St. George which it is said England borrowed from Genoa in the old crusading days. On a marble tablet a long Latin inscription tells, in rather pompous language, what levelling of rock and filling up of valley and diverting the channel of the mountain stream were undergone at the expense of the citizens before this splendid building could be raised, and of the vast sums it cost to make it what we see it. Inside, the halls and passages and landings are filled with statues and busts of the greatest and wealthiest of Genoese merchant princes and prelates. Yet no king or duke or noble ever inhabited it. These men are commemorated here because they were benefactors to the poor. This marble palace is the proud city's home for her paupers. In England we should call it a workhouse; in Italy they call it by a kindlier name, the '*Albergo dei Poveri*,' that is, the Hostelry or Inn of the Poor.

"I enter with the friend who has undertaken to show me over the building; he tells me the strange story of its erection.

"Some two hundred years ago there was a great famine in the city of Genoa. Multitudes died, and whole families begged their bread starving in the streets. The compassion of the city was aroused; it was determined to provide a home for the poor, where for ever after they should be lodged, fed, and clothed. Large sums were contributed, and the site was cleared after the fashion described in the inscription. When all was ready to begin the building, another grievous calamity befell Genoa— a terrible pestilence. People died faster than ground could be provided to bury them. There was no available space outside the walls but this which was already set apart for the Home of the Poor. This ground then became the last resting-place of the plague-stricken. Nine thousand corpses were buried upon the hill-side. Years passed on, and at last it was thought safe to resume the work; and over the resting-place of the dead arose, after long delay, the marble Palace of the Poor.

"It is a great square with a cross intersecting it. One side is set apart for men, and the other for women. It is planned for 1800 inmates, and about 1200 are now inhabiting it. They are admitted upon the recommendation of some respectable person,— about this no difficulty is made; and once admitted, they are provided for till death, from the funds of the Institution. There is little comfort, according to our English notions; and in winter the cold is intense, for Genoa is scourged by bitter north winds from the mountains, and no provision is made for warming the vast passages and stairs. In summer it must be pleasant enough; and the old men and women sun themselves, as Italians love to do, in the many balconies on which their windows open, and look out upon the gardens, and the city, and the mountains, and the sea.

"In the centre of the whole building is the chapel. Thither my friend led me, saying, 'There is one thing only which you must look at here; keep your mind undistracted for that.' So we stopped before an altar, behind which, let into the wall, is a circle of marble about two feet across. Before this we stood long, hushed and awe-struck. Two heads only, that of the dead Saviour and the mourning Mother bending over Him, as she supports Him on her arm. Her face is very quiet, there is no theatrical display of grief; she is not meant to attract you by her beauty, though a beauty beyond description seems to pass from the face to your heart as you look. The Christ lies dead; the damp of death seems almost to stand upon His brow, but all pain and agony are passed out of it. It seems as if the mother's face had grown calm by long gazing into His. The sword has pierced her soul, but already the wound has begun to heal. It is not yet Hope, but it is perfect Peace even in the deepest depth of her darkness. The accompanying illustration, from a photograph taken from the original, may help to illustrate my description—it can do no more.

"The history of this piece of sculpture is unknown, except that it belonged to a great Cardinal long ago, and that at his death his family gave it to the Home of the Poor. It is often said to be by the great Michael Angelo, but no one really knows. The Italians have had a careful copy made of it, and placed in the new Museum of Michael Angelo's works at Florence. In England I am afraid the original would have been sold for the benefit of the Hospital Funds, and the copy left in the chapel. But it is not so here. And surely of all the gifts that in her proud and ostentatious munificence this city of palaces has lavished upon her poor, one of the kindest and tenderest was this, the setting up where these old men and women creep in daily to pray to God, this precious memorial of the sorrow which none other sorrow was like, which has purified, hallowed, and transformed all other, to turn it at last into joy."[1]

In April Mr. Ellerton and his family left Pegli, but before turning homeward he seized the opportunity of visiting Florence. The impressions which that city—itself a poem—made upon his poetic mind are best gathered from his own words in the following letter:—

To a Friend in Venice.

"*Florence, April* 22, 1885.

"MY DEAR ——

" * * * * Yes, it is nice to think that you and I clasp hands in Italy, and hear the same soft language, and see the same dark faces, full of pathos or mischief, or anything but stolid

[1] *Dawn of Day*, Oct. 1885.

content or dull weariness; and see great buildings
and famous pictures, and are living through the
Past of great historic cities, under this cloudless
sky and this bright moonlight. And as I saw
sunset on Fiesole and on Giotto's Tower, and the
lovely Campanile, where the old 'Vacca' of the
Palazzo Vecchio still hangs, so you saw it perhaps
on St. George of the Seaweed, or on the doves of
St. Mark, and the long fretwork of the Ducal
Palace. How shall we match the two Queens
against one another—Arno against Adria! But I
won't give up my Lady of the Flowers even for
your Queen of the Sea! Never was so fair a gem
in so beautiful a setting. You will be able to tell
how impossible it is to describe, when one is simply
overwhelmed with all one sees. To sit in the awful
Baptistery where Dante was baptized, and look up
at the great mosaics of Christ enthroned, and the
dead rising to judgment, as his baby eyes saw
them; to see sunrise and sunset and moonlight on
Giotto's Tower—such a wonder of colour as nothing
can paint; to go from church to church covered
with those great mosaics which take hours to
appreciate—one had rather say *days;* to see with
one's own eyes the places sacred to such immortal
memories; to stand in the Loggia dei Lanzi and
think of that awful Palm Sunday, and that still
more awful June day in the great square below;
to people with one multitude the vast area of the
empty Duomo where the Prophet[1] so often spoke;
to stand by the graves of Pico and Galileo, and
Antonino, and Michael Angelo—no! there can be

[1] Savonarola.

no place like Florence. And then there are the Galleries, of which we have as yet seen only three or four rooms of one, and that contains more precious things than I ever saw before. I really don't know where to begin. I think, however, some distinct impressions are coming upon me.

"First, of the wonderful greatness of Giotto. He is as saintly as Fra Angelico, and far more human. Oh that you could see his fresco in Santa Croce of the spirit of St. John rising up to join the Blessed One so many years parted from him. The friends and disciples are looking into the open grave, in quiet, peaceful sorrow, knowing all is well, but feeling that the last of the Apostles is gone, and the first age of the Church is over. But one looks up in faith, and this is what he sees: the old man's form is being drawn upward, with such a look of peace and joy and love upon his face, which says, 'At last I am to be with Him and see Him again.' And from heaven He stretches down in very human love, holding out both hands to welcome John, as one would welcome a dear friend or brother coming home from abroad. And behind Him are the other ten—James's young face looking over His shoulder — Peter almost inclined to press forward even before his Master, but keeping back, only thrusting his arms out saying, 'Dear John, I must have the next embrace'; it brings happy tears to one's eyes. Scarcely less lovely are the two I have just seen at S. M. Novella, the *Joachim and Anna*, and the *Birth of Mary*—the sweet, placid baby face, and the nurse and servants wondering at the little thing; and the old Mother lying pale and with half-shut eyes, but so happy and thankful, with her cheek on her hand. Cimabue's Madonna is very hard to see, but it is indeed worthy to make the street where it was painted the Borgo Allegro.

"We are working very slowly, but as thoroughly as we can; resting for two or three hours at midday, and only walking or strolling in the evening, for the mornings are tiring. We are putting off San Marco till Sunday, finding each of the greater churches more than enough for a day, and there is so much! S. M. Novella alone would fill *volumes* of lovely photographs, were it possible to photograph all, and Santa Croce another. Except the great statues and a few Titians, we have as yet seen no art that is not Florentine. What a place!

"Well, I must stop now, for we must go for our drive. Tell me all about Carpaccio's Sta. Ursula, the Paradise, and the Scuola di San Rocco *especially*."

In May 1885 the party returned to England, and shortly after his arrival Mr. Ellerton, vastly renovated in mind and body by his delightful visit to the continent, was presented by Sir Spencer Maryon Wilson, Bart., to the Rectory of White Roding, Essex.

CHAPTER VI

1885—1893

WHITE RODING

Hymns Ancient and Modern—The Last Hymns—The Close

SHORTLY after his return from the continent Mr. Ellerton was presented to the Rectory of White Roding, one of the nine villages to which the Roding gives its name [1] as it winds between the hills and flats of Essex to join the Thames near Barking. This piece of preferment he owed to the kind mediation of his old friend and fellow-worker, Bishop Walsham How, who represented to Sir Spencer Maryon Wilson, the patron, that "the best living hymn-writer," as he himself calls him, was at that time without a benefice.

White Roding is a scattered parish lying on a bleak Essex hill, amid scenery totally devoid of any special interest, and being five miles from Sawbridgeworth, on the Great Eastern Railway, the nearest station, was inconveniently situated for a literary man. The rectory is a substantial old

[1] Roding-Abbess, Roding Aythorpe, Roding-Beauchamp, Roding-Berners, High Roding, Leaden Roding, Margaret Roding, and White Roding, with its hamlet Morrell Roding.

house, with a large garden surrounded on three sides by a moat, and the church stands close by, its little spire forming a landmark for many a desolate mile. But the new rector rejoiced in the place as affording a welcome retreat after the toil and turmoil of populous Barnes. The demands of the parish on his time were not excessive, leaving him leisure to devote his pen more freely than before to the service of the Church.

In a very charming and characteristic letter to his friend, Professor Attwell of Barnes, he thus describes his new home:—

> "*The Rectory, White Roothing, Dunmow,*
> "*July* 15, 1885.
>
> "MY DEAR PROFESSOR,
>
> "I have deprived myself of a pleasure in neglecting so long to write to you, for your last letter was provocative of a reply, and I hope this will bring me before long another in return.
>
> "I am rapidly discovering the pleasure of returning to my old vocation of a country parson; and certainly this delightful summer weather presents the life to us all on its brightest side. It is very pleasant to have what I have always longed to have—an old church with some historical interest about it, and thoroughly English looking; and I never see its shingled spire peeping through the elms and limes, or its grey tower with a foreground of corn-fields and a background of dark trees, without a fresh pleasure in thinking of it as something full of true English beauty and charm, of which one can never tire. We delight also in our green

and very unconventional garden, just one of those which arose before people knew how to separate use from beauty, or to fancy they could be separated; so that you scarcely know where your roses end and your cabbages begin. The greater part of the house is I should think seventeenth century, one or two rooms perhaps older, with a very ugly but comfortable addition made some thirty-five years ago by an old rector—a great Evangelical and Calvinist light in his day, the Rev. Henry Budd, of whose (successive) wives, nightcap, sermons, tithe-taking, and perambulations of the parish there are many stories. Evidently a very worthy, pious, simple-minded old man, with a propensity for writing somewhat Johnsonian epitaphs upon his wives, curates, and parishioners. In 1877 my excellent predecessor, Jacob North, a scholarly, liberal-minded, genial man, and a very admirable clergyman, came with his wife and family. He soon lost his sight; but his mind directed everything, and his children were the saving of the parish. Their personal influence upon old and young, and their indefatigable energy in both work and play, were the greatest blessing to the place.

"We like our neighbours very much. . . . . I need scarcely say they are all very shy of my alleged politics, but I think I am beginning to reassure them. Our Conservative candidate is a more than respectable member of the party, Sir H. Selwin Ibbetson, a very typical good squire, church restorer, master of hounds, and a most kindly and considerate landlord to his poorest cottagers—just the man one would look to see among these quiet old-world villages and comfortable farm-houses. It requires an effort to call to mind that the men who seek to represent us in Essex are not typical embodiments of the principles at stake. In fact, I never felt more independent of party sympathies, I think, than now.

"I have been rather too busy with housing books to have time to read them of late. My old friend Dr. Hort came here for two nights at the close of term, and brought with him Harnack's pamphlet about the now famous Faioum fragment, the facsimile of which he showed me, as well as some interesting photographs of the 'Didache.' He is strongly of opinion that Bickell's fragment, if it is indeed third century, is a fragment not of a 'Gospel' properly so-called, but either of a collection of *Logia*, or sayings of our Lord, or else a treatise in which the writer certainly cites the narrative, from memory, in a purposely abridged form. He relies a good deal on the substitution of the ordinary words for 'cock' and 'crow' for the less usual—indeed almost unique—ones employed by the Synoptists;—just what a man would do who was writing from memory, and had to mention the conversation. He was very much edified by the *Times* describing Harnack as a 'fervid Roman Catholic.' Bickell is, I believe, a convert to Rome, but Harnack, though I believe rather 'fervid' as a critic, is a *very* decided Protestant indeed.

"I have just read rapidly about half the first vol. of *Croker's Correspondence*—a case in which the typical Georgian office-jobber does, I fear, show through all the whitewash still. But it raises one's impression of Croker's shrewdness and ability. I hope you will get the book, if only for a deliciously witty letter from Peel about Babbage's calculating machine. Pattison and Mozley I have not yet seen, being not yet *en rapport* with Mudie again, but only with an old-fashioned so-called 'Clerical' Book Club, which gives one but barren fare."

Again, in a letter to the writer of these lines, he says, "I have said nothing of the house, which is an odd, rambling old place, with, however, an excellent drawing-room and dining-room, and a quaint little den for myself where I am writing, of course with a cat on the chair beside me, and with the door open on a sunny lawn. The garden is most delightful, and quite took me by surprise. It is very rough and old-fashioned, but I hope we shall make a παράδεισος[1] of it by a fair amount of Adam and Eve's work. As my predecessor—good and holy man as he was—lost his sight, and his wife and daughters were absorbed in curate's work, the house and garden have suffered a good deal of late, but I hope we shall be able to get them in a tidy state without neglecting the parish."

To his great delight he found the church provided with a very good organ. The choir was mixed, and it was a pretty sight to see the village maidens in their white choir dresses in the front row, with the boys and men in surplices behind.

By this time—1885—his hymn-work was practically done. *Church Hymns* had been completed in 1881, and the *Children's Hymn-Book* the same year. All the hymns on which his fame mainly

[1] Paradise.

rests had now been written, and henceforward his work was chiefly correspondence with other editors, and the occasional writing of a hymn. The compilers of *Hymns Ancient and Modern* had frequently consulted him, but it was not until the preparation of the "Complete Edition" was in hand that he became one of the Committee. His leisure was now devoted mainly to prose, and it was at White Roding that he wrote *The Great Indwelling, or Thoughts on the Relation of Holy Communion to the Spiritual Life*, a work small in volume but full of deepest insight into the mystery on which it meditates. It contains too the graceful little poems on 'The old in their relation to the young,' '*Down the lane at evening time*,' and a sonnet on 'The evening service of Man,' beginning—

> "I would not linger idly by the strand
> Of that dim water which I soon shall pass."

It was here too that he composed *The Twilight of Life*, his *De Senectute*, as he playfully called it, "full of helpful and cheering thoughts on the special conditions, trials, encouragements, and blessings of advancing life, and rich in bright and beautiful teaching founded on Holy Scripture and reason on the hope of reunion with our beloved ones in the world above."[1] The book, published by Cassells, is considerately printed in large type. He also about this time made his translation of Thomas à Kempis's *Imitation of Christ*. But the largest and most important work at White Roding was his editing the *Manual of Parochial*

[1] Obituary notice in *The Christian Age*, June 28, 1893.

Work, a series of articles "by writers who have special knowledge or experience in the subjects of which they treat."[1] Of the twenty-nine chapters or sections which the book contains, six, and part of a seventh, are from his own pen. It was published in 1888, and has had, we believe, a large sale.

Occasionally Canon Ellerton would allow his muse to lead him into other fields than those devoted to hymns. He could when he chose write very elegant sonnets, two of which are given here. The earliest is written in a volume of Keble's sermons given to his wife; the other is a New Year's greeting to his friends from White Roding.

C. A. E. Feb. 18, 1875.

TAKE, dearest, this, thy Lenten thoughts to guide,
   The precious words of Hursley's well-loved saint:—
   Not here the Poet, weaving garlands quaint
Of verse devout, for every holy tide;
Not here the Champion, on his Master's side,
   Skilful to ply his Logic's keen-edged sword,
   Stern to avenge the honour of his Lord;
Not here the Scholar, gathering far and wide
   The classic lore which once he held so dear:
This is the Pastor, yearning o'er his flock,
To call them to the shadow of the Rock.
   Still from his rest those accents calm and clear
Tell of the Narrow Way which led him there,
The Cross borne for us, and the Cross we bear.

"We wish you Good Luck in the Name of the Lord." Psalm cxxix. 3.

O FRIENDS, from under skies of ashen grey
   What tokens can we send you o'er the snow,
   While not a flower as yet has leave to blow,
And early we shut out the short dark day?

---

[1] Preface.

Yet thoughts are free through curtained panes to go
  And find you out and bring you unawares
  Memories of brighter days, and silent prayers,
With power, methinks, to set your heart aglow.
Fain would we send you, ere the year expire,
Some word that tells you of our hearts' desire.
Hark! from their tower the midnight bells proclaim
In changing tones the One Unchanging Name:
Then in that Name, O friends, both far and near,
Good luck we wish you in the new-born year.

So far back as 1870, while Mr. Ellerton was at Crewe Green, he had been applied to by the Rev. E. H. Bickersteth, now Bishop of Exeter, for permission to insert his hymn, "Saviour, again," in the first edition of the *Hymnal Companion*. His letter in reply is well worth preserving, as it shows his opinion on the frequently discussed question respecting the guarding of hymns by copyright.

"*Crewe Green, Crewe,
"Jan.* 31, 1870.

"MY DEAR SIR,

"You are most welcome to use the hymn you mention. The new S. P. C. K. Appendix has the longer form of it, but I shortened and revised it for Sir Henry Baker, and I think the shorter form is the better, but you can choose either.

"Thank you much for your own hymns. Some of them I know well, others are new to me.

"I entirely sympathize in your feeling about hymns as a gift to the Church of Christ. If one is counted worthy to contribute to His praise in the congregation, one ought to feel very thankful, and very humble. So any of my hymns which are in my own power I always give freely, but a few have been written for friends and at their request, and these I cannot dispose of. I am also busy with two friends in compiling a book, and of course those of my writing or translating which are done for that book are joint property. However, I am glad to say that the hymn you approve of is free to any who ask for it.

"I am, my dear sir,
"Yours very faithfully,
"JOHN ELLERTON.

The success which attended the first and second editions of the *Hymnal Companion* led in 1889 to the preparation of a third, and again we find the right reverend compiler applying to Mr. Ellerton for permission to make a still larger use of his hymns than before. The following is the answer which the Bishop received:—

"*The Rectory, White Roding, Dunmow,*
"*April* 24, 1889.

"MY DEAR LORD BISHOP,

"I thank you very much for the kind way in which you have put your request for more of my hymns. Your judgment respecting them is a great solace to me, for I know that your Lordship can enter into the feelings with which some of them were written; and that you know how often one's own hymns rise up in condemnation of one's coldness and faithlessness. So that there are times when it does really cheer one for a Father in God to say, 'I think God helped you to write that, and

I think He has made it a blessing to one and another.'

"I need hardly say how gladly I would place at your Lordship's disposal any of my hymns which you think useful. I never have made any of them copyright, so that the *Hymns Ancient and Modern* compilers will have no reason to complain of your selecting from the Appendix the two you mention in addition to the others. The text in the supplement to *Hymns Ancient and Modern* contains a few variations which I shall be glad if your Lordship will look upon as my latest revision of them. That for teachers originally began,

> 'Break Thou to us, O Lord,
> The Bread of Life to-day,'

but I think that is an inappropriate use of our Lord's metaphor, which is never applied to *teaching*, so that I have altered it.[1]

"I am writing to Skeffington to ask him to send your Lordship my little volume of collected hymns, which I hope you will do me the kindness to accept, in return for much enjoyment of yours. I am most grateful for those you have been so good as to send me. I read with delight in the *Church Missionary Intelligencer* your translation of Xavier's

---

[1] The revised version runs—

> "Shine Thou upon us, Lord,
> True Light of men to-day."
> *Hymns Ancient and Modern*, 580.

The original, however, is preserved in the *Collected Hymns*, p. 64.

hymn,[1] but the hymn for Holy Communion, and that for the House of Mercy, are both of them quite new to me, and you will pardon my saying how *very* beautiful I feel them to be.

"I am so glad that 'Peace, perfect peace' and its tune are in the *Hymns Ancient and Modern* supplement. Beyond all your hymns I think it has brought blessing to many, and I *know* how it has helped the faith of some of God's sorely-tried children. Our Essex poor folk love it dearly."

"*The Rectory, White Roding, Dunmow,*
"*Nov.* 14, 1889.

"MY DEAR LORD,

"I can only to-day just acknowledge the receipt of your Lordship's very kind letter. If I can be of any service in looking over the proofs you send me, it will be a great pleasure to do so. I feel thankful for the opportunity of being still of some little use now that God has given me in my declining years a quiet sphere of work that leaves me some leisure.

"I am so glad to see your translation of *O quanta qualia.* I had two days ago a MS. translation sent me by Mr. Pott; but I like Neale's *metre,* and the lovely French tune; and I shall like to examine your version in detail.

"As to your Lordship's other request, I scarcely know what to say. If the power seems given to

---

[1] "O Deus ego amo Te,
   Nec amo Te ut salves me."

The Bishop's version begins, "O God, I love Thee; not that my poor love," and is included in the last edition of the *Hymnal Companion.*

me to make anything of so great a subject which can be at all useful, I shall be very thankful; but I do not know whether I shall be able. I will keep it standing in mind during the next week or two.

"Do you know Vinet's marvellous hymn *Sous ton voile d'ignominie?* It is in the S.P.C.K. Channel Island book of French hymns, as well as in the *Chants Chrétiens*, and in the book used generally in the Canton de Vaud. I want to try my hand at it for a hymn for Good Friday.[1] May I send it you to criticize if I seem to succeed? It is, I think, a *very* great hymn in its own way, as a meditation on the Love of the Atonement.

"Believe me, my dear Lord,
"Very sincerely yours,
"JOHN ELLERTON."

How highly the Bishop valued the assistance of Canon Ellerton, the late Sir Henry W. Baker, and of Dr. Walsham How, Bishop of Wakefield, may be gathered from his graceful acknowledgment of their services in his Introduction to the *Hymnal Companion*, where he says—

"Nothing could exceed the true brotherly kindness, for I can express it by no other word, with which they have met my requests and helped my work."

Feeling that his work as a hymn-writer was now practically done, he collected all that he had composed and translated into a volume entitled *Hymns Original and Translated*, a copy of which, as we have seen in his letter of April 24, he pre-

[1] The translation is given p. 150.

sented to his fellow labourer and brother poet, Bishop E. H. Bickersteth. It contains seventy-six pieces, including the longer and shorter versions of "Saviour, again." Of them, eight were written in his Essex rectory, namely—

1. "O Father, bless the children." For Holy Baptism; scarcely so much a hymn in the full Augustinian sense of the word as a very beautiful invocation addressed to the Three Persons of the Holy Trinity on behalf of the baptized.

2. "O Jerusalem the blissful, Home of gladness yet untold." For the restoration of a church, translated from *O Beata Hierusalem*, a Mozarabic Breviary hymn at least as old as the eleventh century.

3. "Praise to the Heavenly Wisdom." For the Festival of St. Matthias. These three hymns were written for, and first appeared in, the "complete edition" of *Hymns Ancient and Modern*. The other hymns belonging to this latest period were the following, none of which are, so far as we know, incorporated into any hymnal.

4. "Thrice Holy, Thrice Almighty Lord." For Trinity Sunday, translated from the French Breviary hymn *Ter sancte, ter potens Deus*, by Claude de Santeüil (d. 1684). Of the version in *Church Hymns*, the translation of the first three verses is by Chandler, and that of the last two by Mr. Ellerton; showing that though the version in the collected hymns is dated June 1, 1886, he must have made a translation at some earlier period.

5. "English children, lift your voices." A most loyal children's hymn, for Queen Victoria's Jubilee,

1887, written for Skeffington's collection of Jubilee hymns.

6. "Again Thou meetest in Thy way." For the Sunday after a funeral.

7. "Spirit of God, Whose glory." A fine hymn for the opening of a parish room, written for the dedication of the Charles Lamb Memorial Buildings, Easter Monday, April 2, 1888.

We may include here a hymn the date of which is lost—

8. "This is the hour when in full brightness glowing." For sext in Passion-tide, translated from Charles Coffin's Paris Breviary hymn *Jam solis excelsum jubar*. A version beginning "Behold the radiant sun on high," by J. D. Chambers, is in the *Hymnary*.

The hymns written subsequent to the publication of *Hymns Original and Translated* (1888), now collected for the first time, are given in full in another place.[1]

It now only remains to give some account of Mr. Ellerton's connection with *Hymns Ancient and Modern*, the last service he rendered to the hymnody of the Church of England.

[1] See p. 138.

HYMNS ANCIENT AND MODERN[1]

THE first edition of this world-renowned book was published in 1861. The idea of reducing the chaotic state of English hymnody which up to that time had prevailed into something like order by the compilation of one book of commanding merit originated with the Rev. F. H. Murray, Rector of Chislehurst, in Kent. The carrying out of the idea was committed to the late Rev. Sir Henry W. Baker, who associated with himself some twenty clergymen, including the editors of many existing hymnals, who agreed to give up their several books in order, as far as might be, to promote the use of one.

Small as the book was in its first edition, it at once gained the confidence of the Church. The lines upon which it was constructed were widely recognized as the right lines. Although only con-

---

[1] Much of the information here given is taken from a paper by the Rev. W. Pulling, Chairman of the H. A. M. Committee, read at the Swansea Church Congress, 1879, from a communication addressed to me by the Rev. G. Cosby White, the present chairman, and from the papers of Mr. Ellerton himself, kindly lent me by his son, the Rev. F. G. Ellerton.

taining 273 hymns, 132 were translations from the Latin, 10 from the German, 119 English hymns already well known and loved, and 12 were original.[1] Thus the hymnody of the Western Church was to a considerable extent represented. It contained, moreover, the vital principle of growth. So favourably was it received that the necessity of an Appendix soon became apparent. This was added in 1868, when 113 more hymns of sterling merit were published, including two of Mr. Ellerton's original compositions,[2] and his translation of the *Alleluia perenne*. In April 1872 the sub-committee reported that "they had carefully digested a large number of answers to two sets of questions circulated as widely as possible ; have considered all new matter hitherto proposed to them, and hope that they may be able after their next meeting to print the first rough draft of the revised book."

The final outcome of this and subsequent meetings was the publication of the Revised Edition of 1875. It contained 473 hymns, of which the following ten, in addition to the three which were in the first Appendix, were either composed or translated by Mr. Ellerton.

1. "Joy! because the circling year." From the Latin.
2. "King of Saints! to Whom the number."
3. "Lift the strain of high thanksgiving."
4. "Now the labourer's task is o'er."
5. "O Son of God, our Captain of salvation."

[1] Julian.
[2] "Saviour, again," and "This is the day of light."

6. " O Strength and **Stay upholding all Creation.**"
From the Latin.
7. " Our day of praise is done."
8. " Thou Who sentest Thine Apostles."
9. " Throned upon the awful Tree."
10. " We sing the glorious conquest."

But although he had been from time to time consulted by the compilers, Mr. Ellerton's formal connection with *Hymns Ancient and Modern* dates from 1885. In the spring of that year he was invited to a Conference of Priests and Laymen to consider the further enlargement of the book, it having been represented to the compilers "that an impression exists that it is desirable to supplement their book from the large stores of new hymns which have been given to the Church since the publication of the Revised Edition in 1875."

The result of this Conference will be seen in the following letter from the Rev. William Pulling, then Chairman of the Committee of Compilers.

"*Eastnor Rectory, Ledbury,*
"*July* 1885.

" DEAR MR. ELLERTON,
"I have the pleasure of communicating to you the resolution passed at a meeting of H. A. M. on Wednesday last.

"That having considered the Report of the Meeting held May 20, at the Army and Navy Hotel, we resolve, in compliance with the almost unanimous opinion expressed alike by those present at that meeting, and by those invited but unable to attend, that some additions be made to H. A. M.

"We are very grateful to you for the kind assistance which you afforded us towards coming to a decision upon the important question discussed at that Conference. And we shall be glad of your further kind help in the steps which we are initiating to carry our Resolution into effect."

A further Meeting was held in October, to which Mr. Ellerton was invited as consultee. The subjects discussed were—

1. Hymns for the seasons not proper for the Festival itself, especially Easter.

2. Hymns addressed to the praise of God the Father.

3. Hymns for Holy Baptism ; Holy Eucharist.

4. General Hymns.

5. Hymns suitable for instructions and Mission Services on Sunday evenings.

6. Hymns suitable for use on Sundays.

So highly were Mr. Ellerton's services esteemed by the compilers, that in the next year the Chairman, now the Rev. G. Cosby White, wrote to him in the following complimentary terms—

"*San Gemignano*,
"*Wednesday, May* 19, 1886.

"MY DEAR MR. ELLERTON,

"You have been so kind in giving your valuable assistance in collecting materials for the Supplement of *Hymns Ancient and Modern*, that we are emboldened to ask a further favour. Would you be so kind as to help us in arriving at a final decision as to the admission or rejection of the hymns which have been suggested:—to strengthen, in fact, as an Assessor our 'Final Court of Appeal,' and if so, would you kindly meet us on the afternoon of Tuesday, June 8, at Arundel House, preparatory to a General Meeting of the Consultees on the following day?"

His eldest son, the Rev. F. G. Ellerton, in a letter to me referring to this period, says—

"From this time he was very much engaged until the publication of the book in 1889, both with the general work of selecting and judging, and also in translating hymns from the Latin. He re-cast two of his own, 'From east to west,' and 'Bride of Christ,'[1] which had appeared in *Church Hymns*, and was for a long time occupied over a rendering of *O Beata Hierusalem*, with suggestions from the Rev. Jackson Mason: these two last hymns he was very fond of. So too he in turn contributed suggestions to the translations of others. The translations were a feature of the Supplement, and he much enjoyed his old work of translating, and his *Daniel's Thesaurus* was often consulted, and he asked me, and you too no doubt, for suggestions. It is no doubt a question whether the translations are popular, but 'Bride of Christ' always seems to me very fine."

The following letter to the Rev. G. Cosby White, accompanying two translations from the Latin, is interesting. As the version of *Puer Natus* never seems to have been published it is given on p. 148.

[1] See p. 84.

> "*The Rectory, White Roding,*
> "*July* 22, 1887.

"MY DEAR WHITE,

"I send you (1) *Puer Natus*, with corrections by Jackson Mason. I rather prefer in v. 2,

> '*Here* in a manger He doth lie.'[1]
> (*Hic* jacet in praesepio.)

But J. M.'s second line is better than mine. His verse about *Bos et asinus* is also a great improvement. Please substitute it for mine. I do not quite like

> 'He comes, yet of our blood in truth.'

But if you prefer it let it be so. It is good to get in *sanguine*. I also prefer J. M.'s Doxology,[2] which is nearly what was on my first draft.

"2. *Sponsa Christi* (*H. A. M.* 618).

"J. M. has seen my suggested alterations, and approves of them all. The only one of importance is—

> 'Blessed Virgin Mother,'

for

> 'Mother Ever-Virgin.'

Do you not think that (apart from our own individual sympathies) the use of the first phrase rather than the second will tend to a more harmonious and general acceptance of the hymn?

---

[1] J. M. suggested—
"He in a manger-bed doth lie,
Who holds unbounded sovereignty."

[2] "Praise we the Holy Three in One,
And thank our God for His dear Son."

I should be so sorry to see the question raised and discussed among those who otherwise would gladly and thankfully receive the book. But having said this to *you*, I shall say no more. To myself personally the phrase would be no stumbling-block. The holy Mother of our Lord is to me for all time the 'Blessed Virgin Mary.'"

The complete edition of *Hymns Ancient and Modern*, that is, the edition of 1875 with a Supplement, was published in 1889. Of the 165 hymns of which the Supplement is composed, no less than 13 are by Mr. Ellerton, namely—

1. "Behold us, Lord, a little space."
2. "Bride of Christ, whose glorious warfare." From the Latin.
3. "From east to west, from shore to shore." From the Latin.
4. "God of the living, in Whose eyes."
5. "Hail to the Lord Who comes."
6. "O Father all creating."
7. "O Father, bless the children."
8. "O Jerusalem the blissful, Home of gladness yet untold." From the Latin.
9. "Oh how fair that morning broke."
10. "Praise to the Heavenly Wisdom."
11. "Shine Thou upon us, Lord."
12. "The day Thou gavest, Lord, is ended."
13. "Welcome, happy morning! age to age shall say." From the Latin. Making the whole number of his contributions to the book twenty-six.

"It would be scarcely possible," in the words of Mr. White, the Chairman of the Committee, "to exaggerate the **value of** the assistance which was rendered by **Mr. Ellerton** in **the** production of the complete **edition.**"

Early in 1892 the body of proprietors of *Hymns Ancient and Modern* invited him to associate **himself** with them still more closely in view of the intervention of Convocation, foreshadowed by the appointment of a Committee. He accepted the invitation, but it came too late; he was never **able** to attend any of the meetings, and **his loss was** felt by the compilers to be irreparable.

THE LAST HYMNS

As none of Canon Ellerton's, composed subsequent to the publication of *Hymns Original and Translated* (1888), have been incorporated, so far as I know, into any hymnal, they are here given. They are of unequal merit, some indeed were written when the author had already felt the first touch of that hand which was commissioned to take him from us. With the exception of the last they lack the fire, the *ring* of his best compositions; still they are all full of holy and beautiful thoughts.

The hymns for the Conversion of St. Paul, First Day of Lent, Ascension Day, and St. Matthew, and the Sunday Hymn for Little Children, first appeared in the *Church Monthly Magazine*, and I am indebted to the editor, Frederick Sherlock, Esq., for permission to gather them into this volume.

1. *Ascended Lord, Thy Church's Head*, is worthy of a place in any hymnal. Perhaps the omission of the second and third verses would render it more suitable for congregational singing; while the second line of the third verse would certainly be improved by *A Son of Man* being altered to

The Son of Man, inasmuch as in the original the definite article is used.[1]

2. *What were Thy forty days?* is not, and does not profess to be, in any sense of the word a hymn; but it is a very beautiful Lenten meditation, one that should find a place in any future collection of devotional poetry.

3. *'Tis come, the day of exultation!*—One of the best of this series. It might well end, however, with the sixth verse, which forms a suitable concluding doxology.

4. *To-day we sing to Christ our King.*—In no point is our national hymnody weaker than in historical hymns, hymns which connect the present age of the English Church with the old heroes of the faith, whose names are preserved, apparently only to be ignored, in our Calendar. We greatly want hymns recording the deeds of what are called the "Black-letter Saints," *e.g.* St. Hugh of Lincoln, St. Richard of Chichester, St. Hilary, etc. This hymn, and the Brighton processional, *Praise our God for all the wonders*, are models for such compositions.

6. *O Holy Spirit, Whom our Master sent.*—In a letter dated January 2, 1890, the Bishop of Exeter writes to Mr. Ellerton, "In your most kind letter of November 14, you were good enough to say you would attempt to write a hymn on charity (1 Cor. xiii.) for me; and I have not seldom breathed a prayer that God would give you one for His Church." This is the hymn composed in compliance with the Bishop's request.

---

[1] τὸν υἱὸν τοῦ ἀνθρώπου, Acts vii. 56.

6. "*Follow Me!*" *the Master spake.*—A very valuable addition to the series of Saints' Days hymns, and one that is sure to find its way into future hymnals.

7. A Sunday Hymn for Little Children, dated August 24, 1891.

8. *Say, Watchman, what of the night?*—Mr. Ellerton's last published hymn. The old fire and vigour seems to have returned, and this noble Advent song will rank with the compositions of his best days.

I—CONVERSION OF ST. PAUL.

ASCENDED Lord, Thy Church's Head,
Thou First-Begotten from the dead,
Thy life is hid in depths of light,
Beyond the world of sense and sight.

Though now withdrawn behind the veil,
Thy Pastoral love can never fail;
And Thou, Great Shepherd of the sheep,
By night and day Thy watch dost keep.

Thy dying Martyr saw Thee stand,
A Son of Man, at God's right Hand;
Thy blinding glory barred the path,
And stayed the persecutor's wrath.

Oh, day of blessings for our race!
Oh, mystery of electing grace!
When that Divine and loving call
Subdued the stubborn heart of Saul!

Thy word the fiery spirit broke;
The strong will bowed to bear Thy yoke;
He rose, the bondman of his Lord,
To preach the Name he once abhorred.

Light of the Gentiles ! Praise to Thee,
For this Thy last Epiphany !
From this great hour the Dayspring shone
On lands unnamed, on tribes unknown.

Victorious Love ! pursue Thy road,
Till all the earth shall see her God ;
And many a foeman yet shall be
A chosen vessel unto Thee !

August 13, 1890.

2—THE FIRST DAY OF LENT.

WHAT were Thy Forty Days ?—
No calm retreat within the holy place ;
No friend to speak one strengthening, soothing word ;
No comfort of a silent, pitying face ;
No voice with Thine in soft responding heard ;
Long hours of thoughts unuttered and unknown ;
Day after day, the wilderness, alone !

What are my Lenten days ?—
The open portals of Thy house of prayer,
With friends and brethren kneeling at my side ;
A low-breathed psalm of mercy in the air ;
A pastoral voice to warn, or cheer, or guide ;
The Bread of Heaven itself, bestowed to win
Fresh strength for battling with my secret sin.

What were Thy Forty Days ?—
The lonely vigil and the bitter fast,
Chastening that Flesh which knew no taint of ill ;
The nights and days in high communion passed ;
The self-surrender to the Father's will ;
And, most of all, the conflict stern and dread,
Which bruised for us the ancient tempter's head.

What are my Lenten days ?—
An hour's retirement from the world's full round ;
A few light pleasures for a while foregone ;
A little pausing here on holy ground,

My God to seek, my sins to think upon ;
A few faint sighs o'er evil thought and deed ;
A few resolves a holier life to lead.

Yet make my Lent like Thine !
No strength have I to climb that lonely height,
Like Thee to wrestle, and like Thee prevail ;
Yet grant me, in Thy guiding Spirit's might,
To follow Thee, though flesh and heart should fail,
Alone with Thee to foil the tempter's skill,
And learn at length to do my Father's will.

3—ASCENSION DAY.

'TIS come, the day of exultation !
  The day for which the ages yearned ;
When Christ, the Hope of all creation,
  The Mighty God, to heaven returned.

God is gone up on high ascending,
  His rightful throne once more to fill,
And all the realms of bliss unending
  Are ringing with His welcome still.

On that great battlefield victorious,
  Where Satan fell, He took His prey ;—
A deathless body, risen and glorious,
  Before His Father to display.

From yonder cloud our King Immortal
  Speaks hope to each believing soul :
His touch unbars the long-closed portal,—
  The gates of Eden backward roll.

O joy, all other joys exceeding !
  The Virgin-Born, our Very Own,—
Past all the shame, the Cross, the bleeding,
  Ascends at last His Father's Throne.

Then to our Champion of Salvation
   All thanks and praises **let us pay**;
Who, Firstfruits of **His** ransomed **nation**,
   Hath borne **our flesh on** high to-day.

For on this day of days 'tis given
   To men to share in angels' mirth,
They joy that He is come to heaven,
   And *we* that He forsook not earth.

Lord, give us grace, as Thou hast bidden,
   In works of love to wait for Thee;
Our life with Thine in God be hidden,
   That where Thou art we yet may be.

4—TRANSLATION OF ST. MARTIN.[1] (*July* 4.)

To-day we sing **to** Christ our **King**
   His valiant soldiers' praise;
The men who bore from shore to shore
   The Faith in ancient days;
Of Martin's work for God we tell,
   Through patient years sustained,
Till thousands heard the Gospel word,
   And life eternal gained.

When **first to** these lone woods **and fields**
   Our conquering fathers **came,**
They gave their new-built house of prayer
   Saint Martin's honoured name;
Because from him their sires had learned
   The tale of Jesus' love,
And so from idol forms had **turned**
   To worship God above.

---

[1] The Patron Saint of White Roding church; this hymn was written for the Parish Festival, 1891. St. Martin is commemorated twice in the Prayer-book Calendar; his death on November 11 (he died November 8, 397), and the translation of his remains on July 4. He died and was buried at Candé, a monastery at the extremity of his diocese, but in 473 his relics were removed to a basilica dedicated in his honour near Tours. In England alone there are one hundred and sixty churches dedicated to St. Martin.

Eight hundred years have passed away
  Since this old church was new;
And still to-day the Creeds we say
  Which Martin taught for true.
Then speed Thy Word, O conquering Lord,
  From rise to set of sun,
Till land and sea shall bow to Thee,
  And praise the Three in One!

5—WHITSUNTIDE.[1]

O Holy Spirit, Whom our Master sent
  Rich with all treasures, from the throne above,
We pray Thee for Thy gift most excellent,
  Thy greatest, Thine unfailing gift of love.

'Tis not for us with one commanding word
  To heal the sick, or chase the hosts of hell;
In tongues unknown to make Thy mysteries heard,
  Or things of God with lips inspired to tell.

Those signs are past; the written word is ours;
  And Satan trembles at the might of prayer:
The shield of Faith can quell the evil powers,
  And Hope's bright helmet save us from despair.

These yet abide; but we would covet still
  One gift, exalted faith and hope above:
Grant us the new commandment to fulfil,
  And even as Jesus loved us, so to love.

Grant us to follow His long-suffering path,
  Joying in truth, yet helping them that fall;
To think no evil, give no place to wrath,
  But bear, believe, endure, and hope for all.

So when at length we know as we are known,
  And all the shadows are for ever past,
He Who is Love may find in us His own,
  And all in Him be perfect love at last.

March 24, 1890

---

[1] Kindly communicated by the Lord Bishop of Exeter.

6—ST. MATTHEW.

"*He gave some* . . . *Evangelists.*"

"Follow Me!" the Master spake,
As He passed beside the lake;
This the fisher brothers heard,
Left their all at Jesus' word.

"Follow Me!" and Matthew, too,
That constraining summons knew;
Cast away his hopes of gain,
Chose the labour, want, and pain.

Oh, the blest exchange he made,
With the Master's pound to trade!
Priceless wealth of souls to lay
At His feet on that Great Day!

Following on where Jesus led,
Gathering up the words He said,
Watching every gracious deed—
So the world might hear and read.

Earliest of the Chosen Four,
He, from out his treasure-store,
Bringing forth things new and old,
Tidings of the Kingdom told.

On the Blessèd Mount He saw
Given the new and holier Law.
On the shore he stood and learned
Mysteries by the few discerned.

So he spake of things he knew,
Type and prophecy come true;
Words of life, and signs of power,
Warnings of the Judgment hour:

Spake of Jesus' Cross and pain,
How His grave was watched in vain;
How on Easter morning He
Led His flock to Galilee.

There the Risen Lord once more
Stood beside them on the shore,
Bade His Church her charge fulfil,
Told her He is with us still.

Praise to Thee, O Lord the Christ,
For Thy first Evangelist!
Praise for all which Thou dost give,
Word of God, by Whom we live!

March 21, 1890.

7—A SUNDAY HYMN FOR LITTLE CHILDREN.

It was early in the morning—
The first bright Sunday morning—
That the dear Lord Jesus rose from the grave in which He lay;
And in the morning quiet,
The holy Angels by it,
Sat waiting for the Maries to come along the way.

The Maries came in sadness,
But the Angels brought them gladness
When they said, "The Lord is risen; He will never die again."
And soon He came to meet them,
With loving words to greet them—
Oh, that Sunday put an end to their sorrow and their pain!

Now the Angels who sit keeping
Their watch while we lie sleeping
Are glad to see us wake when the Sunday morn is here;
For they know their Lord rejoices
To listen to their voices,
And the praises of the children to Him are always dear.

Then let us take our places
With gladness on our faces—
With hearts and voices ready our Sunday hymns to sing;
For it is coming one day,
The best and brightest Sunday,
When all His children rise again to meet their glorious King!

8—"SAY, WATCHMAN, WHAT OF THE NIGHT?"

"Say, watchman, what of the night?
  Is it shrouded in darkness still?
Are there no pale streaks of the dawning light
  O'er the crest of the Eastern hill?"
"Yea, the stars are glittering clear;
  Nor yet does the East turn grey;
But the night is waning, the dawn is near,
  The dawn of a cloudless day."

"But, watchman, what of the night—
  The night of our sorrow and pain—
Will the darkened life never more grow bright,
  Nor the joy return again?"
"Yea, sorrow and pain for awhile,
  Are the burden upon you laid;
But soon on your tears shall the sunrise smile,
  With the brightness that ne'er shall fade."

"But, watchman, what of the night
  Of evil, and wrong, and woe?
For dark is the time, and fierce is the fight,
  And unyielding is the foe."
"Yea, the battle is sore and long,
  Through the night of the troubled years,
But the Advent morn brings the Victor song,
  And joy when the Christ appears."

The following Translations and Hymns were found by the Rev. F. G. Ellerton among his father's papers. None of them, so far as I know, have hitherto appeared in print. Some, especially the *Puer Natus* and *Sous ton voile d'ignominie*, have evidently a future before them. Although all are in the Canon's handwriting, Nos. 6 and 7 are believed to be by Dr. Monsell, No. 8 by Emma Toke, and No. 10 by Joseph Anstice.

1—PUER NATUS IN BETHLEHEM.

A Child is born in Bethlehem,
And gladness fills Jerusalem. Alleluia!

Here in a manger He doth lie,
Who reigns for evermore on high. Alleluia!

His crib the ox and ass have known,
And in this Child, their Lord they own. Alleluia!

From Saba comes a train of kings,
Gold, frankincense, and myrrh it brings. Alleluia!

Each kneels in turn upon the floor
The new-born Sovereign to adore Alleluia!

Born of a Virgin undefiled;
No earthly father calls Him child. Alleluia!

Untainted by the serpent's tooth,
Yet one with us in very truth. Alleluia!

Like unto us in flesh is He,
But unlike us from sin is free; Alleluia!

That so in man He may restore
God's likeness and His own once more. Alleluia!

In gladness for this wondrous Birth,
Bless we the Lord of Heaven and earth. Alleluia!

[Glory to Thee, this happy morn,
O Jesu Lord, the Virgin-born! Alleluia!]

To Thee, most Blessed Trinity,
All thanks, all praise, all worship be. Alleluia! Amen.

2—TIBI CHRISTE SPLENDOR PATRIS.
(IMITATED)

Lo, the Angel squadrons muster; lo, the armies of the sky!
Round the sapphire Throne they gather, worshipping the Lord most high;
Holy, Holy, Holy Sovereign King, Almighty God, they cry.

Saviour Christ, the Father's glory, life and strength of loving souls,
While the tide of adoration round Thy Feet in music rolls,
While the anthem of the blessed Thy beloved Name extols.

With the choir of mighty angels we our lowly hymns would raise ;
Here with psalm and song responsive swell the torrent of their praise ;
Till at last with them united on Thine unveiled Face we gaze.

Thou art worthy, Thou hast conquered ; grant us, Lord, to conquer too,
Though our foes are strong and crafty, and our forces scant and few ;
Lord of armies, Thou wilt aid us ; faithful is Thy Name **and** true.

3—HOLY COMMUNION BEFORE A JOURNEY.

(O ESCA VIATORUM.)

"O taste and see how gracious the Lord is."

O MEAT for travellers on their road,
O Angel's Bread on men bestowed,
   O Manna, Heavenly food !
Fill Thou our hearts that faint for Thee,
Forbid us not to taste and see
   That Thou, O Lord, art **good.**

O Fount of Love, which long ago
From one pure Source began to flow—
   The SAVIOUR'S wounded Side ;
Refresh the thirsting in their need ;
For Thee we crave, in Thee indeed
   Our soul is satisfied.

O JESU LORD, Whose Face Divine
Here through the veils of Bread and Wine
   Believing we adore,
Grant us in Thine eternity
With open eyes to gaze on Thee,
   And love Thee evermore.

4—SOUS TON VOILE D'IGNOMINIE.

O Sacred Head, beneath Thy veil of shame,
Beneath Thy crown of pain I know Thy Name;
Through the dim cloud of blood mine eye can trace
The quenchless majesty of that marred Face!

Oh, never in the realm of light till now
Did light so heavenly shine upon Thy Brow;
Never in Beauty's home, Thy Beauty's ray
Beamed with such glow as here on Golgotha.

Ye who adore the Father in the Son,
Where life and worship are for ever one,
Say, did He ever seem so fair to see,
Angels, as here upon the atoning Tree?

His death hath crowned the honour which was His
From everlasting in the land of bliss;
And with the humbling of the Son of Man,
The glory of the Son of God began.

The Father's voice proclaimed it—I am Love;
And Jesus, stooping from His home above,
Bore the glad news to earth, to every one—
Lo! I am Love; I am the Father's Son.

Yes, He is Love; the God we see, we know;
The God in whom God blesses man below,
Where is the Throne of Love, but where we find
Brother and Victim in our God combined?

Love is the highest; Love the joy of heaven;
Love the true Crown to our Emmanuel given;
Poor dreams of power away! henceforth for me
There is no greatness but in charity.

My reason worships Thee, O Love Divine,
Come, fill and change this empty heart of mine;
Come, that my soul Thy Light and joy may share
And carry Eden with her everywhere.

Mine eyes on Thine, Divinest Brother, fix !
My life with Thine vouchsafe to intermix !
Pour into mine Thy heart, and so destroy
All longing in my soul for other joy !

JOHN ELLERTON
(From *Chants Chrétiens*).

[I have translated the whole of the verses, but it obviously requires much curtailment.]

5—NEW YEAR'S EVE.

"Thou art the same, and Thy years shall have no end."

THE years pass on. We name them good or bad :—
This brought us hope and love and bright success ;
That other left us empty, dark and sad ;
Now both are past, the joy, the bitterness :
Glory to Thee for both, from Whom they came ;
        Thou art the same !

The years bring change. The fires of youth grow old :
We half forget the names we once revered,
Smile at the hatreds and the loves of old,
And dwell in peace among the things we feared.
Glory to Thee, the One Unchanging Name :
        Thou art the same !

The years bring doubt : we count them up and see
Our wisdom all at fault, our forecasts vain ;
Nothing that hath been tells us what shall be,
No past experience makes the future plain.
Thee only can we trust ; we know Thy Name ;
        Thou art the same !

Not with high hopes, yet not with weak despair,
We cross the threshold of another year ;
Silent we enter in, we know not where :
All that we know is only, Thou art here ;
Because Thy years, O Master, Guide, and Friend,
        Shall have no end !

1889.

6—ADVENT.

Lord, to Thy holy temple
　Return, return again;
Come back and fill with glory
　The ways and hearts of men!
Not now a lowly Infant,
　Unnoticed and unknown;
But in the royal splendour
　Of Thine eternal throne!

Come back and fill Thy temple,
　Built up of human hearts,
With that abiding Presence
　Which never more departs!
Thy Spirit send before Thee,
　Till, by His life restored,
Thy people all adore Thee,
　Their only King and Lord!

7—ADVENT (Second Sunday).

Blessed Lord, Who till the morning
　Of Thine Advent shall appear,
Words of hope hast left and warning,
　Souls to strengthen, guide, and cheer;
Left them written for our learning,
　Pointing out the one true way,
Lest our hearts with all their yearning
　After home, should go astray.

Grant us in the sacred story
　Of the deeds which Thou hast done,
Grace to catch those gleams of glory
　Which on saints and martyrs shone;
Grant us faithful hearts to linger
　O'er the steps which Thou hast trod,
Where Thy Cross with silent finger
　Points the upward way to God.

Fill us, as we read the pages
  Traced by holy men of old,
With the hope which through the ages
  Did our fathers' hearts uphold;
Still to be, by wisdom learning,
  Kept in patience by Thy word,
Faith still bright, and love still burning,
  Servants, ready for their Lord.

8—LENT.

O Lord, Thou knowest all the snares
  That round our pathway be;
Thou knowest how both joys and cares
  Come between us and Thee.

Thou know'st that our infirmity
  In Thee alone is strong:
To Thee for help and strength **we** fly;
  Oh, let us not go **wrong!**

Oh, bear us up, protect us now
  In dark temptation's hour;
For Thou wast born of woman, Thou
  Hast felt temptation's power.

All sinless, Thou canst feel for those
  Who strive and suffer long;
Then still 'midst all our cares and woes
  Oh let us not go wrong!

9—"PRAISE WAITETH FOR THEE, O GOD IN ZION."

In gladness to Thy House, O Lord,
  Thy children come to-day,
To bless Thy Name with one accord,
  And with one mouth to pray.

High praise in Zion waits for Thee,
  Where that New Song unknown
Is borne across the glassy sea
  From saints before the Throne

For Thee our lowher worship waits,
  Whene'er with duteous feet
We stand within Thine earthly gates,
  Thy glorious Name to greet.

For if Thy grace our hearts inspire
  With faith and love and fear,
The simplest hymn of village choir
  To Thee we know is dear.

Then help us, Lord, while here we live
  To offer Thee our best ;
Do Thou our ignorance forgive,
  And perfect all the rest.

Praise to the Father's Name is meet ;
  Praise to His only Son ;
Praise to the Blessed Paraclete,
  The Three for ever One.

October 9, 1891.

10—O LORD, THY PRESENCE IS REVEALED.

O LORD, Thy Presence is revealed
  By mountain and by flood,
By woodland, and by quiet field,
  And homes where dwell the good.

Yet Thou art with each faithful heart
  That pure would still remain,
And do its firm yet gentle part
  Amidst the bad and vain.

Dear Lord, through this world's troubled way
  Thy children's footsteps guide ;
And lead them onward day by day,
  Unspotted at Thy side.

Be ours to do Thy work of love
  All erring souls to win ;
Amid a sinful world to move,
  Yet give no smile to sin.

II.

"For the Son of Man is as a man **taking a far journey, who left his house,** and gave authority to his servants, **and to every man his work,** and commanded the porter **to watch.**"—St. **Mark xiii. 34.**

WHEN to the far-off country
  The Master took His way,
This charge He gave His servants :—
  "Take heed, and watch, and pray :
Lo, here your tasks appointed
  Until I come again ;
And ever let the watchman
  Look forth across the plain."

Great is His house, and many
  The guests within the hall,
Because from street and highway
  He bade us welcome all ;
The servants' tasks are heavy,
  They ply them might and main ;
And through the gate the watchman
  Looks forth across the plain.

Long doth the Master tarry ;
  And murmuring voices cry,
"Vain all our care and labour,
  His coming draws not nigh ."
And slothful dreamers prattle
  Of pleasure and of gain ;
Yet still the faithful watchman
  Looks forth across the plain.

Soon shall he mark, some midnight,
  The longed-for sign of fire,
Or hail in redness dawning
  The morn of his desire ;—
The day when home in triumph
  The Master comes again,
And He shall haste to open
  The Gate towards the plain.

June 23, 1891.

THE CLOSE

THE publication of the "Complete Edition" of *Hymns Ancient and Modern* in 1889 may be said to mark the close of Mr. Ellerton's hymnological labours. One little thing indeed he undertook for the S. P. C. K., but this was an amusement rather than work: he thought that *The Children's Almanac*, published annually by that Society, might be made more interesting by interweaving a Calendar of Nature, after the manner of that in White's *Selborne*, with the chronology of the months, at the same time introducing a short notice of a few well-known birds. These last papers he asked the writer of these lines to prepare for him. The Almanac was ready for 1891, but did not appear till the following year. Thus his last work was, as his first had been, for children.

And now the time drew near when he must rest from his labours. On the morning of December 11, 1891, the first of the three warnings which paralysis usually gives reached him. Further work was impossible, and appointing a trustworthy priest to continue to feed his flock at White Roding, he withdrew to Torquay. For a time he seemed to rally, and still talked cheerfully to his friends, and took a great interest in Dr. Julian's magnificent *Dictionary of Hymnology*, which had just been published. On May 5, 1892, the second summons was received at Torquay, which crippled him still more seriously, and he immediately began to make arrangements for resigning White Roding, now that all hope of ever returning to his beloved work as a parish priest was taken away.

And now it was, as he was lying disabled, waiting his Master's call, that he was nominated to a prebendal stall in St. Albans Cathedral Church. But the promotion came too late; the installation never took place. One cannot contemplate without pain, that he whose one ambition it was to have a church possessing historical interest, an ambition which was never attained until he came to White Roding, and then only very partially, should never have experienced the satisfaction of sitting in his own stall in that glorious abbey, and feeling himself one of its incorporate body—*cujus a singulis in solidum pars tenetur.*

It appears to be the custom of St. Albans Cathedral for the Prebendaries to receive the title of "Canon," which in some other foundations is restricted to the Residentiaries, so for the last year of his life he received the empty and honorary address of "Canon" Ellerton.

White Roding Rectory was bidden farewell to in the following October, the stricken poet returning to Torquay, where, however, he had the burden of feeling that he was still Rector, of which he was not relieved until March, after he had taken to his bed.

He was able to attend the services at St. John's Church up to the Feast of the Epiphany, January 6, 1893, after which he grew rapidly worse. His mind became overclouded, and as he lay peaceful and happy there came back to his memory in endless succession fragments of the hymns he so dearly loved. Gradually he grew weaker, and ever less conscious day by day, until on June 15 those around him witnessed the realization of his own words—

> " The brightness of a holy deathbed blending
> With dawning glories of the eternal day."

Those who had the privilege of following him to his grave, a sunny spot in the cemetery of Torquay, on Tuesday, June 20, attended a funeral service such as can but very seldom have been witnessed before. He was buried amid his own hymns. At the burial of many a departed Church poet his own hymns have been sung, but when John Ellerton was carried to his bed of hope all the hymns, six in number, were from his own pen.

The clergy and choir met the body at the porch, and proceeded up the church chanting the processional sentences. The coffin, covered with flowers, was placed in the chancel, and Psalm xc. was sung. The Lesson was read by one of the poet's oldest friends and companions in hymnology, the Rev. R. Brown-Borthwick; after which was sung, " God of the living, in Whose eyes." Then followed the celebration of Holy Communion, fully choral with Merbecke's music, the Vicar, the Rev. Basil R. Airy, being the celebrant. The Introit was—

"Rest eternal grant to them, O Lord, and let light perpetual shine upon them.

" Thou, O God, art praised in Sion, and unto Thee shall the vow be performed in Jerusalem.

"Thou that hearest the prayer, unto Thee shall all flesh come.

"Rest eternal," etc.

As a sequence was sung that hymn of tenderest beauty, "When the day of toil is done." And during Communion the last verse of "Saviour, again to Thy dear Name we raise" (*Hymns Ancient and Modern*, 31)—

"Grant us Thy peace throughout our earthly life,
Our balm in sorrow, and our stay in strife;
Then, when Thy voice shall bid our conflict cease,
Call us, O Lord, to Thine eternal peace."

After the last prayer—"Now the labourer's task is o'er."

The coffin was then borne from the chancel during the chanting of *Nunc dimittis*, and thus the poet passed out of the church. The six pall-bearers were representatives of the chief works to which Canon Ellerton had devoted so much of his life: *Hymns Ancient and Modern* by the Rev. C. W. Bond, in the absence of the Chairman of the Committee, the Rev. G. Cosby White; *Church Hymns* by the Rev. R. Brown-Borthwick; *The Children's Hymn-Book* by the Rev. Herbert Harvey, deputed by Bishop Walsham How, who was unable to attend; *The Hymnal Companion* by the Rev. C. E. Storrs, in the place of Bishop E. H. Bickersteth, who was unavoidably absent; Colonel Acton represented the Society for Promoting Christian Knowledge, and Mr. W. M. Moorsom the parishioners of Crewe Green. The procession neared the grave singing, "O shining city of our God."

The Vicar committed the body to the ground, the choir singing the verse "I heard a voice from heaven," etc., while after the concluding prayer the choir broke out into the loveliest of all the departed poet's translations, "O Strength and Stay, upholding all creation."

Thus amid the singing of his own hymns was the beloved poet laid in his honoured grave—"Not dead but living unto Thee." Over no one, be it king or conqueror, prelate or statesman, could it be said with greater truth than over the priest and poet now left to sleep in his Father's gracious keeping, that "his body is buried in peace; but his name liveth for evermore."[1] For as the Church of to-day counts among her choicest treasures the hymns she received from her ancient singers, from Ambrose, Venantius Fortunatus, Adam of St. Victor, the two Bernards, and many others, so will the Church of after ages, until the coming of her long-absent, long-expected Lord, preserve and treasure those which have been given her by John Ellerton.

[1] Ecclesiasticus xliv. 14.

CHAPTER VII

CRITICAL ESTIMATE OF CANON ELLERTON'S HYMNS

IF a critical estimate of the value of any hymn-writer's productions is to carry weight, it must first of all be clearly stated what those principles and canons of criticism are upon which such an estimate is based. Mere personal preference is absolutely worthless; in fact, the greater the respect and affection felt for any particular author, the greater becomes the difficulty of regarding his compositions with a calm and unbiased eye.

Before then presuming to offer any opinion upon Canon Ellerton's hymns, we must bring forth the standard by which we would measure them, and then see how far they come up to or fall short of it.

1. Now if we are going to speak of hymns, we must begin by defining what we mean by the word "hymn." The definition was given long ago by St. Augustine. Commenting upon the supplemental verse of Psalm lxxii., he says, "*Hymni laudes sunt Dei cum cantico, Hymni cantus sunt continentes laudes Dei. Si sit laus et non sit Dei, non est hymnus. Si sit laus et laus Dei et non cantetur, non est hymnus. Oportet ergo ut si sit hymnus, habeat haec tria, et laudem, et Dei, et*

canticum."[1] This often-quoted definition may be enlarged and paraphrased, but its central principle remains unchanged. We may enlarge it by saying that a hymn is praise to God grounded upon His revelation of Himself in creation and redemption, upon His dealings with mankind collectively or individually, or upon His promises. The essential element of a hymn, its primary object, is praise; the hymns of heaven are pure praise,[2] adoration, thanksgiving.[3] So also the highest hymns of the Church, "Benedicite," "Magnificat," "Nunc Dimittis," "Gloria Patri," "Te Deum laudamus," "Gloria in Excelsis."

But when we assent to the principle that a hymn to be a hymn indeed must be a song of praise, we must not restrict the term praise to any narrow limit. There is a subjective as well as an objective praise. A hymn may contain the element of praise without mentioning the word. For example, no one will deny that "Sun of my soul" is a hymn, and a most beautiful hymn too, but there is not in it a single word of direct, objective praise; but who does not feel that in its simple clinging to the Saviour, and commending all to His love and compassion, there is an infinite amount of indirect, subjective praise? There are multitudes of so-called hymns which are merely

---

[1] "Hymns are praises to God sung; hymns are songs containing praise to God. If, therefore, there be praise but not to God it is no hymn. If it be praise, and even praise to God, yet not sung, it is no hymn. A hymn, therefore, if it be a hymn, must have these three things—praise, praise to God, and praise to God sung."

[2] *Enarr. in Ps. lxxii.*   [3] Isaiah vi. 3; Rev. iv. 8.

metrical prayers, but these are for the most part weeded out from collections designed for congregational use. In fact, we may assert without fear of contradiction, that where the element of *self* prevails, the element of *praise* departs, and where self is lost sight of there praise is supreme, although it may be underlying the words and not on the surface. There is no finer example of indirect praise in any language than "Now the labourer's task is o'er."

Hence it follows that we cannot condemn or reject a hymn because it contains the personal pronoun in the singular number, or where would be "*My* soul doth magnify the Lord"; "For *mine* eyes have seen Thy Salvation"? The individual experience of one may be, and often is, the general experience of others, and when this is the case let the others take the language of the one and make it their own.

2. Again, a hymn is a song of praise and thanksgiving offered to God the Father through the Son, according to St. Paul's precept "giving thanks to God and the Father by Him." Of course no one will venture to affirm that hymns, like prayers, may not be addressed to the other Persons of the Holy Trinity; the "Te Deum" itself, although a hymn of praise to the blessed Three in One, seems in its opening verses to address itself to the Second Person, "Te Deum laudamus," *not* "we praise Thee, O God," but "we praise Thee, the God," or "we praise Thee as God." "That hymns were addressed to Christ as God as early as the first and second centuries, is not only sug-

gested by the well-known passage of Pliny's letter to Trajan (x. 96), but asserted apparently by St. Hippolitus, who speaks of Psalms and Odes of the brethren 'written by faithful men from the beginning, which hymn Christ the Word of God calling Him God.'"[1] In fact, the new song of the redeemed, united afterwards to the full chorus of heaven, is addressed to the Redeemer—"Worthy is the Lamb that was slain." The same holy instinct of the Church which constrained her to offer prayers to the Son,[2] compelled her also to direct to Him her praises; still it should be borne in mind, that it is her *normal* principle to offer both to the Father by, through, in the Name of, the Son.

3. Again, hymns of praise offered to Him Who is the God of Truth, must be true to those who sing them. Nothing can excuse false sentiment in a hymn. To hear a whole congregation professing before God feelings which only the most saintly can truly know, and they perhaps but very feebly; or still worse, to listen to them making "passionate entreaties for death, that there may be an immediate attainment of glory," is inexpressibly shocking; it is standing before God with a lie in their right hand.[3]

4. Another essential necessity in a hymn is a soundness of doctrine. The particular point in

---

[1] Julian, *Dictionary of Hymnology*, Art. "Te Deum," p. 1125.

[2] Three of the Collects are thus addressed—Third Sunday in Advent, St. Stephen, First Sunday in Lent.

[3] Isaiah xliv. 20.

which many fail is the utter ignoring of the intermediate state. Their teaching is that at death the godly go straight to heaven and the ungodly straight to hell. This mistake is very serious, for it not only is a practical denial of the words of the Saviour to the penitent malefactor, "To-day shalt thou be with me in Paradise," but it obscures the Scriptural doctrine of the Judgment of the last great day.[1]

5. A good hymn should be congregational. It is by no means a bar to its reception into a Hymnal that it is written in the singular number. We have the warrant of many Psalms for this; but the Psalms express, whether in the singular or plural, feelings which are, or should be, common to a congregation of Christians; and if a hymn embodies the same, it is not sufficient cause for its banishment from congregational use that it is in the singular number. At the same time this is a hymnic licence which should not be indulged in too freely. There is a wide difference between hymns suitable for public and those for private use. A hymn may be eminently beautiful and perfect as a composition yet totally unsuitable for congregational purposes. How many so-called hymns are simply metrical prayers. If all compositions which embody private and personal Christian ex-

---

[1] As an example see the opening verse of a popular hymn by the Rev. Samuel Crossman (d. 1683)—

"Jerusalem on high
My song and city is,
My home whene'er I die,
The centre of my bliss."

perience, together with all metrical prayers, were gathered out of our best Hymnals, and incorporated elsewhere, there would be room in the former for many a fine hymn now lying under sentence of banishment.

Praise, addressed chiefly, though by no means exclusively, to our Father in heaven ; truthfulness, soundness of doctrine, forgetfulness of self, these are some of the points by which we judge of the excellence of a hymn. Now if we judge Mr. Ellerton's hymns by these standards we shall find that they will well bear the test. It is true that his hymns are never pitched in the highest key of adoration and praise; there is none of them that attempt such a seraphic flight as Heber's " Holy, Holy, Holy, Lord God Almighty," but the element of praise is powerfully felt in many. With what a noble outburst of praise does one of his evening hymns open—

> " Father, in Thy glorious dwelling,
> All Thy works Thy praise are telling,
> Resting neither day nor night ;
> With the hymns of Thy creation
> Let our evening adoration
> Rise accepted in Thy sight."

Most of the Latin hymns he selected for translation are jubilant with praise, notably the " Alleluia perenne."

It is impossible to study the volume entitled *Hymns Original and Translated* without being struck with the frequency with which the hymns it contains are addressed to the First Person of the Holy Trinity. There are many exceptions ;

necessarily those on the Passion, including the magnificent "Throned upon the awful Tree," the Christmas hymns, and several of those for the other Festivals and Saints' Days, and the lovely hymn for Sunday evening, "Saviour, again to Thy dear Name we raise." Otherwise his finest hymns are addressed to the Father, *e. g.* "Father, in Thy glorious dwelling," "God of the living in Whose eyes," "Lift the strain of high thanksgiving," the translation "O Strength and Stay upholding all creation," and especially the two exquisite funeral hymns, "When the day of toil is done," and "Now the labourer's task is o'er."

It is almost superfluous to say that all Mr. Ellerton's hymns are as conspicuous for soundness of doctrine as they are for truthfulness. They are eminently sober and reverent; contain no fulsome and familiar addresses to the Divine Being such as spoil so many of the hymns of the last century, no exaggerated sentiment. Indeed, the intense devoutness and reverence of their author made this impossible. A spirit of deepest reverence runs through them all, and no writer was ever more careful not to put into the lips of a congregation words which, as Christians, they could not make their own.

Hence it is that Mr. Ellerton's hymns are eminently congregational. A well-known writer[1] has said, "What makes Mr. Ellerton's hymns especially valuable—over and above their high poetic merit—is their congregational character. A too common fault of modern hymns is that they

[1] Henry Attwell, K.O.C.

are suited to private devotion rather than to public worship, or that they assume in those for whose use they are destined a degree of spiritual experience which is impossible in the young, and very rare in the average adult worshipper. And not only so; their diction is often marred by peculiarities of structure and by obscure metaphors that render them unfit for mixed congregations. Mr. Ellerton's hymns are not chargeable with either of these defects. Whether their tone is sad or jubilant, they appeal to the faith and feelings of young and old alike, while they are couched in language of such simple grace as will ensure them a lasting place in hymnal literature."

Not all Mr. Ellerton's hymns have as yet been incorporated into the great Hymnals; some perhaps never will be, for they vary much in quality. Some, however, the Church, having once counted them among her jewels of praise, will keep and guard to the end. "This is the day of light" will for many a year stand side by side with "Jam lucis orto sidere," and Bishop Ken's "Awake, my soul." "Saviour, again to Thy dear Name we raise," has already taken such deep root wherever throughout Christendom English hymns are sung that its immortality is secured. The older hymns which saw little or nothing beyond the physical agony of the Cross, must allow that the profoundly pathetic "Throned upon the awful Tree" stands higher than they among the hymns on the Passion, far higher than the *Stabat mater dolorosa*, which makes the central figure of Calvary to be, not the Son of God bearing the sin of the world, but the

Blessed Virgin Mother. When we remember that before Mr. Ellerton began to write, the Church of England did not possess one really fine funeral hymn, for the *Dies Iræ* is rather a meditation on the Day of Judgment; when the stock hymn for such an occasion was "Oft as the bell with solemn toll," we cannot but thank God Who put it into the heart of His servant to write "Now the labourer's task is o'er," a hymn which brings almost daily, wherever graveside tears are falling, peace and comfort and assurance of hope.

As Canon Ellerton's reputation spread he was continually receiving requests from all parts of the world for permission to use his hymns, an act of courtesy which was not strictly necessary, since, as we have seen in his letter to Bishop E. H. Bickersteth, he absolutely refused to protect them by copyright, regarding himself not so much their author, as the channel through which God had given them to the Church.

As the following letter appears to concern the Authorized Hymnal of the American Church, it is of sufficient importance to quote in part.

"*Boston, U.S.A.*
"*February* 24, 1892.

"REV. AND DEAR SIR,

"At the last meeting of the Commission appointed by the General Convention of the American Episcopal Church for the revision of the new Hymnal, I was appointed to obtain of authors whose hymns it is proposed to include in the collection the permission for their publication.

"I therefore take the liberty to ask your permission for the publication in the new Hymnal of the hymns beginning—

"God of the living.
"Hail to the Lord Who comes.
"In the Name which earth and heaven.
"King of Saints, to Whom the number.
"Lift the strain of high thanksgiving.
"Now the labourer's task is o'er.
"O Son of God, our Captain of salvation.
"O Thou in Whom Thy saints repose.
"Our day of praise is done.
"Praise to the Heavenly Wisdom.
"Saviour, again to Thy dear Name we raise.
"Sing, ye faithful, sing with gladness.
"Thou Who sentest Thine Apostles.
"We sing the glorious conquest."

The letter contains a long postscript, asking for the addresses of seventeen lady hymnists, and how to obtain leave to use their hymns.

In the Hymnal as published the first of the above was omitted, and the following were added—

"O Father, bless the children."
"Shine Thou upon us, Lord."
"Sing Alleluia forth in duteous praise."
"This is the day of light."
"Welcome, happy morning."[1]

It is remarkable that the list does not include several which we on this side of the Atlantic count among the best, *e. g.*—

"Father, in Thy glorious dwelling."

[1] Note by Rev. J. Mearns.

"From east to west, from shore to shore."
"O Strength and Stay, upholding all creation."
And above all—
"Throned upon the awful Tree."

The following characteristic letter from another American applicant is worth inserting, as showing the estimation in which Mr. Ellerton was held by Transatlantic hymnologists.

"*Iowa City,*
"*April* 29, 1878.

"MY DEAR SIR,
"I have a semi-professional occasion for troubling you with a letter. In addition to ordinary parish labours, I have for many years exercised an obscure and unprofitable trade, which, from the help you gave in compiling the C. K. S. collection, may obtain some sympathy or commiseration from you. In these Western wilds I am supposed to be something of an authority upon hymn-matters, and I plead guilty to the eccentricity of owning by far the largest Cisatlantic library of that sort—some 2300 vols. Pursuing these devious paths, I have been gladdened by the late and rapid rising of your star, which I hail as one of high magnitude. You are doubtless aware that some of your hymns are known and loved in America. Our present Church Hymnal contains but four of them, but these are among your best. 'Saviour, again to Thy dear Name we raise,' is a great favourite. 'This is the day of light' is the best

of Sunday hymns, far beyond all others except Bishop Wordsworth's,[1] and as much above Watts's famous 'Welcome, sweet day of rest,' as a cultivated Churchman of to-day is different from the average Nonconformist of one hundred and seventy years ago.

"'Our day of praise is done' I esteem very highly: it is perhaps too delicate and subtle to be extensively popular. The other is 'Sing Alleluia forth.' I wish our not-too-well-posted compilers had admitted more. 'Welcome, happy morning,' goes into the new Methodist collection which will presently appear. The Report, just printed, of their Committee gives it twelve lines, chiefly from your note in Borthwick's collection. I must thank you especially for 'O shining city of our God.' I know nobody else, except Palgrave, who has done that kind as well; and surely in the hymnody of the future, pure Robertsonian strains like this must displace the coarseness of what Mr. Martineau calls 'the Messianic mythology.'

"All I know about you comes from a dissenting book, Stevenson's *Hymns for Church and Home*, 1873. He says you were 'born in London, 1826. Rector of Hinstock, Salop. Hymns appeared in Nantwich Choral Festival Book, 1866; ditto, 1867; Chester Cathedral Hymn-book, 1867; Brown-Borthwick's *Select Hymns*, 1871; S. P. C. K. *Church Hymns*, 1872.' With the two latter I am familiar, the others I never saw. I found you first in the Appendix to *Hymns Ancient and Modern;* you

[1] "O Day of rest and gladness."

did not begin in time to get into Josiah Miller.[1] I have no English books since the revised *Hymns Ancient and Modern*, 1874, and don't know what you may have done in the last five years.

"May I beg for any information you choose to give about yourself, and specially of your hymns in other collections than those mentioned? I do not ask from idle curiosity. I have made it a sort of duty to be informed on these matters, and to use what I acquire.

"Two hymn-papers I would send you if I thought you would care for them; one in the last number of our *Church Review*, and another soon to appear in a new magazine, *Sunday Afternoon*. And just now I am writing some lectures on English Hymnody, to be read under the auspices of Bishop Perry, in some sort of connection with a little Church College he is trying to revive at Davenport on the Mississippi. In these I wish to do justice to you.

"If I can make any return for the favours I am, perhaps immodestly, asking, I beg you will command me. If you are a collector as well as a writer of hymns, my duplicates are very much at your service. They are always more or less numerous, though mostly trashy. We have no hymnic originality, and very little hymnic knowledge over here.

"With thanks and congratulations, I am,
"Faithfully yours,
"FREDERIC M. BIRD."

[1] The second edition of Miller's *Singers and Songs of the Church* was published in 1869. At least fourteen of Mr. Ellerton's hymns had appeared before that date.

Among the dozens of letters found among Canon Ellerton's papers from unknown correspondents, many from places which are positively trying to ordinary geographical knowledge, the following is selected as being typical of its kind.[1] There is something quite pathetic in the thought of this ardent student pursuing under so many disadvantages in his northern solitude his favourite subject.

"*The Parsonage, Burravoe, Yell, Shetland,*
"*September* 7, 1894.

"REV. SIR,
  "Please forgive me taking the liberty of writing to you, but for many years I have been very anxious to know if you have published any collection of hymns, or any work on hymnology, and as I do not know to whom I should apply, I have thought it better to write directly to yourself.

"For several years hymns and hymnology have had a great attraction for me, but living so far out of the world as I do, I have not had the chance of adding much to my knowledge of so delightful a subject.

"It is superfluous of me to speak of the beauty of your hymns in *Hymns Ancient and Modern*, especially Nos. 12, 30, 31, 37, 118, 401, 406, and 413; and I cannot tell you how glad I was to see so many by you in the new Supplement. I have Mr. Thring's Hymnal, which contains several beautiful ones by you. I have been told that there are

---

[1] Showing that *Hymns Original and Translated*, published in 1888, had not reached the island of Yell by 1892.

some by you in *Church Hymns* (S. P. C. K.), but unfortunately my copy of that splendid collection does not have the names of the authors. I have heard that it is probable that *Church Hymns* may be enlarged.

"I read with great interest your sketches of Hymn Writers in the *Parish Magazine* last year. I there saw for the first time the portraits of J. M. Neale and Isaac Williams. Might you not republish these sketches,[1] and add some more of other hymn writers, in book form with portraits? I am sure there would be a great demand for the work. I also read some years ago your able article in the *Church Monthly* on 'Some famous Easter Hymns,' and I was especially interested in 'Jesus Christ is risen to-day.'[2]

"Again requesting to be forgiven for troubling you so much, and hoping that at your convenience you will favour me with a reply, and tell me about your hymn and hymnological publications,

"I am, Reverend Sir,
  "Yours very respectfully,
   "THOMAS MATHEWSON."

Another enthusiastic admirer, writing from Chicago, begs for "one of your hymns in your handwriting and over your signature"; adding, "If I were to suggest my preference, it would be for your hymn beginning, 'Saviour, again to Thy dear Name we raise.'"

It is no slight testimony to the affection with which Mr. Ellerton's hymns were regarded that

[1] See p. 301.   [2] See p. 391.

some should be translated into Latin. The following elegant version of "The day Thou gavest, Lord, is ended," is rendered still more valuable by the complimentary letter which accompanied it.

"*Malvern House, St. Albans,*
"*August* 9, 1892.

"My dear Sir,

"I have interested myself when laid by for a month through ill-health with a study of English hymns, and I venture to send you one of your own in a Latin dress. If it interests you for a few moments I shall be paying back some of the pleasure with which I have read and re-read the beautiful lines of the original.

"I must beg you, if you find time to look at my parody, to remember that the central thought of the hymn is unclassical, and consequently hard to make intelligible in Latin.

"Believe me,
"Yours very faithfully,
"Harry W. Smith.

"Canon Ellerton."

"THE DAY THOU GAVEST, LORD, IS ENDED."

"Jam, Deus, accepit lux a Te praebita finem,
   Processit jussu nox tenebrosa Tuo.
Te matutino grati celebravimus ore,
   Inque Tuâ solem condere laude juvat.
Nos somnum petimus: terrarum hic maximus orbis
   Volvitur interea persequiturque diem:
Nunc hic nunc illic Ecclesia sancta perenni
   Pervigilat, laudes attribuitque, vice.

Jam rapit hic Aurora diem, mox suscitat illic,
 Et cunctos sensim mobile lumen adit ;
Consequitur cum luce chorus laudesque piorum,
 Atque ubicunque dies panditur, hymnus adest.
Qui nobis abiens requiem tulit, excitat idem
 Hesperios surgens sol, oriturque novus.
Hora ut mutatur, vocum mutabilis ordo
 Laudem auscultanti dat sine fine Deo.
Media succubuit : periit Romana potestas :
 Christe, Tuus nullo limite crescit honos.
Regnabis, donec—nullo non hoste subacto—
 Quidquid fecisti, pareat omne Tibi."

H. W. S.

CHAPTER VIII

CONCLUSION

IN the foregoing pages we have endeavoured to give a sketch of Canon Ellerton's literary work, in which hymnody of course holds the most conspicuous place. From the days of his curacy at Brighton to the last fatal attack which told him that "the labourer's task was o'er," his devotion to this one object was unceasing. He was the chief compiler and editor of the two important hymn-books, *Church Hymns* and the *Children's Hymn Book*, and joint compiler of the last edition of that great hymnal which, above all others, is dearest to the heart of the English Church, *Hymns Ancient and Modern*. He edited or assisted in editing *Hymns for Schools and Bible Classes*, the *Temperance Hymn-Book*, the *London Mission Hymn-Book*. His advice was sought in the compiling the last edition of the admirable *Hymnal Companion to the Book of Common Prayer*; in fact, it is no exaggeration to say, that his hand may be traced and his voice heard in every hymn-book of importance published during the last thirty years; while no less than eighty-six hymns, original or translated, proceeded from his own pen.

We have seen, too, that his prose works were both numerous and valuable; and if we were to add to these the mass of sermons he wrote during his ministerial life, we must own that few ever dedicated the talents committed to them more unreservedly, more faithfully to the Master's service than John Ellerton.

It is a comparatively easy thing to speak of a man's work, for indeed that speaks for itself; but to speak of the man himself, to endeavour to make others see what he was to those who knew him, this is a far harder task. John Ellerton was the truest and sincerest of friends, and his friendship is a golden memory to those who were privileged to share it. He was the most delightful of companions, and no one could be long in his company without being struck with the vast range of his information; it seemed impossible to bring forward a subject in which he felt no interest, or on which he had not bestowed some thought and study. With the entomologist he was as much at home with the Tineæ and Tortrices as with the Sphinxes and Fritillaries; with the geologist he would delight in a collection of fossils, and in their silent forms his poetic imagination would see the creatures which lived and enjoyed their lives in bygone ages. He was a zealous antiquary, and the ruins of an abbey or a collection of coins would elicit from him remarks which showed the largeness of his acquaintance with history; in fact, he thoroughly came up to that well-known standard of an educated man—to know something of everything, and everything of something, and this last "something" was hymns. Hymns were his joy and delight. It was impossible to mention a hymn, whatever its origin

—Greek, Latin, English, French, German, or Danish—but at once he told you its author and history. When lying half-unconscious on his death-bed, hymn after hymn flowed from his lips in a never-ending stream. But his poems, as we have seen, were not all hymns. "He could write," says one who knew him, "charming sonnets, all of which proved his command over English, his admiration for the beautiful in Art and in Nature, purity of thought, and tender sympathy combined with manliness." But the most remarkable trait of his character was his intense lovingness—always making the best of and doing his best for others, never thinking of himself. All good men loved him, and his friends generally spoke, indeed speak of him still, as "dear Ellerton."

What he was in his own family, how thoroughly he entered into the amusements and recreation of his children, showing his love for and sympathy with young people, it is not for these pages to unveil. What he was in his parish would be best understood by hearing him spoken of by those among whom he ministered; all who so remember him love to speak of his tender sympathy with them in all their troubles and trials, identifying himself with them alike in their joys and in their sorrows. It has already been mentioned how, when he held a Mission in Brighton in 1890, the old people who remembered him thirty years before flocked to see his beloved face, to hear his kindly voice, once more. In the pulpit—calm, thoughtful, scholarly—he had few equals; while his reading had a peculiar charm, and the pathos he threw into such passages as the last chapter of Ecclesiastes, or David's lament over Saul and Jonathan, will never be forgotten by those who heard him. As a missioner too—and during his seven years at White Roding he conducted many Missions and Quiet Days, notably one to the Chichester Theological College in 1889—his devotional addresses were deeply impressive.

Yes, dear Ellerton, would that I could offer a worthier tribute to thy memory than these poor words, in which thy pure and holy life is so feebly sketched. To have been thy friend and fellow-worker is indeed a privilege on which it will ever be a delight to look back; the thought that we may meet again, if indeed I should be accounted worthy to rest where thou art resting, gives renewed energy to press forward to that home where, as thou didst sing, there is peace, and light, and joy, and love, and life for evermore. To thee, whose chiefest joy it was to put words of praise and thanksgiving, resignation and peace, into the lips of God's children here, as midst temptations and sorrows they journey onward towards the golden gates of the city where they would be; surely in that day, when the multitude of the Redeemed which no man can number shall mingle their voices with those of cherubim and seraphim in the great seven-fold ascription of salvation to Him who sitteth upon the throne and unto the Lamb, to thee will be given a place of high honour in that celestial company, where the joy which thou hadst on earth in the voice of praise and thanksgiving shall be fulfilled.

PAPERS ON
HYMNS AND HYMN-BOOKS

CHURCH CONGRESS AND OTHER PAPERS

MAINLY ON THE SUBJECT OF AN AUTHORIZED HYMNAL.

The first four of the following papers are among the earliest of Canon Ellerton's contributions to Hymnology. They appeared in the *Churchman's Family Magazine*, a periodical since defunct, in 1864. The first is introductory to the second, tracing the history of English Hymnody down to the publication of *Hymns Ancient and Modern*. The second discusses the question whether one Authorized Hymnal would be of advantage to the Church or otherwise, and the answer is distinctly in the negative. The third discusses fully the canons of criticism by which a hymn should be judged. The fourth contains practical suggestions concerning congregational singing and the choice of hymns and the tunes, although the excellent hymnals now in use render some of the remarks somewhat obsolete.

Of the date or occasion of the concluding paper, "Modern Theology as shown by Modern Hymnody," found among the Canon's MSS., I can learn nothing; but as a just and thoughtful review of Nonconformist hymns it is well worth preserving.

No. I

ON SOME PECULIARITIES IN THE PAST HISTORY OF ENGLISH HYMNODY

THERE is scarcely any event in the history of our Church worship during the past sixty years so great and so remarkable as the substitution of Hymns for metrical Psalms. It is great, because it involves a change in the whole character of our Common Praise as important as that which the adoption of a new Office for morning and evening service would make in that of our Common Prayer. It is remarkable, because we English Church people hate all innovation, especially unauthorized innovation, and this is entirely unauthorized; because we hold fast to the traditions of our Reformation, and this is wholly contrary to its traditions; because we like in such matters to be led by our rulers in Church and State, and they have been the last, instead of the first, to sanction this. It came to us from an unwelcome source—from the Dissenters, eminently from the Methodists; it was first adopted by those of the clergy who sympathized most with them; for many long years it was that dreaded thing, a "party badge"; but it held its ground until wise men of all parties began to recognize its value. First as supplementary to the New Version, and then as replacing it, hymns found their way into hitherto inaccessible quarters; and the revolution is at last complete.

I regard this movement with unmixed thankfulness; and I would fain hope my readers do so too. Besides the greatest benefit of all, that our service of praise is so much more distinctively and specially Christian than before, as being based upon the truths we confess in our Creeds, there are two other advantages, scarcely less important, which have resulted from it. This substitution of Hymnals for a metrical Psalter is valuable, not as a disuse of the Psalms, but as a restoration of them to their right use. I believe that we shall now more than ever learn the true value of our *really* authorized Psalter, that matchless fragment of our lost "Bishops' Bible," not as an edifying lectionary, but as an exhaustless treasury of praise; and that its use in song will not be limited to "Choral Services" and large churches, but will become in course of time a regular part of the Sunday worship of nearly every village congregation. And if, by the means of good and simple chants, we learn thus to use our Psalms, we shall, I hope, in due time, get to use them less rigidly. Foreign ritualists (Protestant as well as Roman) smile at our clumsy English way of cutting up our Psalter into sixty equal bits, and binding ourselves down under heavy penalties to sing or say precisely the same words upon the same day of the month, whether it be in Advent or Easter—whether it be a service of supplication or of thanksgiving, a "Lent Lecture," a School Feast, a day of local or national mourning, or a Harvest Festival, an Episcopal Visitation, or a gathering of choirs. But the rule has something to say for itself; of this, as of many of our peculiar usages, we can give a good practical account. If, however, the "custom which has become a rule" permits us to sing hymns selected for the occasion at "special services," may we not hope that selections of specially suitable Psalms will ere long follow?

But there is yet another reason why we may rejoice in this great change. Our Prayer-book has been hitherto our great link with the worship of the Past. Through it we are heirs of the best devotions of Christ's Church, from the time of the Apostles to the day in which the last revision was made. But there, as a matter of necessity, the golden chain has stopped. I do not think we can add any more links of the same shape. Even if we need additional services, it is hard to conceive of modern forms which we could endure to hear within the same walls as the old. But the work which our prayers began, our hymns must now supplement and continue. One whole storehouse of ancient devotion, of which the key was lost with the Latin Offices, is unlocked anew. Cranmer could render their prayers so felicitously that our versions are better than the originals. The dross was purged away, and the metal moulded into forms more beautiful than ever. But the gift of translating their hymns was denied him; melodious English verse was then unknown.[1] On the other

---

[1] Cranmer's version of Venantius's processional Easter hymn "Salve Festa Dies" (a great favourite with our fathers; see Latimer's contemptuous reference to it, Serm. xii. 207), attempted "for a proof to see how English would do in a song," was sent to Henry VIII. in 1544 (apparently), with other "Processions, to be used on festival days." But he evidently mistrusted himself; and he worked against the

hand, while the English Church now has none who could adapt mediæval prayers like Cranmer, she has already produced, within the last twenty years, most admirable versions of nearly every great mediæval hymn ; versions constructed if not with the skill, at least exactly upon the principle on which our collects were adapted from the Leonine, Gelasian, and Gregorian sacramentaries, of silently dropping or modifying the word or phrase here and there inconsistent with the Reformed doctrine, while that which is a witness for our real unity of faith is carefully preserved.[1] While we thus have

---

grain, and at Henry's express desire. Cranmer's *Works*, vol. ii. p. 412, ed. Parker Society. This hymn has now been translated by Mr. Neale, *Hymnal Noted*, 79. See p. 50.

[1] See on this point the interesting essay on "Ancient Collects in the Prayer-book," appended to Mr. Bright's *Ancient Collects*. As examples of hymns treated in the same spirit with great success, I may notice St. Thomas Aquinas's "Adoro Te Devote" (in *Hymns Ancient and Modern*, 206), and Venantius's "Vexilla Regis" (in the *Church Hymnal*, published by Bell and Daldy, No. 71). I need not remark that there is no *dishonesty* in this adaptation of ancient hymns ; the object is not to show what Aquinas or Venantius really wrote (which any one who wishes to find out may easily ascertain), but to present the leading ideas of their hymns in such a form as it may be fit for a Reformed Church to offer to God. But the extent to which it is either fair or wise to depart from the actual text of a hymn, whether in translating or merely transcribing it, is a question which I must reserve for further discussion. Venantius's hymn was written for a procession carrying a relic of the "True Cross." It is translated very literally, but with great vigour, in *Hymnal Noted*, 22. Those who have the right clue to its comprehension will see that, as it there stands, it is quite

fresh ties to bind us to the ancient Church, we can now at length avail ourselves of the spiritual development of the Universal Church since the Reformation. Whatever hindrances there may be to external communion with foreign Churches, we are surely drawing near to our brethren in a most real and blessed way, when we thus draw near to God with the words of their wisest and holiest men. The same may be said of those who have separated from our own communion. The voice of Christian life among them has chiefly found expression in sacred song; and when we take the best of their hymns into our own service books, we take that which is most precious and most lasting in their religious utterances. And lastly, the living and growing Church of our own day pours her spiritual life into her hymn-books. Long did that fresh stream chafe and beat against the rigid barrier of an imagined authority, which kept out from our churches all but the two "allowed" versions of the Psalms. Some small leakage indeed there was; one or two hymns found their way in. Even Tate and Brady could not keep

---

inconsistent with the spirit of our services; to those who have not this clue, it must appear simply unmeaning. Again, there is a far more famous hymn of Aquinas's, the "Pange lingua gloriosi Corporis Mysterium," which has now been translated and revised many times, but will never be tuned to harmonize with our own Communion Office; and it would be strange if it could, seeing that it was written by the most acute theologian of his day to express precisely that very form (the Paschasian) of Eucharistic doctrine which our Church has deliberately repudiated.

Ken out of our churches. And when, by a bold stroke, it is said, of some pious University printer,[1] one or two of Wesley's and Doddridge's hymns ("Hark! the herald angels sing," "High let us swell our tuneful notes," "My God, and is Thy table spread") were appended to an edition of the New Version, they were tacitly accepted as covered by the authority which was supposed to sanction the Psalter. Now however, that, not by State enactments, Order in Council, or vote of Convocation, but by the quiet yet irresistible influence of the good sense and Christian feeling of her congregations, the Church stands committed to the use of hymns, the warmth and power of her worship is felt to be enormously increased. It is cheering to hear of a foreign observer like M. Taine (*Histoire de la Littérature Anglaise*) speaking with respect and astonishment of English hymns, and the enthusiasm with which we sing them. What Frenchman's heart would have warmed to us over the New Version?

As an illustration of the spiritual wealth we have acquired by breaking through our old traditions, let us, before proceeding farther, compare the materials for our thanksgivings at this Easter season forty or fifty years ago, in an "orthodox" church, with those which are to be found now, in three or four of the best of our hymnals. The Easter Anthems, the Proper Psalms, the Eucharistic Preface, are still the same. But for metrical hymnody, that which, as Sir F. Ouseley has well

[1] *Oxford Essays*, 1858. *Hymns and Hymn Writers*, by Rev. C. B. Pearson.

shown,[1] is especially the part of the *whole* congregation in the service of praise, we had our one quaint and well-known "Jesus Christ is risen to-day," and two very prosaic paraphrases of the anthems already sung. But what is the case now? The Latin Church may be represented by two of its very noblest hymns, "Aurora Lucis" and "Ad cœnam Agni" (*Hymns Ancient and Modern*, 126 and 127), as well as by the "Victimæ Paschali," which the Lutheran Church has always retained (*Hymns Ancient and Modern*, 131), and by several others of less interest; the Eastern Churches by (let us say) Mr. Neale's two hymns from St. John of Damascus—"'Tis the day of resurrection" and "Come, ye faithful, raise the strain;" the ancient Bohemian Church by "Christus ist erstanden" (*Hymns Ancient and Modern*, 136); the Reformation by Luther's "Christ lag in Todesbanden" (*Mercer*, 104); later Lutheranism by several excellent hymns, conspicuous among them Gellert's "Jesus lebt" (*Hymns Ancient and Modern*, 140). Wesley supplies us with one of his best hymns, "Christ the Lord is risen to-day;" Watts with "Hosanna to the Prince of Light;" Kelly with "Come, see the place where Jesus lay;" Montgomery with "Songs of praise the angels sang;" and, of course, very many more might be enumerated. Is it possible to over-estimate the influence of such a change upon the next generation of Churchmen?

The result of this general acceptance of hymns by worshippers of every school in our Church is,

[1] *Churchman's Family Magazine*, July 1864.

of course, that just at present her Hymnody is in a state which may be well termed chaotic. No one has authorized the use of any hymn-book whatever, though most of our Bishops have now recommended, or at least approved, some one or more; the field is open to unrestricted competition, or at least restricted only by the law of copyright; each clergyman may compile a fresh Hymn-book for his own congregation, if he have time, money, and patience; the five or six best-known selections, especially those which are printed as Chorale books with music, have each its following of enthusiastic supporters. Thousands are now interested in the subject of hymns, where but hundreds a few years ago knew of any but the two or three above mentioned, which had strayed, no one knew how, between the covers of the "New Version"; the bolder spirits are searching high and low, from the Oratory to the Camp Meeting, for fresh materials; while the more cautious are eagerly imploring, with English love of law, the authorities in Church and State to give the National Church her one Common Hymn-book, to be bound up with her Common Prayer-book, and so to put a stop to the confusion.

I purpose, in the following papers, to consider how this movement may be best turned to account for the glory of God and the edification of His Church; whether it is possible or expedient that our Church should have one general hymn-book; what are the sources available for such a book, and the principles on which it ought to be compiled; and what may in the meantime be done by individual Churchmen, and especially by the clergy, towards directing and consolidating the improvement in our service of praise.

But before entering on this investigation, I must call the attention of my readers to some peculiarities in the past history of English Hymns.

I said at the outset of my paper that the use of hymns in our public worship, as distinguished from metrical Psalms, was wholly contrary to the traditions of our Reformation. And this brings me to the first peculiarity in the history of our Hymnody, *its comparatively recent growth.*

Now I am quite aware that the statement I have just made as to our Reformers is very likely to be questioned. There is no doubt that, at the beginning of the Reformation, the feeling was in favour of continuing the use of the ancient hymns, and that with this view attempts were made to translate them into English. In Henry VIII.'s Primer of 1545, eight of the Ambrosian hymns for the Canonical Hours, translated probably by the king himself, were inserted in their proper places, with the other offices for the Hours. These were reprinted, Mr. Clay tells us,[1] several times down to 1552. But in 1553, when Genevan influence had become powerful over our Reformers, a new Primer was put forth, from which these hymns disappeared. They were revived in two or three Primers published early in Elizabeth's reign, but not, it would seem, later than 1575. And these, of course, were not for church singing, but for use

[1] *Private Prayers put forth by Authority during the Reign of Queen Elizabeth.* Ed. Parker Society. Preface, p. 10.

in private devotion. The only metrical hymn authorized for use in church was the Veni Creator in the Ordinal of 1549, retained, with a good many alterations, to our own day. It is interesting, by the way, to compare this with the shorter Long Metre version, inserted in the Ordinal at the last revision, 1661—a remarkable improvement upon the diffuse and prosaic Edwardian hymn, both in vigour and accuracy; if to these we add the versions usually appended to Tate and Brady's Psalter, and finally Mr. Caswall's version [1] (*Lyra Catholica*, p. 103), we shall have a very fair specimen of the

---

[1] As the *Lyra Catholica* is now a scarce book, I subjoin the most literal of Mr. Caswall's versions—

> "Come, O Creator, Spirit blest!
> And in our souls take up Thy rest;
> Come with Thy grace and heavenly aid,
> To fill the hearts which Thou hast made.
>
> Great Paraclete! to Thee we cry:
> O highest gift of God most high!
> O fount of life! O fire of love!
> And sweet Anointing from above!
>
> Thou in Thy sevenfold gifts art known;
> Thee Finger of God's hand we own;
> The promise of the Father Thou!
> Who dost the tongue with power endow.
>
> Kindle our senses from above,
> And make our hearts o'erflow with love;
> With patience firm, and virtue high,
> The weakness of our flesh supply.
>
> Far from us drive the foe we dread,
> And grant us Thy true peace instead;
> So shall we not, with Thee for guide,
> Turn from the path of life aside.

powers of the sixteenth, seventeenth, eighteenth, and nineteenth centuries respectively, in translating an ancient hymn.

The taste for metrical psalmody sprang up rapidly among us in the sixteenth century. But the question to be decided was, whether the words to be sung should be strictly versified Psalms, as those of Marot and Beza, or hymns, as those of Luther, sometimes translated Catholic hymns, sometimes paraphrases of Psalms or other portions of Scripture, or rather free imitations of them, sometimes purely original hymns. Germany had already the old hymns of the Bohemian brethren, and a few others. They became the nucleus of her subsequent collections. Luther encouraged, by every possible means, the multiplication and use of good hymns; and the Evangelical Churches became pre-eminently the hymn-singing Churches. In imitation of Luther, Coverdale published *Goostly Psalmes and Spirituall Songes*, many of them translations from Luther, some of them from Latin hymns, some versified Psalms, and a few original. These were published with music, purposely for social and domestic use; but they were at once forbidden by Henry VIII. in 1539. On the other

---

> Oh, may Thy grace on us bestow,
> The Father and the Son to know,
> And Thee through endless times confess'd
> Of Both th' eternal Spirit blest.
>
> All glory, while the ages run,
> Be to the Father, and the Son
> Who rose from death; the same to Thee,
> O Holy Ghost, eternally."

hand, Sternhold, Henry's Groom of the Robes, began, in evident imitation of Marot, his version of the Psalms, thirty-seven of which were published in the year of his death, 1549, ten years after Coverdale's hymn-book. Psalm-singing became popular; suppressed under Mary, it revived at once under Elizabeth. In March 1560 Jewel writes to Peter Martyr:—"As soon as they had once commenced singing in public, in only one little church in London, immediately not only the churches in the neighbourhood, but even the towns far distant, began to vie with each other in the same practice. You may now sometimes see at Paul's Cross, after the service, six thousand persons, old and young, of both sexes, all singing together and praising God."[1] This popular movement soon gave rise to a warm controversy; one party advocated part-singing, the re-introduction of organs, and, in the larger churches, what we now call Choral service. The others were zealous for metrical tunes only, sung in unison, and unaccompanied, as Jewel describes.[2] It would seem that Queen Elizabeth's well-known Injunction, permitting "that at the beginning of common prayer, either at morning or evening service, there may be sung an hymn, or such like song, to the

---

[1] *Zurich Letters*, i. p. 71.

[2] *Ibid.* p. 164. Cartwright, in 1573, in his *Defence of the Admonition*, shows us that the Puritan demand was specifically for "no other singing than is used in the Reformed Churches (*i.e.* the Calvinistic), which is, the singing of two psalms, one in the beginning, and another in the ending, in a plain tune."

praise of Almighty God," was really a concession to the advocates of *metrical* as against *chanted* psalms. The mention of a "hymn" must not mislead us; the two names were as yet among the people used interchangeably. No new translations from the Latin service books would now have been tolerated by those who were fresh from the days when these service books had been forced upon the people by the terrors of the stake; and the many who still clung to the old faith clung also to the old language, and did not want that new Protestant thing, congregational singing. Thus it came to pass that, even if our people would have sung hymns, there were scarcely any for them to sing. I say, scarcely any, for we have a few real hymns of this age. A few were appended to the Psalter of 1562, our Old Version. Among these we find metrical versions of all the canticles (a proof of the popular dislike of chanting them, stupidly misunderstood by Tate and Brady, who proceeded to versify them anew in the eighteenth century) as well as of the Lord's Prayer, the Apostles' and Athanasian Creeds, and the Ten Commandments. We have also Mardley's "Humble Suit of a Sinner," and the better known "Lamentation of a Sinner;" another "Lamentation"; the Veni Creator of 1549; a really beautiful "Prayer to the Holy Ghost, to be sung before the sermon," and a long "Thanksgiving at the receiving of the Lord's Supper." In some editions was inserted a translation, by Robert Wisdome, of Luther's "Song against Pope and Turk," beginning "Preserve us, Lord, by Thy dear Word." To the Accession

Service, issued by authority in 1578, were added three hymns, the best of which, "As for Thy gifts we render praise," has been lately admitted by Dr. Kennedy into his *Hymnologia Christiana*; another is an acrostic on "God save the Queene," "to the tune of the 25th Psalm"! A few more might be mentioned, but they are exceptions which prove the rule. No hymns were furnished for the great Church festivals, or for the course of Church seasons; none appeared with that power which seems to belong to almost every really great hymn, of provoking imitations and sequels. The sacred poets of Elizabeth's reign vied with one another in versifying Psalms, and the rising school of composers in setting those Psalms to music. In short, the Church of England followed the lead of the Calvinist rather than of the Lutheran Churches. This is the true explanation of the reproach sometimes cast upon us, that we are two centuries behind Germany in hymns.[1] It is vain now to speculate on what might have been; how Sidney, and Sandys, and, above all, Milton, might have given us immortal hymns instead of very disappointing versions; how Drummond might have continued his good work of putting the songs of St. Ambrose and St. Gregory into an English dress; how Herbert might have served yet better the Church he loved so well, had he been able to offer some contributions to her worship; how Ken might have become the Angelus of England, could he have foreseen that his holy words would have

---

[1] See an interesting paper by the Rev. W. F. Stevenson in *Good Words* for 1863, p. 538.

been auxiliaries, not to the bedside devotions of a few scholars only, but to the congregational singing of thousands. But the opportunities were lost. Those two great centuries, the sixteenth and seventeenth, so rich and fruitful for the Church and the nation in all else, the ages of our noblest Christian poetry, of our best theology, of our profoundest learning, of our highest pulpit eloquence; ages of conflict and suffering for the faith and the order of the Church; ages abounding in ardent, loyal, devout men; ages in which religious questions were the most deeply felt and most passionately discussed of all questions; yet have contributed nothing, or next to nothing, to the permanent store of the Church's songs.[1] While, on the other hand, the true Hymnody of England begins in the much-abused eighteenth century, the age whose poetry, as Hare says, was prose, as the prose of the seventeenth had been poetry; the age of scepticism in religion, frivolity in taste, laxity in morals; the age of evidences, not of convictions; of toleration, not of enthusiasm; an age which sentimentalists think a dead level of dulness; when the devout Churchman had become a tiresome formalist, and the brave and earnest Puritan a prudent and prosperous Dissenter. Then it was that, from the

[1] From a tolerably extensive knowledge of English hymns, I have been led to the conviction that, of the many thousands now in use, not above a hundred at most are of an earlier date than 1700; and I doubt whether half of these were written for public worship. Of course I leave out of count translations, and the curious Welsh hymns of Rees Pritchard and others.

pleasant arbour of Sir **Thomas** Abney's suburban villa, his invalid guest, the gentle Nonconformist minister, sent forth at intervals the first really congregational hymns which had appeared since the reign of Elizabeth. The Church, for the most part idle and corrupt, through the earlier years of that melancholy half-century, took small heed of what the little Doctor wrote, and what the decorous tea-tables of Stoke Newington admired; but to the Dissenters the work of Isaac Watts was a greater boon even than they thought, and the Church in due time came to recognize its value. He was, if I may so speak, the founder of a school of hymnists, of which Doddridge is the most illustrious member. I have never myself felt much affection for this school; I have little sympathy with Watts's theology; and his verse seems to me sadly encumbered with the artificial conceits and tinsel ornaments, now grievously tarnished, of his age. Yet there is in many of their hymns a power of faith and love which still lives and glows. Even in our own Church, some of them, we may venture to say, will never be forgotten or superseded.

The new fashion, it is to be observed, was strictly Nonconformist. I do not know how soon our Church adopted it, though I am acquainted with a parish church in which Watts's Psalms and Hymns were sung more than a hundred years ago, and are in use to this day. Among the few devout and ascetic Churchmen the observance of the Canonical Hours, which the Nonjurors had revived, and which perhaps had never wholly been laid aside since the days of Cosin, had led to the private use of the hymns of Austin and Ken. It is probable, also, that the custom of introducing special anthems on the occasion of charity sermons and the like, may have early led to the adoption of an occasional hymn or ode to be performed by the singers. But this was not congregational worship; and even among the Dissenters the hymn was still subsidiary to the metrical Psalm. Doddridge's hymns were written each with reference to one of his sermons, and intended to be sung before or after it; a fashion which John Newton afterwards introduced for a time at Olney.

But a greater movement was at hand. In 1738 John Wesley returned home from America, and he and his brother Charles began to found their Societies. As is well known, they were for a time intimately associated with the United Brethren, and this connection had an important effect both upon the form which the Wesleyan discipline assumed, and upon the means by which its devotional fervour was sustained. For the first time, men bred up in the English Church, and men bred up in the Lutheran Churches, learned to understand and value one another; and though too soon their friendship came to an end, yet to that brief intimacy, more than to any other single cause, the Church of England owes the revival of her hymnody. From the Moravians the Wesleys borrowed not only the text of many good German hymns, but the precedent for their abundant and continual use; and one of the two brothers, at least, was nobly inspired by their example. Charles

Wesley, living and dying an English clergyman, loving to the last the Church from which he at least had never dreamed of separating, produced, during the fifty years which followed, a store of hymns from among which we may select not a few that will bear comparison with those of any age and any country. He is the true founder of our second great school of hymnists, more fervent, thoughtful, and subjective than the first; a school which includes not only his own immediate co-adjutors and even his rivals, but many an honoured name besides, both within and without our Church, from Cowper to Montgomery.[1]

The third school belongs to our own day, and is the result of the influence of Ancient, as the second was of German hymns. I forbear to speak of it here, because I am not now writing the history of English hymnody, but merely commenting upon a few of its peculiarities. The fact of its recent origin is of importance to us, in our estimate of the stage we have now reached in our hymns, and in our investigation of the possibility or desirability of an authorized Hymnal.

But connected with this late maturity there is another feature in our Hymnody worth notice, its *peculiarly personal and subjective character*. Compare an Ambrosian morning hymn with one of Watts's or Charles Wesley's. Ken's is indeed

---

[1] Toplady, the doctrinal antagonist of the Wesleys, yet really, as a devotional poet, belongs to Charles Wesley's school. The hymns of the one have been frequently attributed to the other. There is a distinct school of Calvinistic hymnists, but it is of little importance.

written for private devotion, but Watts's "My God, how endless is Thy love," and Wesley's "Christ, Whose glory fills the skies," were each of them included by its author in an avowedly congregational collection. "Jam Lucis" (*Hymns Ancient and Modern*, 1) is childlike in its simplicity of feeling, for it belongs to the childhood of the Church. Not merely the plural number, but the generality of its expressions, shows that it was written with a view to being sung by many worshippers, who had indeed a sense of common wants and trials, dangers and sins, but had not yet learned to estimate the individuality of each separate soul, its difference from its kind, its personal responsibility to God. The very allusion to that which is so private a matter for each one, as the habit of abstinence in food, shows that there had not yet dawned upon the Church the thought of how differently each one is constituted from his neighbours, physically as well as spiritually, and of how little avail general rules and prescriptions can be in that inner world of consciousness which is the battle-field of the carnal and spiritual will. But the spirit of self-dedication and dependence which animates Watts's hymn, and the yet deeper cries of the dark and cheerless heart for the light and warmth of communion with its Lord, which breathe through Wesley's, though they belong essentially to all true worship, yet could scarcely have found utterance in congregational worship, till the time was come when the direct responsibility to God of the individual conscience, and its true dignity as the means by which His Word acts upon the human will, were recognized and acknowledged by all.

How strongly this subjective character is marked in the later German hymns which are now becoming so common among us, a cursory glance at any collection of them will show. But in some of our English hymns of the second school—notably in some of Cowper's written under deep religious depression—it assumes a form which makes it necessary, I am convinced, that they should be excluded from the worship of the congregation, and reserved to guide and elevate the individual in moments of private meditation and prayer. Because a hymn may be in itself true and beautiful, it is not therefore of necessity fit for use in Church ; and cannot be made so, as some compilers seem to think, merely by the substitution of the plural for the singular in its personal pronouns. To this point, however, I shall have to recur hereafter ; for it is one of the most important and one of the most difficult questions connected with our future hymnody, what place this later element must find for itself ; how we can best combine hymns ancient and modern and thoughts ancient and modern, in our united worship. On the one hand, we cannot but feel, after long dwelling among the pathetic and introspective hymns of later times, a craving for the simpler and calmer language of the Ancient Church ; for hymns which draw our minds outward and upward, which make the Trinity and the Incarnation, rather than the Atonement, their central thought ; which tell of the source, rather than the process of sanctification. We cannot do without the bracing and refreshing influence of the ancient hymn. And on the other hand we cannot ignore the growth of the Church out of her childhood, the actual presence among us of thoughts unknown to the ancient worshippers; and therefore no mere collection of ancient hymns, be their translations as spirited as Neale's and as melodious as Chandler's, will satisfy the Church now. Experimental religion, as the last generation called it, must be represented in our worship. But surely no part of our task requires such sound judgment, such refined taste and feeling, such clear spiritual insight, such a combination of wisdom and charity, of honesty and reverence, in him who would undertake it, as the adjustment of these conflicting claims. He must indeed be a scribe instructed unto the kingdom of heaven, who shall be able thus to bring out of the Church's treasury things new and old, and to blend them in due proportion for the service of his brethren; who shall recognize the actual point of her spiritual history at which the Church of our day has arrived, and discern her true voice among all the artificial tones she is made to utter; who shall know when language the most venerable must be rejected, because it has ceased to find any response in the Christian consciousness of our people; and when language the most attractive must also be rejected, because it cannot by any possibility express their actual feelings; and so its very beauty would only make it the more dangerous, in that it would tempt men to come before the God of Truth with superficial emotions and unreal words.

No. II

ON THE POSSIBILITY AND DIFFICULTIES OF AN AUTHORIZED HYMNAL

My last paper was written with the view of bringing before my readers two things—the reason why the Church of England has never yet had an authorized Hymnal, and the peculiar character of the materials for such a purpose at present in our hands. I now proceed to an inquiry naturally suggested by my first point, namely, Ought we to take steps to obtain such an addition to our formularies? What are the reasons for and against our doing so?

The first argument that occurs, I suppose, to everybody, is that, as a matter of practical convenience, one authorized Hymnal, for use in all our churches, is much to be desired. The multiplication of such compilations, in an age when travelling has increased to an unprecedented extent, has become a very great annoyance. How few of my readers, among the many who this summer or autumn, let us say, are worshipping as strangers in some church at a distance from home, will be able to make use of the hymn-books to which they are accustomed? Nowhere is the confusion worse confounded than in our fashionable watering-places. One such is in my thoughts now, with its fifteen churches, all crowded during the season; in those fifteen churches, a few years ago, twelve different collections were in use, and a thirteenth in preparation; six or seven of these being peculiar to the congregation in which they were used. Such diversity as this is a real hindrance to common worship; it seals many a tongue which would readily take part in the service of praise; it obtrudes upon the stranger the sense of separation and distance, where all ought to tell of unity. And if it is hard upon the stranger, it is no less hard upon those who are even more to be considered, the poor of the congregation. For the immense number of hymn-books in existence necessarily limits the circulation of each, and thereby raises its price. Some books are sold for half-a-crown which contain less matter than is furnished in others more widely used for threepence. And what is yet more provoking, the two collections are probably very nearly alike. In hymn-books put forth by clergy of similar views, the same hymns will, as a matter of course, constitute the great bulk of each volume. For most compilers go over the beaten track; their libraries are seldom rich in originals; they are the copyists of copyists, and wield in the service of the Church the scissors not the pen. Generally speaking, new hymns of real value find their way into collections made by a considerable body of compilers, covering a large area, and procurable therefore at a small cost. A hymnal which was used in every congregation of our Church would command such a sale that, even if bulky, it could be offered at a rate which would bring it within the reach of the poorest.

An authorized Hymnal, moreover, would secure us uniformity in the wording of our hymns. The worst result of the great number of collections in existence is the unsettled state of the text of many of our most valuable hymns. Each private compilation, though it may not produce any new hymns of more than tolerable merit, yet is sure to present us with a rich crop of various readings in old ones. Any one who is accustomed to the use of different books knows the distracting effects of these perpetually-recurring changes; and, I may add, any one who is accustomed to one particular form of a hymn is not only disturbed, but in some measure indignant at each innovation. It seems to be precisely the case in which the judicious interposition of authority would do good. Let the best form of each hymn be carefully selected, its use in this form be sanctioned, the authorized volume find acceptance, and in a few years other readings will silently disappear, even from unauthorized collections, and finally be forgotten.

Let me, however, so far anticipate the subject of my next paper as to say here, once for all, that by the *best* form I do not mean necessarily the *original* form of a hymn. There is much confusion of thought upon this point. A hymn-book—a book for congregational use—has one only object; and everything in it ought to be made subservient to that one object. It is the material for Common Praise. It is not a "treasury" of religious poetry; it is not a collection of the opinions of four or five hundred men and women upon religious subjects put into metre; if real poetry is to be found there, the reason is only that, *cæteris paribus*, poetic language is better adapted for song than prosaic. Now it is plain that a composition may have in it, as it leaves its author's hands, the elements of a valuable hymn; while yet it may need to pass through other hands, perhaps through many, before it reaches its best shape. The author may have intended it only for private use, or only to express his own passing thoughts; his work may be deformed by the effects of imperfect education, of a dull ear for rhythm, of narrow religious prejudices, of a vulgar or rhetorical style; and yet a wise and devout Hymnologist will at once detect in it the true metal, which, properly purified, will, it may be, circulate in the Church to the end of time. Ought we to reject this because it is blemished? ought we to carry our veneration of relics so far as to admit it, blemishes and all, into a Church Hymnal, because we love and revere the memory of the author? Why should Prudentius's Holy Innocents still play with their palms and crowns through a dozen different versions, because that ecclesiastical Della Cruscan was silly enough to think the notion a pretty one? Why should Dr. Watts's angels clap their wings and sweep their strings in our churches? Why should the noble last verse of "Rock of Ages" be disfigured by a physiological blunder, pardonable in a Devonshire vicar a hundred years ago, but in our ears only ridiculous?[1] Why should a well-meaning compiler, like the excellent Rector of Bath, have taken so much pains to restore to the 545 hymns in his book all the little bald and rugged patches which the kindly hand of time, or the taste

---

[1] "When mine *eye-strings break* in death." It is fair to say that this is not restored by Mr. Kemble.

of more judicious editors, had concealed?[1] Why should Mr. Neale, in preparing *Vexilla* (*Hymnal Noted*, 22) for English congregations—if, indeed, English congregations must needs sing *Vexilla*—

[1] Mr. Kemble's Hymn-book is so extensively used, and its claims upon the attention of the Church are so confidently put forward, that I cannot refrain from directing attention to another mistake, of an opposite kind, in its construction. Here is a most conscientious and painstaking man, who lays down for himself a rule, wise in itself, but not without many exceptions, only to adhere to it where he ought to have departed from it, and to depart from it where he ought to have adhered to it. He has restored many turns of expression which were better forgotten; but he has exceeded most editors in the liberty he has taken of abridgment. The fatal scissors have not indeed been employed in the appropriation of the fruit of his neighbour's toils, but they have made sad havoc of his own. I will give one example. Professor Carlyle wrote a hymn for the beginning of Divine Service, expressing, in devotional language, the part which each of the three great Christian graces—Faith, Hope, and Charity—fulfils in public worship. Mr. Kemble professes to give us this hymn (442, "Lord, when we bend before Thy throne") in the very words of the author. But, alas, he leaves us but the beginning and end of the hymn, and "Love" has entirely disappeared from it! It is true other compilers have done the same thing; but then they make no profession of giving us hymns *as the authors wrote them*. There is, indeed, one conceivable explanation of this strange curtailment. Mr. Kemble proposes we should sing this hymn to "St. Matthew's." Now a suburban organist, who thinks that a tune is nothing unless it is drawled "to bring out the harmony," and garnished with proper preludes and interludes, takes a long while to get through a somewhat heavy D.C.M. tune in "triple time." Possibly Mr. Kemble thought that two verses in this style would exhaust the patience of any congregation; and perhaps he was right. But it was cruel to cut his picture to fit his frame.

first reproduce with "Chinese exactness" a mere mistake in a reading of the Psalms, and then append a note to warn us that it *is* a mistake? Let us, indeed, take all due care of the text of our hymns. Let us do for them what Bunsen has done for those of his own country, or Daniel and Mone for Ancient and Mediæval Hymns. Let us have an English "Thesaurus" to contain, in chronological order, all but the greatest writers; and of these let us have good uniform editions. Gladly would I see reprinted all those hymn-books of Charles Wesley's, of which few persons but Mr. Sedgwick[1] know even the names; and gladly would I welcome the publication by the Wesleyan body of his Psalter, and those hundreds of his hymns which, we are told, still lie in manuscript. But this will be quarrying, not building. When we have got our "Thesaurus," we shall still have to construct our National Hymnal, and not altogether without the sound of axe and hammer.

I hesitate to say, as some do, that an authorized Hymnal would supply a want in our Church system; for the want is already supplied by voluntary efforts. There are surely but few churches now, and those chiefly village ones, where some Hymn-book is not used, either as a supplement to, or a substitute for, metrical Psalms. Still there are, no doubt, some congregations by which hymns would be sung for the first time, when they enter under the sanction and patronage of our rulers in Church and State. The authorization of a Hymnal would be the *coup de grâce* to

[1] See p. 276.

Tate and Brady. But the real meaning of those who look to it for the satisfaction of an acknowledged want, is that the whole material of the devotions of her children would thus be supplied by the Church as a Church, speaking through her legitimate channels, and none of it left to the selection of the individual clergyman. It is fair to suppose that a work so important would be undertaken, if at all, with such care as to ensure the production of a better hymn-book than any now in existence; that from its very nature it would be the most comprehensive of hymn-books; that its merits would secure it ready acceptance; that thus it would become permanent, and take its place at last in the affections of our people, as a part of the Common Prayer-book to which it was appended. Congregations would not then, as now, be disturbed by each new pastor—I had almost said, each new curate—bringing with him his favourite Hymnal; the familiar lesson-book of the child would become the solace of the aged man; the tunes sung at the old church of his boyhood would be linked with words to which the worker, the sufferer, the wanderer in after life might recur with unspeakable affection; and the Hymn-book of the English Church might be a bond of union no less powerful than her Prayer-book for her scattered children, an instrument effectual beyond all other to maintain her hold upon her people, and to promote her extension. Nevertheless, this argument will, I admit, only carry weight with those who wish to abridge rather than extend, the discretion now allowed to each clergyman in the conduct of Divine Service.

Yet even those who demand for him the utmost possible liberty may be reminded that it is the voice of the congregation, not of its pastor, which would be controlled by prescribed forms of praise; that the choice denied to him would be merely the choice, made once for all, of a book, not the continual selecting of portions; and that it would be practicable, and even, I hope to show, desirable, where circumstances might seem to require it, considerably to relax even this slight restriction.

But great as would be these and the like advantages arising from the adoption of an authorized Hymnal, the difficulties in the way of such an undertaking appear to me truly formidable; and it is the consideration of these difficulties which has been my chief inducement to the discussion of the subject in these pages. It is not enough to speculate on the beauty and pleasantness of a National Hymn-book as excellent as our Prayer-book, as much venerated and beloved, combining the dignity of the Ancient, the holy associations of the German, the popularity of the Methodist Hymnody; we must ask ourselves calmly whether it is possible for us to get this, or anything like this? whether we can get anything at all without great danger? and whether, when we have what we have asked for, we shall like it, and welcome it, as much as we fancy?

The first question that arises is as to the body from which an authorized Hymnal ought to proceed. To place a Hymnal on exactly the same footing as our Prayer-book, it ought, of course, after having been prepared, to receive the approval of the Convocations of both Provinces, of both Houses of Parliament, and of the Crown. A special Act would be required, repealing so much of the Act of Uniformity as bears upon the subject. Further, if the Hymnal is to be literally of equal authority with the Prayer-book, its use must be compulsory, under penalties similar to those which enforce the use of the Prayer-book; and it must be specified in the declaration of unfeigned assent and consent required of every incumbent at institution. No one, I suppose, dreams that all this is either possible or desirable. That Parliament should sanction the imposition of new formularies of any sort upon the Church is highly improbable; that it should impose upon it a vast body of hymns gathered from all sources, to be forthwith adopted to the exclusion of many hundreds of rival collections, in which great numbers of persons have considerable pecuniary interest, and to the use of one or other of which thousands of Church people of all ranks are warmly attached, is simply incredible. Were it possible to pass such an Act, the agitation of the whole Church would ensure its speedy repeal. All that we can ask, then, in the way of authorization, must be simply an Order in Council, permitting the use of one particular collection, in the same way as that which allowed Tate and Brady's Psalter; or at the utmost, giving the sort of authority for its use which sanctions the use of the Accession Service. This might be done upon an address to the Crown from Parliament, which, though not probable, it is at least possible might be voted, if it were known beforehand that the measure would be generally acceptable to the Church. But this could only be if the Hymnal had been prepared by a body of compilers which commanded general confidence; if it had been sufficiently long before the Church to invite and profit by free criticism; and if it had been to some extent tested by actual experience. An Order in Council allowing such a book would doubtless be, to a considerable extent, at once acted upon. It is probable that the authorized Hymnal would be adopted by the Cathedrals, by the Universities, by many Colleges and schools, by the Royal Chapels, and by a large number of the churches of our towns and cities. Vested interests would not be hastily and alarmingly interfered with. If the Hymnal were really good, it would gradually make its way. But how much depends upon its compilers! To whom shall we look?

The subject has been mooted in Convocation once or twice; an address from the Lower House to the Upper has been suggested, praying the appointment of a Committee to compile a Hymnal. But of whom is such a Committee to consist? Not surely exclusively of the members of one or both Houses of the Convocation of the Province of Canterbury. Such a work is too great to be undertaken by any body, however venerable, so limited in numbers, representing but one province of the United Church, and composed of members not necessarily very conversant with this subject, and already largely occupied with other business. It is to be questioned whether the result of the labours of a Committee of Convocation would be likely to be a better Hymnal than some which the Church already possesses. It must be obvious indeed, that such a task as the preparation of an Authorized Church Hymnal ought to be entrusted, as was the preparation of the Authorized Version of the Bible, to a body of men specially chosen for the task from the whole Church upon the one ground of fitness for this peculiar duty; and, moreover, left at liberty to avail themselves of the services of any persons, of any nation, and in any religious communion, whom they may think competent to render them assistance. It is only thus that there can be any hope of collecting all the materials available for the purpose, for procuring the best judgments upon their selection and arrangements, and of producing a result which shall disarm hostility, overcome prejudices, and enlist the hearty sympathies of the Church at large. That the book, when prepared, ought to be admitted to the Convocation of each Province for approval, before being allowed by the Queen in Council, I do not question. But I confess it appears to me that our efforts ought in the first place to be directed to the obtaining a Royal Commission of clergy and laity for the purpose of preparing it; and that the wisest course would be for Convocation to petition the Crown to that effect.

But suppose these preliminaries adjusted; suppose a Commission appointed, so largely constituted as to represent fairly every school of religious thought within the Church, and so judiciously as to command general confidence in their piety, learning, moderation, and good taste; still the difficulties would be but beginning. The task of the Commissioners is to provide for the Church a Hymnal which shall obtain from hundreds of congregations, each using its own favourite collection, at least the sort of suffrage which the Athenian general of old is said to have gained from his colleagues. Each hymnist must at any rate acknowledge that the new book is only second to his own in merit. And those who bear in mind how long the Prayer-book was unpopular — how long the Genevan Bible maintained its footing against King James's in general esteem, will not be very confident as to the likelihood of even this amount of success. Such persons will think of the many popular hymns which must be called to the bar of the Commission, tried, and condemned; of the still more numerous ones, which will be nearly up to the mark of approval, and yet, perhaps, on a final revision be rejected, from the dire necessity of compression; of the strange new faces that will surely take the place of familiar old ones, ancient and mediæval hymns finding their way for the first time into ears that were accustomed but to Watts, Newton, and Wesley, or *vice versâ;* of the certainty that the very comprehensiveness of the new book will make it disagreeable to those who are familiar only with one type of hymn; its very Catholicity be mistaken by too many for a cold and unspiritual neutrality. It must, indeed, be a sanguine temper that has not many misgivings as to the success of an undertaking which cannot fail to provoke abundant criticism, which must of very necessity wound many deeply-cherished prejudices, break in upon many hallowed associations, and claim to disturb, even though with the view of reforming, the devotional language of thousands.¹

But an authorized Hymnal would have to make its way, not only against a strong current of prepossession, but one still stronger of pecuniary interest. The manufacture and sale of hymn-books is now a department of British industry with which a prudent Minister may well deem it unadvisable for a Royal Commission to interfere. In any case, the law of copyright, the dread of which has chilled the ardour of so many a hymnologist, who fondly hoped he could gather into one collection every good and popular hymn of the day, will confront in all its terrors the compilers of a hymnal which aspired to supersede all others. What are they to do? Are they to help themselves freely, and then ask for an Act of Indemnity? Are they to try the question of copyright in the Law Courts? Are they to go round to each publisher in turn, soliciting, in the name of the Church of England, permission to make use of his property, in the hope of being able to combine the contributions thus begged from door to door in a volume, which, if successful, is to make all that property worthless? Will

¹ I have not questioned the probability of the Commissioners being able to agree among themselves. Yet there is no species of composition with regard to which the judgment of a devout man is more likely to be warped by early associations and prejudices than a hymn. Who shall ensure our compilers against the catastrophe which is said to have befallen the clergy of one of our university towns, who resolved some years ago to unite in the compilation of a hymnal for use in all its churches, but differed over one single hymn, quarrelled, and separated, *re infectâ?*

Parliament give them power to purchase all the copyrights they require? Or must they be content to construct their hymnal out of materials which are accessible to every one; in other words, to forego almost all the rich accumulations of the last thirty years; to pass over nearly every good translation from ancient or from German sources, and, with such exceptions as the liberality of authors may furnish, the whole hymnody of the Church of our own day? What prospect would so meagre a selection have of fulfilling the requisite conditions of success? And if it be replied that the State can surely do what private individuals or associations have done with considerable success, let the reader remember that the permission hitherto very generously accorded to compilers whose competition was scarcely dangerous, is hardly likely to be extended to a book which, under the patronage of the Crown, is to come before the public with such high claims to universal adoption.[1]

But there is another difficulty to be encountered. The advantages of uniformity in our books of Prayer and Praise are many and obvious, but uniformity has its disadvantages too. Admirably as our offices of prayer are suited to the habitual devotions of the "faithful," they are deficient, we all know, in the power of adaptability to irregular, occasional services, to unforeseen exigencies, to congregations

[1] No one can complain of publishers for protecting their own property, though the idea of *property* in a hymn designed for the public glorifying of God would surely have been thought an unseemly one in any days but those of proprietary chapels.

of a type differing from the ordinary one. Hitherto this deficiency has been the less felt, because the free use of hymns has in a great measure supplied the requisite elasticity ; and of course no one would now think of making a Church Hymnal as rigid in its structure as the Prayer-book, or as the Hymnaries of the Ancient Church. Yet, considering how varied is the character of our Church's work, it seems hard to conceive of one sole book which shall be fit for all times and places of her worship.

The Wesleyans have indeed *their* one book ; but then their congregations are chiefly of one class, accustomed to one very definite type of worship and ministry. But can we indeed produce a Hymnal suited alike to the Court, the Cathedral, the University, and the village Church; to Belgravia and Bethnal Green ; to the mission vessel in the Channel, the Staffordshire pitmen's open-air services, the Londoner and the rustic ; to Yorkshire, Sussex, Lancashire, Cornwall, Wales ; nay, if we hope to see it co-extensive with our Prayer-book, we must add, to Ireland and the Colonies? The Ancient Church, with all its love of uniformity, never ventured upon such a scheme. It is only modern Ultramontanism that seeks to impose upon all congregations and all lands the one inflexible Roman Breviary.

Of old, each diocese, even each great religious house, had its own collection of hymns, and in France, at least, much liberty in this respect is still allowed ; and though it suits our English notions of propriety that " all the realm shall have but one

Use," yet the experience of three centuries has taught us, I think, that this eminently Tudor rule had better not be pressed too far. Some amount of diversity then must be tolerated in our Hymnals, not merely for the present, until uniformity can be attained, but permanently.

There are various ways in which this might be provided for. The best would probably be the permitting each Bishop, if he shall think fit, to allow the use, in his own diocese, of a local supplement to the National Hymnal, containing such additions to its contents as he and his clergy may judge suited to their circumstances. This would be better than a distinct book for each diocese or neighbourhood. A few exceptional cases, such as prisons, or penitentiaries, or public schools, or sailors' churches, might be left to provide their own hymnals ; and possibly a small book for " mission " and other irregular services might be desirable. This would be better than encumbering the general collection with hymns only useful in a few cases, or peculiar to certain localities.

Lastly, there is one more difficulty, the thought of which has deterred many among us from desiring an authorized Hymnal ; the difficulty of providing for the future development of our Hymnody. Noble as it is, it is yet far from complete, and is in full growth at this day ; fostered mainly by its free and unrestricted use in all our churches. So long as the present state of things continues, and the Church demands fresh hymns, fresh hymns will be produced; most of them, no doubt, feeble and ephemeral, but here and there one of great and permanent value.

But if an authorized Hymnal is to settle finally and unalterably the Hymnody of our Church, the fount of inspiration will be choked up; and our third school of hymnists, the only one which belongs specifically to the English Church as such, will come to an untimely end. And there are yet many deficiencies to be supplied. We have no hymn of first-rate excellence for the New Year, for a Baptism, or (saving the prose version of Notker's, incorporated in our Burial Office, "In the midst of life") for a Funeral.[1] Can we then yet venture to gather our stores together, and virtually forbid, or at least discountenance, any subsequent addition to them? May we not fear lest, in a generation or two, our National Hymnal appear almost as inadequate to the spiritual life of our people as that of the American Church; that melancholy compilation of dull respectability, which now, neither old nor new, resembles nothing so much as the compo-Gothic of a suburban chapel-of-ease of five-and-thirty years ago? Some provision then must be made for a periodical recasting, for the admission from time to time of new matter, if our Church's service of song is truly to be the utterance of her inner life, the witness and the helper of her growth. Our uniformity must be organized development, not lifeless inflexibility. Like the inspired Hymnal of the Old Testament Church, ever growing from

---

[1] Even *Hymns Ancient and Modern* can find no fitter vehicle for the faith and resignation of mourners than the terrible "Dies Iræ"; certainly one of the greatest of hymns, but, pathetic as it is, ill suited to the calm and unexciting language of our English Burial Service.

the Tabernacle to the Second Temple, speaking to successive generations of Egypt, of Horeb, of Sion, of Babylon, receiving the voice of Psalmist and Prophet from Moses to Ezra; even so must our Church be free to sing from age to age the eternal Song of Moses and the Lamb; even so must our Hymnal carry on in its pages the unfolding history of God's dealings with us; and be to our children's children, "far on in summers which we shall not see," the heir-loom of a fruitful Past.

No. III

ON THE PRINCIPLES ON WHICH A HYMN-BOOK SHOULD BE CONSTRUCTED

THE great task before every one who desires to see the Church of England furnished with a National Hymnal worthy of her, is to do all in his power to prepare the minds of his fellow-Churchmen for its reception. For it is doubtful whether even yet our people are ripe for it; whether the Church would really welcome a Hymnal of the very best character. This is a doubt which must often suggest itself to the thoughtful hymnologist when he sees how vague are the notions of Churchmen in general as to what constitutes a hymn, and wherein its merits consist. Few people take pains to judge of a hymn. Lovers of Church music too often treat it as the mere *libretto* of a tune; if it has an easy refrain, or a lilting rhythm, if it "goes well to music," they are satisfied. If I were to send my copy of *Hymns Ancient and Modern* round to all the parsonages within the district embraced by our Association, with a request that my friends would mark for me their favourite hymns, I know very well where the stars and crosses would cluster thickest; not round the best, but round those which Mr. Monk and Mr. Dykes and Mr. Jenner have adorned with new and pretty melodies. I myself think there is no better hymn-book in print at present than this; but yet I can see with sorrow that its great popularity (apart from that of its music) depends upon its weakest rather than its strongest features. Let my readers put me to the test; let them take a copy of the book without the music, and try to dissociate words from tunes; then let them fairly compare some of the unnoticed and unpraised hymns—such ancient ones as 45, "Creator of the starry height"; or 95, "O Christ, Who art the Light and Day"; or 173, "O Love, how deep! how broad! how high!"; or 273, "O Lord, how joyful 'tis to see"; or 431, "Disposer Supreme"; or such modern ones as those of Heber (241), Keble (143), or Anstice (276)—not the best, or the best known, of their respective authors; with a corresponding number of the universally popular verses in the volume, with the sensuousness, the effeminacy, or the empty jingle of such hymns as "Oh, come and mourn with me awhile" (114), "Jesu, meek and lowly" (188), or "Nearer, my God, to Thee" (277). And even when hymns are estimated independently of tunes, too often the ear catches at some pretty turn of words, or some favourite phrase, without regard to its true value, or its fitness for the service of the sanctuary. In short, the majority of readers, learners, buyers, and singers of sacred lyrics do not know what a hymn is, or when it is really good, still less whether, supposing it good, it is suitable for congregational use. I shall therefore in this paper endeavour to lay down a few principles of criticism, and in the next try to teach my readers to apply them.

What then is a hymn? Now I will not supply any answer of my own to this question; I will go back to the age in which the metrical hymnody, of the Western Churches at least, began. I will take my definition of a hymn from one of the greatest theologians, the friend and disciple of the greatest of Christian hymnists—one, therefore, whose judgment on such a matter few will call in question. St. Augustine, commenting on the words, "The hymns (Authorized Version, 'prayers') of David the son of Jesse are ended," asks, as his manner is, what a hymn means, and answers, "Hymns are 'the praises of God with song'; hymns are songs containing the praise of God. If there be praise, and it be not God's praise, it is not a hymn. If there be praise, and that God's praise, and it be not sung, it is not a hymn. To constitute a hymn, then, it is necessary that there be these three things —*praise*, the praise *of God*, and *song*."[1]

Certainly this definition is sufficiently clear and precise; but is it too narrow? Has not the

[1] Aug., *Enarr. in Ps. lxxii*. See also p. 161.

practice of the whole Church, as well as in many cases the authority of particular Churches, sanctioned the use in public worship of very many compositions which fulfil none of Augustine's requirements but the last? And in so doing, has not the Church the Divine precedent of the Psalter to fall back upon? Now, first, as to this precedent, let it be observed that the Book of Psalms is much more than a hymnal. It is a manual of private as well as public devotion; it is a prophetical book; it is an inspired record of the spiritual experiences of saints under the Old Covenant; it embraces compositions corresponding (so far as the utterances of the Divine Word can correspond with the merely human) with the historical ballads or patriotic songs of other nations. Therefore in structure it is not to be compared with any collection of hymns formed expressly for congregational use. There is absolutely no evidence whatever that the whole Psalter, as we have it, was so used by the Jewish Church. Had this been understood at the time of the Reformation, the absurdity of attempting to versify it from end to end for the congregation would have been seen, and the Church would not have groaned for three centuries beneath the incubus of successive Metrical Versions. But it is to be observed, that wherever we have distinct evidence, or even reasonable probability of the use of any Psalm in the Temple services there we shall find Augustine's three essentials of a hymn. Such are the Dedication Psalms of the Tabernacle of David (xcvi., cv., cvi.), that of his house (xxx.), those (probably) of the Second

Temple (cxliv., cxlv., cxlvi.),[1] the Processional Hymn of the Ark (lxviii.), the Paschal Hallel (cxiii.—cxviii.), a portion of which was probably the "hymn" of the Upper Chamber, and others which might be named. And further, even if the devotional public use of all the Psalms, penitential as well as laudatory, by the Jewish Church, could be proved, it must be remembered that the Psalter was its Prayer-book as well as its Hymnal, and was not used, as ours, to supply merely the jubilant half of public worship. I have already spoken of the use of chanted psalms in our service, a practice concerning which we may take many hints from ancient service-books. But I am far from denying the great value of metrical paraphrases of the Psalms, judiciously selected, and properly adapted to the needs of the Christian Church. Who would willingly give up "All people that on earth do dwell"? Who does not love to recall some of the happier even of Tate and Brady's verses? of which I rejoice to see a few interspersed among *Hymns Ancient and Modern;* not, of course, classed separately, as if they were something else than hymns—a mistake into which many of our compilers still fall. Indeed, some of our best hymns are adaptations from the Psalter. Several of Watts's so-called "Psalms" are better than any in his other volume; Lyte's *Spirit of the Psalms* has enriched the Church with a few hymns of great beauty, and

---

[1] It is but fair to say, that Hengstenberg includes Pss. cxxxvii. to cxlvi. in the cycle of "Dedication Psalms," some of them being old and some new. Still, though not all Psalms of praise, these are all addressed to God.

there are many isolated instances which might be named. So in Germany, the finest of some of Luther's *Spiritual Songs* are free adaptations from the Psalter, among them the noblest of all, "Ein feste Burg," a version of Ps. xlvi. Such a use of the Divine pattern of devotion is surely more real, more intelligent, and therefore more truly reverent, than any feeble attempt to turn its mere words into metre, and to pour into old bottles the new wine of Christian thanksgiving.

But yet undoubtedly the Christian Church in all times and nations has sung hymns which are not strictly acts of praise to God. It is obviously impossible and undesirable to keep closely to the letter of Augustine's definition. The Church has her penitential days and seasons, her times of trial and chastening, her longings for her absent Lord; and she has a mother's true sympathy with all the varied sorrows and wants of her children. Her very music, then, cannot be all alike; her Hymnody must find a place for the low tones of the fast-day and the house of mourning, no less than for the glad songs of the "night wherein an holy solemnity is kept." A Hymnal which was *all* praise would never be human enough to find a place in the hearts of the worshippers. And indeed there is a sense in which the lowliest cry of a broken heart is praise, for God is glorified by it.

Every feeling, then, which enters into any act of true worship, may fitly find expression in a hymn. But here we must fix our limit. Hymns may express adoration, thanksgiving, commemoration of God's mercies; they may be prayers, penitential, supplicatory, intercessory; they may be devout aspirations after God; but in any case they must be forms of worship. It is not enough that they *suggest* devotion, they must be capable of *expressing* it. The observance of this rule would clear the ground at once of much irrelevant matter with which the Hymn-books of every Church and sect are at present encumbered. The whole multitude of didactic and hortatory verses, the addresses to sinners and saints, the paraphrases of Scripture prophecies, promises, and warnings, the descriptions of heaven and hell, the elaborate elucidations of the anatomy and pathology of the soul; all these, whatever be their value in the chamber, the study, or the pulpit, ought utterly and for ever to be banished from the choir. But simple as this principle is, that a hymn is a form of worshipping God, it is violated afresh in almost every Hymnal that is published. Hymns addressed to saints departed, for instance, though of course abundant in the unreformed times and Churches, should have no place among ourselves. Yet these have been restored to some collections (*Hymnal Noted*, 15, 16; *Hymns Ancient and Modern*, 65, 432).[1] This, however, if mis-

[1] The Reformation, effecting as it did a complete revolution in the teaching of the Churches which accepted it, with regard to the saints, has of course closed to us all, or nearly all, the sources from which we might have been inclined to draw our Saints'-day hymns. But, in truth, few mediæval hymns to the Saints have much merit as compositions to counterbalance that which is wrong or defective in their theology. The best appear to me to be two Gallican ones, translated by Mr. Isaac Williams (*Hymns Ancient and Modern*, 414 and 431—the latter a difficult but very noble

directed devotion, is still devotion, not mere profane rhetoric. But what are we to say of Bishop Heber offering to the Church as an Epiphany hymn an imaginary address of the Magi to the Star of Bethlehem? What of the compilers of the *Hymnal Noted*, proposing to us to address ourselves to the devil (53), or to the wood and iron of the Cross (24)? Babies are the objects of a good deal of domestic idolatry, but why should a venerable Church Society invite a whole congregation to sing to a baby in church (*S. P. C. K. Hymn-book*, new ed., 227)? To match this baptismal "hymn," Dr. Kennedy has a wedding "hymn" to a bridegroom (*Hymnologia Christiana*), successively as "lover" and "husband," and Mr. Blew a funeral

---

hymn), the "Exultet orbis gaudiis" (*Church Hymnal*, 176), and the famous hymn attributed to St. Ambrose, for Apostles' days, "Æterna Christi munera" (*Hymns Ancient and Modern*, 430). So that our Saints'-day hymns have yet to be written. Canon (Bishop) Wordsworth has some valuable remarks upon this subject in the Preface to his *Holy Year*, pp. xviii, xix, but his efforts to supply the deficiency on which he comments do not seem to me very successful. We have, however, some few English Saints'-day hymns of great excellence. Heber's two on St. Peter and St. John, and Mr. Keble's on St. John (written for the *Salisbury Hymnal*), it seems almost impertinent to praise. They exactly fulfil the idea which these Festivals in our Church are intended to express—commemorating the Saint to the glory of his Lord. Some of Bishop Mant's are valuable. The hymn for St. Matthew's day (I suppose by Mr. Anstice) in the *Child's Christian Year*, and one by Mr. Thrupp, on the Brethren of our Lord, St. Simon and St. Jude (assuming the truth of his theory), are both very beautiful, but rather too elaborate and meditative for Festival hymns.

"hymn" to the earth. The American Church sings Pope's Ode to a departing soul (191), and one of her funeral hymns is a remonstrance with a "joyous youth" (126). Mr. Kemble prints stanzas to "angels," "mortals," "sinners," and (in one case) missionaries; to a "believer," an "afflicted saint," and to the Bible. Even Canon (Bishop) Wordsworth, reverent and careful as he is, falls into the mistake of apostrophizing Sunday, instead of praising the Lord of the Sabbath (*Holy Year*, 1), and (if I read him aright) exhorts St. Bartholomew not to "repine," because none on earth can tell the story of his life (100).

But is every hymn to be condemned which is not directly addressed to God? This would obviously be too narrow a rule. The spirit rather than the form of the hymn is the test of its devotional character. Hymns inviting to the praise of God, on the model of Psalms xcv. and c., form a large class, containing many eminently fitted for public worship. Another important class comprises hymns which "rehearse the righteous acts of the Lord," which celebrate the Incarnation, the Epiphany, Passion, Resurrection, or Ascension. Such are most of our good hymns for the Christian seasons. These two elements are magnificently combined in the "Adeste Fideles," the noblest of Christmas hymns, which, now that we are familiar with it in its English dress, as we have long been with John Reading's beautiful tune for it, bids fair to become the most popular also. To this class belong hymns which are confessions of faith. Such was formerly what is now called the "Creed of St.

Athanasius." In fact, all our creeds are hymns, to be "sung or said." Canon (Bishop) Wordsworth insists strongly on the value of hymns as vehicles for doctrinal teaching. "A Church," he says, "which foregoes the use of hymns in her office of teaching, neglects one of the most efficacious instruments for correcting error, and for disseminating truth, as well as for ministering comfort and edification, especially to the poor." This is most true; but it is important to notice that the doctrinal element must always be kept in due subordination to be devotional; the type of the hymn must be a creed, not an article of religion; a confession before God, not a definition to men. Hence those doctrinal hymns are always the best which, if not addressed to God, pass, ere they close, into a direct utterance of prayer or praise.

I will illustrate my meaning by an example. Let the reader compare the two following hymns. They are both doctrinal; the subject of both is Faith; the views expressed in both as to the source and work of faith are identical. The difference is in the mode of treatment.

> "Mistaken souls! that dream of heaven,
>   And make their empty boast
> Of inward joys, and sins forgiven,
>   While they are slaves to lust!
>
> Vain are our fancies, airy flights,
>   If faith be cold and dead;
> None but a living power unites
>   To Christ, the living Head.
>
> 'Tis faith that changes all the heart,
>   'Tis faith that works by love;

> That bids all sinful joys depart,
>   And lifts the thoughts above.
>
> 'Tis faith **that conquers** earth and hell
>   By a celestial power;
> This is the grace that shall prevail
>   In the decisive hour."

This is from Dr. Watts (i. 140). There are three more verses, which, as Watts himself bracketed them, I omit. They do not alter the character of the hymn. Compare it with the following:

> "O God of our salvation, **Lord**,
>   Of wondrous power and **love**,
> May faith, salvation's holy **seed**,
>   Be sent us from above!
>
> 'Tis faith that gives **us** strength to fight,
>   That we our foes may quell;
> And with the shield of faith we quench
>   The fiery darts of hell.
>
> By faith we make our prayers to Thee
>   In that most holy Name,
> On which, for mercy and for peace,
>   Hope rests her steadfast claim.
>
> **For that** Name's sake assist **us, Lord**,
>   **To run** our heavenward race;
> And oh! may no unholy life
>   **Our** holy faith disgrace.
>
> To Father, Son, and Holy Ghost,
>   Be praise and glory given;
> Who pour into the hearts of **men**
>   True light and heat from heaven."

This is the Hymn for Vespers on Thursdays from the *Parisian Breviary*, translated by Mr.

Chandler. I do not know the date or the author,[1] but most of these Gallican hymns are of a comparatively late period; some of them written by men, such as Coffin and Le Tourneaux, who were actually contemporary with Watts, although the hymns are all classed together by Chandler as "of the *Primitive* Church." This is not a particularly good specimen of Mr. Chandler's volume; I chose it simply because of its subject. Watts's first verse is in very bad taste, but on the whole his hymn is homely, lucid, nervous English; it grasps at a great truth, and states it clearly. But Watts simply turns this truth over in his mind, and reflects upon it. He has sat down to make a judicious protest against two opposite errors, and he does it. But it is not a hymn; there is not a particle of devotion in it. To use it in church would be like reading a tract in place of the Liturgy. It is the prevalence of compositions like this which gives to so many hymn-books of thirty years ago that air of cold and wearisome wordiness which pervades them, as contrasted with more recent collections. The Gallican, on the other hand, is less clear about faith than one could wish, but he has read his Psalter and his Augustine. What he knows he feels. He does not think about convincing men, but about glorifying God. He cannot meditate upon faith without praying for it. He promotes devotion while he teaches doctrine. He gives us a true hymn, not very lucid or vigorous, but simple and real.

Another class of hymns, embracing many of the

[1] Charles Coffin, b. 1676, d. 1749.—H. H.

most popular, consists of meditations upon the glories of heaven, and aspirations after them. As to the admissibility of such hymns into church, I am far more doubtful than most hymnologists seem inclined to be. They have, indeed, abundant precedents in their favour, but those chiefly of a bad period; they are liable to be tainted by some of the worst vices of modern hymns—softness and sentimentalism; they afford a dangerous opening to unreality and sensuousness. Still there are some genuine hymns of this class, of undeniable beauty and power, the best being the least detailed, such as the exquisite "O quanta qualia" (*Hymns Ancient and Modern*, 235), or the well-known "Jerusalem, my happy home." But "Jerusalem" hymns might well have a paper to themselves.[1]

Once more, from among the immense multitude of modern hymns which deal with the relations of the individual soul to God, some, as I intimated in my first paper, must keep the place they have won for themselves in our public worship. Not merely are they necessary in order to make a hymnal

[1] The beautiful rhythm of Bernard of Morlaix, with the latter part of which Mr. (Dr.) Neale has made us all familiar, has doubtless done much of late years to bring the "Jerusalem" hymn once more into fashion, so thoroughly do its plaintiveness, its softness, and its lusciousness, harmonize with the habits of our day, and the peculiarities of modern thought. But in its very popularity lies its danger. It is as wrong to build castles with the imagery of the Apocalypse as to denounce opponents in the language of the prophets. Both the one and the other have been done by many true saints and heroes; both are mischievous habits, nevertheless. Yet we recoil from the fanatical, while we tolerate the sentimental use of Holy Scripture.

acceptable to all, but they represent a condition of thought which has become, under the influence of Protestant theology, more or less common to all worshippers who have any sort of true religious enlightenment. To admit them into a national hymnal now is therefore simply obedience to the law, that forms of common worship must express such thoughts and feelings as are, or ought to be, common to all worshippers. This law I take to be the true guide in the compilation of a national hymnal, and the true test of what ought to be admitted into it. Such a rule is wanted. No one doubts that Heber's "Holy, holy, holy," is eminently congregational; no one now, I suppose, would include Cowper's "Far from the world, O Lord, I flee," in a congregational collection. Somewhere between these two extremes lies the boundary line of a Church Hymnal. It may never be possible to draw that line very clearly; because a hymn of first-rate excellence, though belonging to a class not generally adapted to public worship, must not be lightly rejected, and will sometimes compel us, as it were, to admit it. Such a hymn as Charles Wesley's "Jesu, lover of my soul," seems to me absolutely to stand *upon* the line. It is a hymn for times of sorrow—of purely inward and personal sorrow, being originally entitled "In Temptation." It was not included by the Wesleys in their general collection, but placed there by the Conference, after the author's death, among hymns for "mourners convinced of sin." I should think that all who have really felt its wonderful power and reality would wish to see it in a Church

Hymnal; yet most clergymen, I suppose, would hesitate before selecting it as the vehicle of the ordinary worship of a mixed congregation. There is less difficulty about "Rock of Ages," because, though a strictly personal hymn, it expresses the very fundamental principles of Christian life, and is, as its author entitled it, "A Prayer, Living and Dying." A third famous hymn, Cowper's "Oh, for a closer walk with God!" must, I think, be rejected altogether from a public hymnal: true and beautiful as it is, it belongs not merely to a secret, but to an exceptional condition of heart; it is plainly impossible that it could be real for a whole congregation at once, even on the hypothesis that the whole congregation were living and faithful Christians. Only a few at any one time would be in the spiritual state indicated in the hymn, and therefore, while to these few its value would be great, to the majority it would be unmeaning, and thus unfit to offer to God. If this seem to any reader hard measure to deal out to compositions so widely and so justly revered, let me ask him to reflect whether the truest use of such a hymn as this of Cowper's is not in private devotion, and to remember that to withdraw such hymns from public worship is by no means to slight them, but only to appropriate them to their right purpose, and to provide for their fulfilling it in the best way.

So much for the subjects which should occupy a Church Hymnal. But there are other considerations still which must determine the acceptance or rejection of hymns. I will not speak of doctrine; it is of course to be assumed that the Hymnal of the Church must harmonize with her other formularies; and if the spirit of each hymn be truly devotional, the traces of the school of thought from which it has been derived, though conspicuous, will not be offensively prominent. When we are really turning to God, we are all looking one way. Such a volume as Sir Roundell Palmer's *Book of Praise* shows us, as he well points out, the essential unity which underlies all truly spiritual utterances of devotion, and it shows us too that hymns of all ages and countries may be blended in one volume without being watered down by timid variations into colourless and insipid neutrality. Much, however, depends upon the moral and intellectual character, so to speak, of hymns. Supposing many alike admissible, which are we to prefer? Let me point out a few particulars in which the excellence of a hymn may be said to consist.

1. A hymn must be sincere. Professing to be a form of worship, it must be what it professes throughout. Covert controversial allusions (too common in the eighteenth-century hymns), or any other evidences of spiritual pride or vanity, are intolerable. So are theatrical displays of emotion, such as disgrace many hymns, both Roman and Protestant, on our Lord's sufferings. The thoughts with which a devout and intelligent believer in our own day dwells upon the Passion can never clothe themselves in the sensuous language of Faber and Caswall; they "lie too deep for tears." In our Prayer-book there are no overstrained expressions either of sorrow or of joy; no invitations to one another to weep, or prayers for "a fount of tears":

why should such things be found in our Hymnal?[1] Yet many have been awakened to spiritual life by the Prayer-book; and none who have used it faithfully have failed to feel the power of its deep reality. The fanatic may think it cold and formal, but it is only as the coldness of health when touched by the hand of fever.

2. A hymn must be vigorous! Not affected or overstrained in tone, it must yet be animated; not too reflective and diffuse; speaking in words which, though calm, are forcible. I place this, the most important intellectual characteristic of a hymn, next to its most important moral characteristic; and the two are nearly connected. Nothing weakens a hymn so much as want of truthfulness;

---

[1] A volume might be written upon the changes in the outward forms of emotion, which climate, race, and civilization bring with them; changes which are in nothing more conspicuous than in the greater calmness of our sorrow as compared with that of our fathers. Uncontrollable grief brought no suspicion of weakness upon the saint or hero of the Middle Ages; nor does it now upon the Oriental. Tears were true signs of repentance then; there was nothing forced or unnatural in inviting people literally to weep at the foot of the Cross. But we have learned now better the Divine philosophy of our Lord's warning not to disfigure our faces when we fast. The sorrow which overflows at the eyes and the lips quickly evaporates, and is already half sensuous; the sorrow which abides within is fruitful and permanent. Besides, too, the penitence of a redeemed man has already begun to be turned into joy. Hence it is that a true English churchman feels the hysterical hymns of the Oratory merely painful and loathsome. I grieve that the editors of *Hymns Ancient and Modern* should have admitted one or two, which forcibly remind me of a certain saying of Mr. Ruskin's about Swiss crucifixes.

unreal emotion runs into inflated and overstrained language, or into tame and spiritless imitation. Numbers of Dissenting hymns are weak dilutions of Watts; Wesley's "Lo, He comes," gave birth to a whole volume of Advent hymns in the same metre; just as in our own day the *Christian Year* has been the model for many a set of verses, like it on nothing but its metres and its Anglicanism. The permanence of a hymn depends more upon its vigour than upon any other quality. The hymns that can be called really great—the representative hymns of the Church—are few in number; they are most diverse in character; but this they have in common, that they had power to embody in themselves the characteristics of the time which gave them birth. The whole faith of the Primitive Church shines out from the *Te Deum;* the whole piety of the Middle Ages is in *Dies Iræ* and *Stabat Mater;* the whole power of the Reformation rings through "Ein feste Burg." So Ken's three hymns, the dying words of seventeenth-century Churchmanship, precisely represent its spirit; as "Rock of Ages" does the Evangelicalism of the succeeding century. Now some of these hymns are very full, and some very brief; they differ most widely in merit; but they have one thing in common—vigour—and therefore they live and speak on to human hearts.

3. A hymn should be simple. Hymns are not for the few, but for the many, not chiefly to be read and pondered over, but chiefly to be sung. And the hymns of a National Hymnal, especially, are meant for all classes in the nation.

While then they should not be vulgar or puerile, they should be easy to understand; the language plain, the thoughts not too far-fetched. Some of Dr. Neale's translations are faulty in this respect. Thus in the *O quanta qualia* before mentioned, a hymn I long to see in every collection, we have such lines as " Wish and fulfilment can severed be ne'er," and " There dawns no Sabbath—no Sabbath is o'er"; and in others of his best hymns, "God the *Trinal*," " *Conjubilant* with song," " *Laud* and honour," and other perfectly needless Latinisms. Other translators, however, particularly Mr. Williams and Mr. Blew, are nearly or quite as guilty. Indeed, the volume of the last-named editor has almost the effect of being written in the days of " Euphues," and might have been conned by Don Armado and Sir Percie Shafton. Even in *Hymns Ancient and Modern* there are too many verses that, as a friend complained to me not long ago, " begin with the verb and end with the nominative case." Complexity of metaphor and imagery is yet more fatal to success. Perhaps if I were to name a model of simplicity, I might fix upon our old Easter hymn, " Jesus Christ is risen to-day," as appended to the Prayer-book. Every word might be understood by a child; yet how well does it commemorate the one great fact of the Resurrection, in language homely indeed, but perfectly sincere and adequate.

4. This leads me further to add—A hymn should be brief. I protested last month against the curtailment of hymns; and whenever a hymn, like the one I then cited, is framed on a definite plan,

it must suffer from abridgment. I am bound to say, however, that a very long hymn, which, like some of Paul Gerhardt's, flows on till it has outgrown its strength, from lack of purpose and concentration on the part of the author, is also a great evil. Many of the German hymns in Mr. Mercer's book, though curtailed, are still too long for our congregations to use. The Mediæval Church, I need not say, constantly abridged long hymns; and with proper precaution, we may improve some of our own by this process. The verses which have disappeared from Charles Wesley's Christmas Hymn, which any one may now see in the *Book of Praise* (34), are better away. Another fine hymn of his, "Soldiers of Christ, arise," has gained by compression, though it is frequently too closely pruned. Indeed, Charles Wesley did not scruple to abridge his own hymns in preparing the present Wesleyan Hymn-book. Watts too bracketed in his own hymns such verses as he thought might be conveniently omitted; and in general, where the object of curtailment is to increase the clearness and vigour of a hymn, it may be safely attempted.[1] Eight four-line stanzas, or thirty-two lines, may be taken as a limit which it is not desirable a hymn should exceed. Even this implies quick singing, which, though generally to be encouraged, is not of course applicable to every hymn and tune.

5. Lastly—to go back to Augustine—we are to remember that a hymn is *cum cantico*, it is to be sung; and therefore it must be *adapted to music.*

---

[1] The compressed version of the writer's "Saviour, again," is a good example of this.—H. H.

The metre, therefore, ought not to be too complex, or greatly varied. The rhythm ought not to be rugged, nor the diction bald and prosaic. We cannot always expect real poetry, even in a good hymn; but we have a right to expect words that lend themselves well to the simple and solemn music which alone is fit for congregational worship. Moreover, certain metres are adapted to certain subjects. The stately march of our Long Metre suits well the dignity of the Ambrosian hymn; but it is not so well fitted for jubilant words. For these by far the best metre would be some form of Trochaic, particularly 8-7, with four, six, or eight lines to the verse. Again, a lengthy hymn in Short Metre, or a penitential hymn in what is called 148th, would be almost intolerable.

These hints by no means exhaust the subject; but they may serve to show my readers that there are principles of criticism other than mere liking, or partisanship, or fashion, by which we may judge of our hymns; principles too, I hope, easy to understand and to apply. I cannot, however, bring this paper to a close without one caution. The Church of the present day may find herself compelled, by the force of circumstances, to sit in judgment upon the Hymnody of the past; but let not her tribunal be the seat of the scorner. Surely the days are past when it was a sign of good Churchmanship to ridicule the extravagances of the Methodist, or the vulgarities of the Dissenter. I think I have been able to select instances of the faults I have pointed out from hymnists of every school. But it is a thankless task merely to point out faults. The Hymnody of our land ought to be criticized in a spirit of reverence, of humility, and of brotherly kindness. Now that the Church is girding herself once more to her long-neglected work, it ill becomes her to sneer at the half-educated men who evangelized England while her clergy were amusing themselves. We are entering into their spiritual labours, in laying our hands upon their Hymnody for our own purposes. We shall find bad taste, vulgarity, rudeness enough. We may smile at Watts bidding us "drop a tear or two," at Newton "hoping to die shouting," at Wesley protesting that "no sight upon earth is so fair" as a corpse; but for a century and a half we went on singing what we call Psalms, which made the Almighty talk to the "conscious moon," and proclaim that birds were "more happy far than" ourselves. And that long-despised Hymnody has done what Tate and Brady never could do; it has awakened, nourished, and sustained the spiritual life of tens of thousands, in every rank of society, in every corner of the earth, under every possible circumstance of trial. Let us handle it modestly, patiently, wisely; seeking for light and guidance in its use from Him who resisteth the proud, but giveth grace unto the humble; grace to separate the good from the evil, to discern the treasure in the earthen vessel—

> "To pierce the veil on Moses' face,
> Although his speech be slow."

No. IV

PRACTICAL HINTS TO THOSE WHO USE HYMN-
BOOKS AT PRESENT

I SHALL throw my concluding observations into a form somewhat different to that which the previous papers on this subject have assumed. For in venturing to give a few practical hints as to the use of hymns, I can no longer address myself to such a mere abstraction as the "reader." I must suppose myself in communication with some of the many friends, between whom and myself a common interest in the training or directing of our Parochial Choirs has become a bond of union.

It is, I need scarcely say, the congregational use of hymns of which these papers have professed to treat; and to those in whose hands the direction of our congregational singing is placed I now speak. Happily for the Church, that direction, at least in our rural parishes, is most frequently the task, if not of the clergyman, at any rate of some member of his family, some friend or associate upon whose taste and direction he can rely, and with whom he can at any time communicate frankly, without fear of giving offence. In large parishes the choir is often of sufficient importance to be under the direction of a paid trainer or leader, who ought, if possible, to be an intelligent and well-educated Churchman. And yet in such cases the need of a strict organization, of definite rules, and of a distinct understanding that the clergyman is really responsible for what is sung, is even more urgent than in a smaller choir. If the singing is an act of worship, and so a means of grace, the minister of the congregation is necessarily the one only right person to see that it is really and effectually what it ought to be.

I have only to do with metrical hymns and their use; let me ask my friends, then, by whom are these to be used? Of course, the answer, in theory, is, by the congregation. Your object, then, is to get your hymns sung by your congregation.

Now a congregation consists of four divisions:— First, those who *can* and *do* sing; secondly, those who *can* and *don't;* thirdly, those who *can't* and *do;* and fourthly, those who *can't* and *don't*. All four of these divisions must be affected by the singing. The first, whether nominally members of the choir or no, are the natural leaders of the service of song, and through them you must influence the rest; the second must be encouraged and cultivated till they pass into the first; the third must be kindly borne with and tolerated, till they are drowned by the first two; while the last will assuredly feel and enjoy the power of true congregational worship; they too will make melody in their hearts, though God has seen fit to deny them the privilege of doing so with their lips, and among them you will often find your chief encouragement, your warmest sympathy, and perhaps your most substantial help. But do not, I beseech you, fall into the vulgar error of thinking that you can promote congregational singing by depreciating your choir, or that it will come right of itself in some inexplicable way, without care or attention on your part. A congregation can no more sing without leaders than a regiment can march without officers. Do not think that the singing among Dissenters, which is often spoken of as being eminently congregational, is purely spontaneous. Any one who is acquainted with the organization of a meeting-house knows what pains are generally taken with the singers, what tempting overtures, on special occasions, are made to members of neighbouring choirs, what importance is attached to the classes for practice within the congregation. And thus, though the hymns may be in wretched taste, the music vulgar and florid, and actually far more difficult than really good Church music, the result is congregational singing, because of the pains taken with the matter. There is not the slightest reason why your congregation should not sing much better music quite as heartily, not for display, but for worship. If you dread a merely sensuous service, if you are anxious that the singing, as well as the prayers, should reflect that spirituality which belongs to all true communion with God, still, believe me, you will never promote spirituality by letting things alone. For what is the result? If you have no choir, you either have no singing, or singing led by one or two untrained voices, children, or teachers. Perhaps a few of the bolder members of the congregation will join in, but they have never practised together; they cannot keep together, except at a pace of wearisome slowness; they are chilled by the silence of many around them; and generally the singing becomes the most tedious and unprofitable part of the whole service; and you yourself will be left to wonder why, after you have preached to them again and again upon the subject, your people will not sing as warmly and heartily as the Dissenters. And yet there is a worse case; the case in which singing is sure to become truly sensuous and profane; when a parish has a choir which is left to its own devices, with no judicious hand to control it, and no pastoral sympathy to encourage it. Then it is that music is selected purposely and avowedly to display the skill of the performers; that chants and tunes are changed perpetually, lest the congregation should learn them; that the words are so entirely subordinated to the music as to render the singers indifferent to the most glaring absurdities; and, finally, that all idea of Church singing as an act of worship dies out of the minds of those engaged in it. The sooner such a choir is abolished the better for the glory of God and the welfare of the congregation. But if a choir be well organized, well trained, and directed by those who have right views as to its true object and functions, and if the music selected be such as congregations generally can be expected to sing, and the words such as they ought to sing, then I maintain that there is no help to congregational singing so powerful as such a choir; and that under its leading the very finest congregational singing may be expected to develop itself. It may seem invidious to cite one particular congregation in illustration of a statement which is now happily being verified in hundreds; but I cannot help remarking that any one who worships on Sunday evening in the parish church of Leeds will be speedily convinced that the grandest and most hearty congregational singing of metrical tunes is perfectly compatible with the existence of a very powerful and skilful choir, and even of music which errs on the side of elaboration rather than of simplicity.

The fact is, that congregational singing depends much upon the selection of the words and tunes of the metrical Hymnody, and upon the manner in which these are sung. Therefore my first advice to a friend who wishes to make his congregation sing is, Be careful as to what you make them sing; and my second, Take some pains to teach them and to help them to sing.

And first, as to the selection of words. Look to your hymn-book; criticize it, ask yourself, not whether you like everything it contains, but whether it is a real help to public worship; whether the hymns are hymns indeed, and whether, upon the whole, they are good hymns. If not, you will never have congregational singing till some change be made. You may not think it wise to abolish the book; it may be quite good enough to be retained, yet deficient in many of the requirements of a hymn-book. In that case you had better try to add to it. If you can print a supplement of your own, and present it to your congregation, you will often conciliate those who would be disturbed by the suppression of the book to which they are accustomed. In that case you may choose freely from existing books, so long as you do not sell a single copy of your compilation. But if you distrust yourself, or dread the expense of this process, or if you have no hymn-book which you wish to retain, you had better fix upon some hymnal already in existence. And here comes in another consideration. If your congregation be large, and tolerably well educated, containing many persons who are likely to sing from notes, it is convenient to select a hymnal which may be obtained in the form of a Choral-book ; *i.e.* with the tunes in short score, on the same page as the words. This is a direct encouragement to congregations to sing, and to those skilled in music to take their own part, when hymns are sung in harmony. In this form you may procure the *Chorale Book for England* (too expensive, however, and consisting exclusively of translations from the German), Mercer's *Church Psalter and Hymn-book* (in which German and Wesleyan hymns predominate), the new Hymnal of the Christian Knowledge Society, Chope's *Congregational Hymn-Book*, Morrell and Hows' *Psalms and Hymns, Hymns Ancient and Modern*, and a few others. The last is also published in the Tonic Sol-fa notation. The words of each of these, of course, can be had separately without the music. The disadvantage of using Choral-books is, that the congregation is tied to a certain set of tunes, and these not always the best adapted to the words, but only the best which the law of copyright, and the judgment of the editor combined, enabled him to set to them. In country churches, and wherever the congregation sing by ear rather than by eye, it is much better that the director of the choir should keep himself free to use tunes selected from every source within his reach, so as to adapt to each hymn the melody best fitted for it.

But another and a much-neglected part of the duty of the director of a choir, is the selection week by week of the hymns to be sung. Let me urge upon you to consider how important a task this is; how closely connected with God's glory is the choosing the form of words in which His Church is to show forth His praise; how largely the spiritual life and health of a congregation may be fostered by care or checked by negligence in this particular. How can a conscientious clergyman ever delegate this task to any one whom he cannot thoroughly trust? How can he be content with permitting his people to sing words which he would not venture himself to utter as an act of personal worship? How can he ever suffer it to be supposed that the hymn exists for the sake of the tune, by allowing an objectionable hymn to be even occasionally used for the sake of the music to which it has been set? The reform of our hymnody is, after all, very much in the hands of the clergy. If you will be firm in your resolve that hymns which ought not to be sung shall never be sung by your congregation; if you will keep your own marked copy of your hymn-book, and determine to suppress every bad hymn, and to give preference to the best and most vigorous, familiarizing your people with them by frequent use, you will do your part towards creating a taste for good hymns, which will soon show itself in the general improvement of existing collections, and be the best possible foundation for a National

Hymnal worthy of our Prayer-book in time to come.

But, alas! it is surprising how thoughtless and unmeaning is the use of even the good hymns we have. Take, for instance, Bishop Ken's Morning Hymn, and consider how ingeniously our choirs generally contrive to spoil it. Look at it as it stands in the *Winchester Manual*, or in the *Book of Praise* (246), or in its earlier form, if you can obtain it, in the *Layman's Life of Ken*. The hymn consists of fourteen verses. It begins with meditation, wholly private and personal, and rises gradually into devotion. First the speaker addresses himself; secondly the angels; thirdly God. The first eight verses are mere preparation; the true worship begins at the ninth. This devotional part, though uttered in the first person, is, in its simple, universal character, perfectly fitted for congregational use, with the exception of two stanzas which are a little tainted with the extravagance and artificiality of the age. And now, how do we generally employ it? First, we seldom use the devotional part at all, except the final doxology, but perversely select the preparatory verses addressed to the soul,—that is to say, exactly the part which is unfit for public use,—and make that an act of public worship. Secondly, we take the words which refer to first waking, and to sunrise, and transfer them from the scholar's bedside to the forenoon service of the congregation, when the sun has been for hours high in heaven. In Ireland, I am told, where "Morning Prayer" usually begins at mid-day, this absurdity is still more glaring.

Thirdly, we sing this hymn on Sunday, and yet avoid those verses which are applicable to every day alike, and use those which specially refer to the "daily stage of duty" which a devout Churchman does not willingly "run" upon the Day of Rest. And yet we flatter ourselves that the Church of England, beyond other Churches, sings with the understanding as well as with the spirit!

But this is only one out of well-nigh innumerable instances of thoughtlessness which grievously impair the solemn beauty of our noble ritual. How often we hear hymns which speak of the daylight being past sung in the full blaze of a summer afternoon; or penitential hymns on festivals? I have heard the fifty-first Psalm sung on Whit Sunday. I know a church in which very great attention is paid to ritual correctness, where at the Sunday afternoon catechizings it is customary for the children to sing a hymn, composed I have no doubt originally for an orphan asylum, in which they are made to lament that their fathers and mothers are all dead! But it is a needless and a thankless task to multiply instances.

Next to the hymn comes the tune. I will not be tempted to wander from the subject of these papers into any remarks upon the character of our metrical tunes. I have at present only to do with a tune as interpreting a hymn. I would then warn my friends who are directors of choirs, not merely to be satisfied with the excellence of a tune as a composition, but to be very careful in noting whether it is really adapted to the words to which they purpose to sing it. And let them not say

Cela va sans dire. Our very best compilers of Choral-books often make serious mistakes in this respect, hence the necessity of studying the character as well as the metre and accentuation of each tune. Let me give one or two hints drawn from experience.

1. Lay down as a general rule, that each hymn should have one tune to it. The converse of course does not follow, that each tune should be sung to one hymn, and no more. But try patiently and carefully to match each hymn with the tune fittest for it, and keep to that. There is only one exception to this rule: when you use the same hymn through the year on any particular occasion—*e. g.* Morning or Evening, Baptism, or Holy Communion—and desire to vary the expression of it in accordance with the season; then you may adopt the mediæval practice of having a penitential and a jubilant melody for it, in addition to the ordinary or "ferial" one. But it is better to change the hymn than the tune if you can do so.

2. In adapting tunes to words, consider the meaning and the metre. For the first, it is well to know something of the history of the hymn. An ancient tune will often best fit an ancient hymn; a German tune a Lutheran, Moravian, or Wesleyan hymn. Each Church season too has its distinctive character, which ought to be reflected in its music. The tune of an Advent hymn ought not to fit a Lent hymn, nor ought that of a Christmas hymn to be used for an Easter hymn. But a Christmas tune will often suit a School Festival, or an Easter tune a Harvest hymn, admirably. And as to

metre, it is not enough to fit note to syllable, and accent to accent, accurately. The place of the rhymes should be noticed, especially in Long Metre and "Sevens" hymns. Some tunes are composed for verses of which the couplets rhyme (as in Ken's hymns); others for verses of which the rhymes are alternate (as in the Hundredth Psalm). And if a tune of the first kind is used for a hymn of the second, there will be a sense of unfitness felt, which will often make it difficult for a congregation, they scarcely know why, to take it up. Thus, besides the "Old Hundredth," "Wareham" and "Angels" ought never to be sung to rhyming couplets. Hymns which require to be sung slowly are the only ones which, as a general rule, should be sung in "triple time." It is better to make this restriction than to change into "common time" a tune originally written with three beats in a bar.

3. No general rule can be laid down as to the pace at which hymns should be sung. There are some good remarks on this subject in the preface to *Hymns Ancient and Modern*. But each hymn has its own proper speed, depending upon its character. By repeated experiments you will discover this in each case; and you may take the opportunity of testing your own judgment by that of some good and carefully regulated choir. Having got the true speed of any hymn, mark in your book the number of seconds which one verse should occupy (as is done in the excellent little collection of "Metrical Tunes" originally published in the *Parish Choir*), and never allow your singers to

fall behind the standard rate. But remember, that rate may very probably differ, not for each tune only, but for each hymn. Generally, however, all ill-trained choirs sing metrical tunes far too slowly, and chant too fast.

Need I add to these hints one more? Give your congregation every opportunity of learning to sing the hymns you select. Encourage classes for practice. Circulate the music you use among those who will play and sing it at home. Do all you can to break down the notion that the choir are to sing instead of the people. This, indeed, is one of the many good reasons for the choir being an unpaid body, that it is thereby more closely identified with the congregation, and less likely to be looked upon as a corps of officials delegated to do that which the general body of worshippers are unwilling or unable to do. I am speaking, of course, of ordinary congregations, not of those whose circumstances permit them, in addition to their own part in the service of song, to decorate the house of God, through the means of a first-rate choir, with a more difficult and elaborate offering of praise. But much mischief is still done by the attempts of village choirs to imitate those of large town churches and cathedrals. This, however, is an evil which I trust the progress of Church Choral Associations in our rural districts will do much to remedy. A judicious choir-master, passing from parish to parish, will teach better than any book what the service of song in a village church ought to be; and the periodical gatherings of country choirs in some central church will show how noble and beautiful, in its own place, such a service may be made.

My subject has led me to dwell largely upon the use of hymns by the congregation. But before I close these papers, let me plead once more for their more systematic use by the individual Christian— their use, I mean, not simply like that of the *Christian Year*, or other religious poetry, but as definite forms of worship, of private prayer and praise. In the ancient Church, the distinction between private and public devotion was so much less marked than is now possible, that the same hymns sufficed for both. The same "Hours" might be said in the Minster and in the Hermitage. But wherever said, praise formed a part of the daily office, and that praise was expressed in metrical language. Each canonical hour, each day of the week, each season, each festival, had its own hymn. I do not ask for so unnatural a thing as a return to this rigid system, or even to the modifications of it which have been again and again attempted in our Church—in the "Primer" of the Reformation, in the devotions of Cosin and Taylor, by the devout Nonjurors, or by like-minded men in our own day. There are, doubtless, some who can follow such a system with profit; but with most of us it is a mere impossibility. Yet this one lesson I think all might learn from such manuals of devotion—the power of hymns as forms of worship. And when we consider the vast hymnody we already possess, really true and beautiful, the result of a great and powerful movement within or around our Church, we can scarcely help feeling that we are neglecting a great gift from God, if we simply reject all which we cannot use in public.

The hymns of the great Evangelical school will doubtless be its best and noblest monument to the end of time. If those which will become enshrined in our Church Hymnal are found to be fewer in number than some among us hitherto have thought, yet, on the other hand, no period of our Church's history has brought to bear upon the sorrows and conflicts of the individual soul a larger experience or a truer sympathy. While, then, the Pre-Reformation ages will always be those which most influence our forms of common worship, the worship of the individual must needs bear most vividly the impress of Protestant theology. The one manifests what all are to God, the other what God is to each. I trust to see the day when each idea shall find its full realization in our worship; when, side by side with the simple, calm, comprehensive, objective Hymnal of the Common Prayer-book, we shall have a Hymnal for the hour when the door is shut, and the heart is unveiled to the Father. For the two can never be one.

There are thoughts which it is dangerous to our strength and sincerity of character to utter before man; there are burdens upon the spirit, and perplexities of the conscience, to which we have now found that no words of common worship can bring relief. There are joys with which a stranger does not intermeddle. The soul has its Lent, its Easter, its Pentecost. Private devotion requires its own especial embodiment; and all who have tried it will own that no form of private devotion (and forms of some sort must be found) is to be compared to a really good hymn, for its expressiveness, its suggestiveness, its soothing or elevating power, —the facility with which it comes to mind, its perpetual and friendly presence to the memory, its witness to a thousand hallowed and peaceful associations, its calming and consoling influence in pain or weariness, in weakness, in death itself. It is not surely a thought to be lightly passed over, it is not without a lesson of deep significance for us all, that our Divine Master sustained His spirit upon His awful deathbed, not with any new utterances of devotion, not with aspirations coming fresh from the lips of Him who spake as never man spake, but with the familiar words of His Church's Psalmody, the broken fragments of the Hymnal of His Childhood.[1]

[1] Psalms xxii. 1 ; xxxi. 5.

SPEECH UNSPOKEN AT THE NOTTINGHAM CHURCH CONGRESS, 1871

THE arguments in favour of an authorized hymnal are very plain and obvious. It is a thankless task to speak of objections and difficulties, even though an objection may resolve itself into a groundless apprehension, and a difficulty may exist only to be overcome.

The very first question that meets us when we speak of an authorized hymnal must be, What does "authorized" mean? From what source is the authority derived, and how is it to be exercised? We may be willing, as loyal Churchmen, to be bound by the judgment of the Convocations of the two Provinces, and to accept for ourselves a hymnal prepared under their auspices; yet I think we can scarcely hope that such an authority is weighty enough to command the universal adoption by the Church of such a book. If "authorized" means authorized by the same sanctions as the Book of Common Prayer, we are landed at once in the midst of difficult and thorny controversies; and the events which have occurred in connection with the far easier task of revising our Table of Lessons may well lead us to despair of a successful issue.

Then what must the book be? Is it to be denuded of all that might offend any school of thought in the Church? Then we shall have a merely vapid and colourless book, and round it there will grow an accretion of highly-coloured supplements; uniformity will be no nearer; and the object sought will be defeated. Or is the book to be comprehensive, so as fairly to represent, on all disputed points, the devotional side of each party in our Church? Alas, the hymns which some will regard as absolutely indispensable are just those which will prove a grievous scandal and stumbling-block to others. Fierce battles will be fought over its construction, and it will come into the world only to meet on all sides the serried ranks of men prepared at all risks to refuse acceptance to it.

But another point. The time is ill-suited for the task of constructing a permanent Church hymnal. There are three sources—

1. The Evangelical hymns of the eighteenth century, and of the first thirty years of this century.

2. Translations—Ancient and Mediæval, as well as foreign Protestant, a mine only very partially explored.

3. The living growing hymnody of our own and sister Churches. It has burst into an almost tropical luxuriance under the glow of revived Church life—tropical often in its beauty and sweetness, sometimes in its rankness and unwholesomeness. And here I come to the main point. Is this rich growth to be arrested—frost-bound I had

almost said—by the spell of authority? Can it be so? A uniform book cannot arrest the free development of our hymns—it would be disastrous if it could. Will all the fervid spirits who almost chafe under the restrictions of our form of prayer, who are repelled by the majestic calmness of our Morning and Evening Offices, and prefer to kneel through our Communion Service, using devotions more suited to their temper of mind than our Liturgy can furnish—or those who call (and not unreasonably) for new forms of prayer adapted to the varying needs of a growing and widespread Church—will these be content to place upon their necks the yoke of an authorized hymnal? I don't think we have any right to ask them; and I fear if we attempt it we shall either totally fail, or achieve a success which is worse than a defeat. There is danger in a move in the direction of restriction just at the moment of a cry for elasticity.

Then again, a uniform hymnal implies a uniform, or nearly uniform, level of Christian life in the Church. But is it so? Can it be that the same hymn-book is equally fit for a neglected country parish, and for a devout and highly-educated suburban congregation; for a Mission Church in some poor district, and for the College Chapel or the Cathedral Choir; for Cornwall and for Lancashire; for London and for Wales? Other sects are indeed, it may be said, provided each with its own hymnal; but with these, just because they *are* sects, there must needs be a more uniform level of religion than in a great and national Church;

uniformity and comprehensiveness cannot consist. Far better surely to let the various shades of theological opinion in our own communion find each its fitting devotional expression in hymns, so long as we can keep our Prayer-book the one common heritage, and the one uniting bond of them all.

But though I think one national hymnal is neither possible nor desirable, yet there is every reason why we should set this before us as an ideal towards which we are to work for the future, and which in some calmer and happier day our children may yet attain. And I must say a word before I sit down as to what we of this generation can do to purify and elevate our hymnody. Now we must all confess that in the new development of our hymnody God of His goodness has given us an instrument of great power to do our work with; and I do hope the time may soon come when we shall be, not merely tacitly but avowedly, permitted to make the fullest and freest use possible of this instrument to quicken and express our devotion, our penitence, our watchfulness, our thankfulness; when no one shall deem it a badge of party to enter into His gates with thanksgiving in our joyous processionals, to fall low on our knees before His footstool in our metrical litanies, or to worship Him in the beauty of holiness in our Eucharistic songs. From all the hymns of the past we may learn some lesson for the present as to their varied use—from the Ambrosians their help in promoting daily and hourly communion with God; from mediæval hymns their power in interpreting the mysteries of our faith ; from Germany their hymns of Christian experience ; from the Wesleyans their evangelistic power. But in our very affluence and freedom there is a special danger. And I do desire to take the occasion of the first free discussion on hymns which a Church Congress has held to appeal most earnestly to my brother clergy and choir-masters to stand out like men against the ever-increasing flood of unreal and sensuous hymns. I know all that is to be said for these : they are so popular—the children like them —their music is so pretty—they make our services so hearty. But what is the popularity of an hour, if it is purchased by the sacrifice of sincerity ? If we are to maintain God's truth our words to God must be true. If we are to win back for Christ the pith and manhood of England we must ourselves be manly. Those who grind among the iron facts of life cannot and will not be fed upon the loveliest dreams. You want to train our children to perfect their Saviour's praise. Ah! but when the saintly prisoner of Orleans[1] gathered the little ones round the window of his cell to teach them their Palm Sunday Hosannas, he did not tell them that banners brightly gleaming would point their path to heaven, but that the praises of their hearts were the palms and flowers that Jesus would accept, and that He Himself would be their Guide into the heavenly Jerusalem.

You want to draw the weary and heavy-laden to the foot of the Cross—yes ; but when the Italian Knight[2] rose up broken-hearted but consecrated

---

[1] St. Theodulph, Bishop of Orleans, *cir.* 820.
[2] Jacobus de Benedictus, cent. 13.

from the grave of his blighted life and buried love, to take refuge in the thought of the more awful sorrow of her who stood beside that Cross, his immortal *Stabat Mater* does not linger upon all the merely physical details of the death of deaths, but goes straight to the heart of the transcendent mystery of love and sorrow. You want to nerve the Lord's champions to fight their battle against the banded powers of evil ; but " the solitary monk that shook the world " [1] did not go forward to meet the devils whom he believed to be opposing him with the challenge of a surpliced train and organ swell, but in the power of Him Who is a sure stronghold in the day of trouble, and Who knoweth them that trust Him.[2]

[1] R. Montgomery, " Luther."   [2] Nahum i. 7.

HYMNS AND HYMN-SINGING

Paper read before the Church Congress, held at Stoke-upon-Trent, *Friday evening, October* 8, 1875.

THE branch of this subject with which I am now about to deal is the present condition and future prospects of congregational hymnody in the Church of England.

All of us, probably, are aware that the present condition of our hymnody is one of rapid—some would say of too luxuriant—growth. That growth is not restricted to our own Church or nation. The old distinction between Lutheran and Calvinistic communions, that the one were singers of hymns, the others of metrical psalms, bids fair to be entirely abolished before the present century comes to a close. Among French Protestant congregations *Chants Chrétiens* in one form or another (some of them translations of English hymns) have all but superseded the psalms of Marot and Beza, just as among ourselves Tate and Brady have fallen into disuse. Even the old Scotch Psalms are slowly giving way before the newer rivals, and each of the chief Presbyterian communions in England and Scotland has its own modern hymn-book in use or in progress. Among ourselves the revolution is now virtually completed. Two results have followed. The first, the vast impulse given to the multiplication of hymns; their free and abundant employment among us,— their interpolation at various points of our regular services, their value in the various special services which have arisen among us—children's services, missions, choir-gatherings, and the like, their evangelistic use, on which I do not now dwell—all this has enormously augmented their power and their popularity, and has, of course, tended to multiply their number. Then while the twenty-five years from 1835 to 1860 will be marked by future hymnologists as the age of translations, the time when Latin, and to a less extent German hymnody was made available for congregational use among us, the fifteen years which have since elapsed have been years of almost unexampled fertility in the production of original English hymns. Doubtless many of these will ere long be disused and forgotten. But it is to be noticed that these new hymns are not mere additions to our stock. They are displacing the older ones to a great extent. While the best of the early Evangelical and Wesleyan hymns ar I am convinced, valued by Church people far ore than they ever were, it is worth while remarking how few of them appear likely to remain in use. I may take as representatives of modern Church hymn-books three of those which now command the largest sale, *Hymns Ancient and Modern*, Mr.[1] Bickersteth's *Hymnal Companion to the Book of Common Prayer*, and the

Now Bishop.

new *Church Hymns* of the S.P.C.K. Out of Watts' 720 hymns, five are in *Hymns Ancient and Modern*, eleven in *Church Hymns*, while but twenty-eight survive even in Mr. Bickersteth's. Of the 348 Olney Hymns Mr. Bickersteth preserves twenty-one, *Hymns Ancient and Modern* but four, *Church Hymns* but six. Notwithstanding the strong reaction in favour of Charles Wesley's hymns, *Hymns Ancient and Modern* gives us out of the twelve great volumes but thirteen hymns, *Church Hymns* twenty-three, and Mr. Bickersteth's thirty-six. Of the other hymn-writers of the eighteenth century, about ten of Doddridge's, two or three of Toplady's, and a few single ones by other writers, are the most that will be found in the books mentioned. Later authors, such as Bishop Heber and James Montgomery, are of course men largely represented. These statistics will show that it is not mere addition, but displacement, which is occurring. I do not mention this with unmixed satisfaction. In the "struggle for life" of hymns it is not always the fittest which survive. Happily, in their case, disuse is not always death. It may be that the calmer wisdom of a future generation will in some cases reverse the hasty judgment of our own day, and restore to our children some of those words which animated the praise, enshrined the experience, and cheered the dying hours of saintly men and women whose names still dwell among the hallowed recollections of our own childhood.

Next—this increased use of hymns has of course brought with it a great change in our hymn-books. But we must not conclude from this that the number of hymn-books published has increased in the same proportion. Local selections, so common in the early years of this century, have almost disappeared. One after another large and important hymn-books for general use have arisen; each of these has killed off many small competitors, and the number in future seems likely to be diminished rather than increased. Such local books as now appear are mostly mere supplements to one of these. Already a clergyman seeking to introduce a new hymn-book into his congregation is likely to make his choice not, as till lately, from among some twenty or thirty, but from among seven or eight at the most.

In turning to the FUTURE, it is natural to ask if the tendency of the Church of our own time is thus to the widespread use of a few large hymn-books? is it possible or desirable to go a step further, and concentrate into one national book the few that seem likely to distance all competitors? Or is it to be desired that at least a certain number of hymns which are common to all these books should be authorized, and congregations be left at liberty to add to these according to the taste of those who are responsible for their hymnody? Each of these questions I feel bound to answer with an emphatic "No."

I do not think we are ripe for the interference, to such an extent, with the free development of our hymnody. A comprehensive hymn-book must do one of two things: either it must contain hymns the language of which would be so repellent to the views of many congregations that they would bitterly resent its being imposed upon them by authority; or it must omit and alter to such an extent, that congregations which use existing books would be no less disturbed by the loss of teaching to which they are attached. We may deplore our present divisions; we may hope and pray that they may be healed; but for all that we ought to deprecate such an attempt at ignoring them as would severely test an obedience which is not too readily rendered even now, and would turn our very songs of praise into watchwords of theological strife.

And as to the selection of certain hymns common to all, I doubt whether it is known how few in number they are. The great and excellent collections of hymns which the last few years have produced are separated from each other by strongly marked lines. Each covers its own ground, each has its own distinctive character. Thus, to refer again to the three books I have ventured to take as representatives, the revised *Hymns Ancient and Modern* contains 473 hymns, *Church Hymns* 592, the *Hymnal Companion* 400; yet out of this large number of 1465 hymns, there are but 129 common to all three books; and of these 129 the text occasionally differs in particulars which the editors of each would probably consider virtually affecting the value of the hymn. It might be convenient to represent these by consecutive numbers common to all three books; but I cannot think that very much would be gained by authorizing so small a fragment of our immense hymnody. It has been urged indeed that an authorized hymn-book would benefit us by fixing the standard text of the hymns we use, especially if the rule were made of restoring every hymn to the exact form in which it was originally written. On any other principle, indeed, uniformity in the wording is under present circumstances as hopeless as unanimity in the selection of hymns. And yet I own I can scarcely imagine an editor of a hymn-book who has carefully investigated the original text of hymns, seriously desiring to print every hymn exactly as it was written. Many of our old friends it would be absolutely painful to recognize in their resuscitated dress. How many of Faber's, for example, could be included as he wrote them in a National Church hymn-book? Hard things are often said by living writers as to the mutilation of their hymns by compilers. May it be permitted for one whose own hymns have not escaped this unpleasant process to say a word on the other side? That any one who presumes to lay his offering of a song of praise upon the altar, not for his own, but for God's glory, cannot be too thankful for the devout, thoughtful, and scholarly criticism of those whose object it is to make his work less unworthy of its sacred purpose. A Church hymn-book is not a statue gallery erected that men may pass through it and admire the skill of each artist; it is a temple for the worship of the Most High, in which every stone, rough-hewn or cunningly carved, is fitted to its place and subordinated to the one Spirit which informs and consecrates the whole.

Must we then be content to give up all prospect of a national Book of Common Praise to match our Book of Common Prayer? If what I have said seems to discourage such an expectation, let us remember that Colonial Churches, or Nonconformist bodies among ourselves, are too small and too homogeneous to be any true precedent for the great and complex Mother Church at home. The true precedent, I fear, would be that of modern Ultramontanism, which seeks to impose upon every country and diocese alike its own inflexible Roman Breviary, and in so doing is destroying a multitude of hymns and sequences far better than its own.

Some appeal to authority, indeed, all will allow. There are frequent public occasions upon which many would welcome the authorization by our bishops of special hymns as well as of special psalms and lessons. There creep into churches now and then hymns which I venture to think ought to be formally prohibited. Above all, the change of a hymn-book is a matter so important and interesting to a congregation, so deeply affecting its life and unity, that it seems only reasonable to require that the sanction of the Bishop should be sought and obtained in all cases by the clergyman who proposes to make the change.

But the true hope for unity in our songs of praise lies, I am convinced, in a very different region from that of law and prescription. It is not pressure from without, but the impulse of new life from within, which alone can draw us nearer. Our hymnody must be the expression of that life, or it is unreal and worthless. As in each congregation, in each soul, spiritual life becomes deeper and fuller, those hymns will be loved and valued, and those alone, which have in them that true inspiration. And those hymns, whether ancient or modern, whether English or foreign, whether Catholic or Protestant in their origin, will be welcomed and used; not all at once, perhaps, not without hesitation and questioning; but if slowly, yet surely and permanently. Look at our greatest hymns; it is not authority and custom that have made them dear to every congregation; it is not always literary excellence; it is not even in every case theological accuracy; it is a true correspondence with thoughts and aspirations that filled the heart of the Church. The whole life of the Patristic Church is in the *Te Deum;* the whole awfulness and pathos of the Middle Ages is in the *Dies Iræ;* the whole gospel of Evangelicalism is in *Rock of Ages.* And whenever a hymn arises which thus says what we want to say, it must make its way, and be heard, and live. When growth in spiritual life shall have brought with it unity of spirit, then our songs will be uttered with one accord. Who would substitute for *that* unity the uniformity of compulsion, of indifference, or of compromise?

My conclusion then is, that the future of our Church hymnody can be but the reflection of our own future. What our congregations are, what the Church is, that our hymns will be; true and strong in faith and love, or false and weak, empty and lifeless. And that, therefore, the way to improve our hymnody, the way to guide it, the way to restrain it, is primarily, and above all, the discipline of our own hearts. This will give us self-restraint in our choice of hymns, it will save us from being carried away by mere fashion and caprice; from being slaves to the latest novelty, the lilting chorus, and the taking tune. But especially I would plead with my brother parish-priests, upon whose choice depends what their congregations week by week, and day by day, shall thus utter before God, to feel the greatness of their responsibility, and to grudge no time or pains in the selection of the words they put into the lips of their people.

Let me urge them to remember how this work of selection, well done, may not merely form the taste, but elevate the religious tone of our congregations. Is it then a task to be hurried over in two minutes, while the choir are waiting to begin practice? Is it a matter to be left to a young school-master, or a group of young ladies? Is our chief care to be that the tunes are pretty and popular, and the words something that will "go with a swing"? Are we thus to sanction the trash which, alas, will find its way even into good hymn-books: artificial bursts of enthusiasm—sentimental complaints of weariness, or sorrow, or even longing for death [1]—feeble and confused dilutions of the

[1] In ridicule of this species of cant, I have heard J. E. delight in telling the following story:—Old Betty was a bed-ridden parishioner, who was for ever calling for death to release her from her infirmities and take her to glory. Whereupon her neighbours resolved to put her to the test,

imagery of the Apocalypse—exaggerations and affectations doing duty for precision in doctrine and sincerity in feeling? Ought we not rather to pray and to strive that the hymns we invite our congregations to sing may be scriptural, not merely in their phraseology, but in their inmost spirit, reverent not in form only but in meaning, definite with the certainty of faith, calm with the consciousness of God's presence, lowly with the reality of penitence, joyful with the sincerity of thankfulness; that so, whether we prepare to enter into His gates with the thanksgiving of our glad processionals, or to speak good of His Name in the quiet hymn of the daily office, or to fall low on our knees before His footstool in the Litany of Penitence, we may be emboldened to say for ourselves and for our people, "Thou shalt open our lips, O Lord, and our mouth shall shew forth Thy praise."

---

and as she was lying alone, one of them knocked three solemn knocks at the door of her cottage. "Who's there?" with the answer—"I am Death, come for old Betty to take her to glory." "Oh no, no, no!" shrieked the old crone, "she isn't here, it is *next door*."—H. H.

HYMNS AND HYMN-BOOKS

Paper read before the Church Congress held at Swansea, *Wednesday evening, October* 8, 1879.

I READ my paper this evening under a solemn feeling in consequence of the death of Miss Frances Havergal, who has passed away from us since she accepted the invitation of the Committee to prepare a paper on this subject for this Congress. The hymns of this lady will long live in the heart of the Church.

When I was invited to read a paper before this Congress on Hymns and Hymn-books, my first question was, What branch of so wide a subject am I expected to handle? and it was suggested to me in reply to give some sort of outline of what an authorized Church hymn-book, if ever we attain it, ought to be.

Let me begin by reminding you of our materials. They are such as no age of the Church ever before possessed. First, for the home-grown hymns. Within the last few months there has passed away an old man, Daniel Sedgwick[1] by name, who kept a

[1] An interesting sketch of his life and work by William T. Brooke, who calls him "the father of English Hymnology," will be found in Julian's *Dictionary of Hymnology*, p. 1036.

tiny shop in one of the darkest nooks of the city of London, ironically designated Sun Street. This good man lived, ate, drank, wrote, and, for aught I know, slept in the midst of piles on piles of hymn-books. His kindly welcome and amazing knowledge were at the service of any one who was interested enough in the study to explore his strange domain. He could reckon up at least 1400 authors who within the last 150 years had written volumes of English hymns, all of whom he has duly catalogued. We may divide these roughly into four great schools, three of them existing side by side, each of them represented by existing books, and all four happily blended, though in differing proportions, in our best hymn-books—the early Nonconformist, from Watts and Doddridge to Conder, Kelly, and Montgomery; the Wesleyan, of which modern revival hymns are an offshoot; the Calvinistic-Evangelical; and the Anglican and Anglo-Catholic of our own time. Each of these four schools must necessarily be represented in any hymn-book which is to be a true help to the devotions of the whole English Church. But we have also, and we need also, hymns from other sources. I am not going to insult the understanding of my hearers by assuming that any one here entertains the strange notion that while the Collects we have translated from the ancient service-books are an inestimable treasure of devotion, the hymns which lie beside them in the same quarry are unfit for our use. What I claim for Latin hymns in general is what I claim for Latin prayers: that many are of exceeding value; that the oldest are generally the best; that the Church of England may well deal with them as she dealt with the Collects—transferring many whole, leaving a certain number alone, boldly altering and adapting others to suit her own requirements. An admirable example of the last mode of treatment is the Bishop of Ely's translation of *Adoro Te Devote*, if only the text be left as the Bishop wrote it; retaining as it does the spirit of humble and believing reverence which pervades the hymn, without any phrases which might clash with our authorized definitions of doctrine. Premising this, I may observe that now all the great Latin hymns have been repeatedly translated, some of them by successive revisions, as well as it is possible to render them. Many have taken root among us; some are as familiar as their kindred Collects, and are sung by all denominations in England and Scotland just as heartily and unconsciously as if they were home-born. We may almost say the same of the few imitations of Greek hymns which Dr. Neale and others have given us. Few would imagine Mr. Chatfield's touching hymn, "Lord Jesus, think on me," to be the work of the fifth-century African squire-bishop,[1] of whom Charles Kingsley has given us so graphic a portrait in *Hypatia*. The rich store of German hymnody has been opened to us mainly by one who has been taken to her rest since the last Congress, Catherine Winkworth. But few of these hymns are fitted for congregational use; yet these few are of great and permanent value. I think, too, that

[1] Synesius, Bishop of Ptolemaïs: he died in 430.—H. H.

we may gain something from the hymns of Protestant France; and to one who may be surprised at this, I would recommend the study of the beautiful little hymnal published by the Society for the Promotion of Christian Knowledge for use in the Channel Islands. Nor must we forget that the Church Congress is welcomed this week among fellow-countrymen who have a hymnody of their own, dating further back than ours. I, as a Saxon stranger, know of the hymns of Rhys Prichard only through wretched translations from which all the poetry has evaporated; yet even so I can well understand how the "Welshman's Candle" of the early seventeenth century, with its manly piety, its practical good sense, and its firm hold upon the great truths of our faith, expressed in the plainest and homeliest language, must have been a true light from God to many and many a lonely home. And our kind hosts have shown us this week how they love, and how they can sing, the hymnody of William Williams, represented in our hymnals, I believe, only by the well-known hymn, "Guide me, O Thou Great Jehovah."

I pass on to consider the far more difficult question, how to use our materials?

We are all agreed that a Book of Common Praise ought to follow the lines of our Book of Common Prayer, and yet, in some sense, to fill up and supplement the Prayer-book. The question is, In what sense? Not, surely, by any inconsistency or even development of doctrine. Whatever the limits of comprehension may be as regards individuals, or even as regards particular congregations, a book which shall appear as an addition to the existing formularies of the Church of England must not differ from these any more widely than they differ from one another. But if it be the case that the different elements of which our Prayer-book consists bring out different sides of the same truth, and set forth the faith from varying points of view, then this amount of comprehensiveness we may fairly claim for an authorized hymn-book. To secure this, it must not be the work of one school, or of a very small body of divines. No existing book ought to become the authorized book. I am glad to support this view by the opinion of one whose loss we are still lamenting, who presided over the compilation of our most popular and widely-used hymn-book. The late Sir Henry Baker, heartily as he rejoiced in the wonderful success of *Hymns Ancient and Modern*, always expressed his conviction that it could never become more than one of two or three hymnals which should ultimately divide our congregations among them. He felt that it was the product but of one school in the Church of England, though a school into which he himself infused a large spirit of comprehensiveness.

We must further remember, that if ever the day comes that our Church possesses an authorized hymn-book, it will be quite as much used out of church as in it; it will grow to be used in the family and in private devotion, by the poor, the sick, the aged, the lonely, the mourner, just as much as the Prayer-book, or even more. It is vain, then, to fancy we can keep out private and what are called subjective hymns. Some such, wisely selected, there must be ; as subjective as the 42nd Psalm, or the 51st, or the 103rd. There are those who gravely tell us that hymns in the singular number are unfit for public worship, and so would shut out " Rock of Ages " and " Sun of my soul "— why not also the " Miserere " and the " Nunc Dimittis " ?

Again, when an authorized selection is made, something must still be left to individual liberty. I have on a former occasion given my reasons for believing that the number of hymns which would be accepted freely by all congregations alike is comparatively small — judging from our most popular hymn-books, not more than about 150. These would be placed in a class by themselves. Others might be allowed by the Ordinary, at least tacitly, if not formally ; and perhaps from time to time additions made to the hymns authorized ; for it would indeed be a grievous mistake to apply an arbitrary rule of finality to the only part of our public worship which retains the elasticity which our changing circumstances demand.

It is possible, then, to conceive of a hymn-book compiled by some Committee or Commission such as might command general confidence ; receiving the recommendations of the Bishops, and perhaps, after the precedent of the New Version of Psalms, that of Her Majesty in Council ; and so, without the dangerous course of an amended Act of Uniformity, making its way by degrees into our congregations. Were this wisely done, we should not all at once, but we may hope gradually, lose many foolish, unsound, and exaggerated hymns, which now pass muster in better company than they deserve, often for the sake of their popular tunes. We should lose the abominable habit of ticketing clergy and churches by the hymn-book they use, and finding party catch-words in the very language of our praise. We should feel a little more formal, a little less free; but we should be drawn into closer fellowship with one another, and find ourselves relieved from some of the hindrances to our fellowship with God. But if I am asked whether these results are likely to be attained, I see but little to encourage me in predicting them. An authorized hymn-book means willing submission to authority, cheerful toleration of divergencies. These are not exactly our strong points just now. And there is one other consideration, which I cannot do more than indicate. I very much doubt whether the tone of our popular devotion, as indicated by the style not merely of hymns, but of other devotional manuals, at present most in demand, is one which it would be wise to stereotype in an authorized hymnal. A Bishop of our own Church recently remarked in addressing some clergy, that it had occurred to him to spend a whole Sunday in a large and influential London church. In that congregation during the day he had heard eleven hymns sung; but in only one verse of the whole eleven hymns was there any allusion to God the Father, and in that verse He was glorified not as the Reconciled Father of our Lord Jesus Christ, but merely as the Maker of this world, and the Giver of its good things. Not till we return to a higher and more really Catholic ideal of worship can we afford to bind **our** devotion by any closer bond of authority; and not till the God of patience and consolation grants us to be more like-minded one towards another, **can** we hope **with one** mind and **one** mouth to **glorify Him.**

AN AUTHORIZED HYMNAL

FRAGMENT OF A LETTER TO ―――?

SIR,

My answer to the question, When are we to have an Authorized Hymnal, is a very simple one—not during the existing state of things in the Church of England, I most earnestly trust.

The advantages of one general hymn-book are obvious—

1. Convenience to travellers. 2. Cheapness. 3. Exclusion of undesirable hymns. 4. The appearance of unity, with hope of approximation to the reality.

Besides this, many people are influenced by the desire to be like "the nations around." Other Churches and denominations have their one hymn-book, why not we?

Thirty years ago there was a good deal to be said for convenience and cheapness, for that was the age of local "selections," sold at a high price, and generally hard for a chance visitor to procure. But now that three or four large and carefully compiled books have really all but starved out the multitude of inferior ones, there is very little difficulty about finding a hymn if one does worship in a strange church; especially now that our people are sufficiently well-trained in the ethics of worship, to wish to see a stranger supplied with a book and using it.

Again, since each of your correspondent's four typical books can be had for a penny, not much need be said about the expensiveness of a variety of hymn-books. If our clergy would adopt the practice in use in such churches as Nantwich, where the clergy *mean* that everybody shall sing, and instead of giving out "Hymn 300," give out *the first line*, afterwards stating the number, then even strangers with books of their own would (with few exceptions) be able to find the hymn the congregation is about to sing.[1]

But I should like those who want an authorized hymn-book to ask themselves a few questions as to what it is they desire. Authorized by whom? By a joint Committee of both Houses of Convocation say some. Well, that committee could draw up a book, but the authorization must come either from the State, which is neither possible nor desirable, and which would provoke tremendous resistance; or from the Bishops, which could only mean that the Bishop of each diocese, if he thought fit, could recommend the book to his clergy: would this avail? Has it been successful in the one diocese in which it has been tried with every possible advantage, and an excellent collection, the diocese of Sarum? Would people who now use the *Hymnal*

---

[1] Mr. Ellerton was strongly opposed to the recent practice of giving out the Scripture text prefixed to a hymn, instead of the first line.—H. H.

Companion, or *Hymns Ancient and Modern*, and like the book they use, give it up because the Bishop suggested a new one? It needs no deep knowledge of human nature—of clerical nature—choir nature —church-going-ladies' nature, to answer such a question.

But the Americans have done it? Yes, when the American Church was a very small and homogeneous body. Now they have enlarged their book, and picked out all our best tunes from *H. A. M.* and elsewhere, having no law of copyright to deter them; yet still I doubt whether their own very dull hymn-book will long satisfy the young American Church. So with the Presbyterian Churches, the Wesleyans, Congregationalists, etc. All these are bodies much more uniform in views, much less comprehensive than the Church of England. We are so large a body, compounded of so many elements, that we must have more freedom than they. Surely they are ill readers of the signs of the times who wish to destroy the last remnant of elasticity in our Church Services for the sake of uniformity. We are complaining of the want of adaptability in our services; we are asking for additional offices, for greater freedom in the selection of forms of prayer. And yet this is the moment that people choose for asking us to put a fresh yoke on our necks, and submit to be restricted to a new measure of centralization! And this while our hymnody is daily growing, and we are all recognizing the need of all the freedom we can get in employing its treasures for the various uses to which our great task calls us.

And there is a fallacy which I must notice in the argument that so many hymns are used by all congregations in common, as to make it easy to authorize them all. People forget the variations of the text, and the adaptations of doctrinal statements to the prevailing colour of the hymn-book. The Dissenters sing Aquinas's hymns, but not what Aquinas himself wrote. Unitarians sing a great many Evangelical hymns; but invocations to Christ are omitted. But people say, Why not revert to the original text? I reply, Because you cannot. Those who use the *Hymnal Companion*, for instance, cannot sing Faber's hymns as Faber wrote them; but Mr. Bickersteth has made a very good and legitimate selection from them. People who talk loosely about the evil of altering hymns are for the most part people who do not know how the original text reads.

I long for unity in worship as much as any one; but I do not think unity can be forced on us from without. The . . .

MODERN THEOLOGY AS SHOWN BY MODERN HYMNODY

I HAVE been asked to put down a few thoughts on a subject which is worth the study of Church people, especially of all who are interested in the question of the future relations of the English Church with the religious bodies which surround her.

Mr. Bayne, himself a Nonconformist, called attention some three years ago, in an able paper in the *Contemporary Review*, to the phenomenon of the widespread existence of a religious sentiment in England which is wholly inorganic—entirely vague and loose, not adhering to any form whatever of doctrine, government, discipline, or method, in worship and fellowship. Such a state of things obviously cannot be measured by any of the ordinary standards of doctrine or of discipline—it owns none. But there is one form in which religious sentiment impresses itself—and that of course is hymnody. Moreover, it may be said of nearly every religious body in the country, that it has been more or less affected by the Catholic revival in the English Church—so far at least as to be thrown into a state of fermentation and controversy. Still more deeply have the Nonconformist bodies been leavened by the Liberal or Freethought movement, so that their divergence from their old standards is in many cases avowed, in many more not the less real for being unavowed.

Now if we want to study and to gauge this state of things, we have a convenient test ready to our hands in modern Nonconformist Hymnody. We all know what is the case among ourselves. Our Hymnody is the only region in which our forms of prayer and praise are elastic enough to reflect the changes in the theology of the Church, or rather in the grasp which the Church of our day has upon her fixed standards of faith.

Thus, early in the century, the adhesion of the High Churchmen of that period to Metrical Psalms represented faithfully their prudent, narrow, Anglican conservatism; the Evangelical hymn-books, almost identical with those of Dissenters, show us that spiritual energy and life was almost confined to that section of the English Church which was most nearly allied to Calvinistic Nonconformity. Again, the rise of the Catholic movement has been signalized by those distinct developments of Church Hymnody. At first it was patristic and scholarly; that was the age of translations of Ambrosian Hymns, and of such Gallican ones as are least Roman in character—of Mant, and Chandler, and Isaac Williams. Then rose the idea of the unbroken continuity of our own rites with the Pre-Reformation period in English—and the *Hymnal Noted*, and all the other translations of the Sarum Breviary hymns, embodied this idea. We were to have in every office its own prescribed hymn, unchangeable, and set to its own traditional melody, however severe and unlovely. These Purists passed away. The younger generation of Catholics began to acknowledge the beauty and goodness of many of the popular Evangelical hymns ; and meanwhile such leaders of the secession to Rome as Faber and Caswall wrote fresh hymns avowedly to catch people's taste, which were readily—almost too greedily—picked up by their old friends in the Church they had deserted. This state of things is well represented by the first edition of *H. A. M.* (1861), and its enormous popularity shows how well-timed the concession was. But *H. A. M.* itself called into being a school of English hymn-writers ; and its second form has shown us that the English Church, while ready to borrow freely good hymns of sound theology from all sources, ancient, mediæval, modern, foreign and English, Catholic and Protestant, has yet abundant spiritual life of its own, and is now capable to a large extent of meeting from within its own resources the devotional aspirations of its children. Our Dissenting friends meanwhile have by no means stood still ; and it is important to notice the changes in the aspect of their hymnody, because while so large a minority of the population are still under Nonconformist influence, it must ever be of the deepest interest to English theologians to inquire how they are taught to worship God and to think of God.

A few words must be said as to the sources of Nonconformist hymnody. We all know it began with Dr. Watts. Till his time the meeting-houses

and the churches alike sang metrical Psalms, with
of course a few exceptions, which I need not
enumerate. Watts, Doddridge, Browne, Beddome,
etc., form the first school of Dissenting hymnodists.
Watts was fond of Latin sacred poetry, and I often
think he must have been familiar with Santeüil
and Coffin. His school are especially the singers
of the Atonement. His Calvinism is of a very
faint and mild form. His theory of sacramental
grace is a good deal like Antoine Horneck—a sort
of modified "Virtualism," by no means so pronounced as Wesley's, but readily lending itself to
Anglican theology; hence Doddridge's "My God,
and is Thy table spread," has never been disused
among us, though we have revived so much Catholic
teaching about Holy Communion. Of course the
level of poetry in this school is wretchedly low;
otherwise doubtless more of their hymns would
have been revived, for its theology, ever chiefly by
defect, except indeed upon the one most important
point—one entire misconception of the Fatherhood
of God, and its work in man's redemption. Yet
another point I would notice. Hymns of direct
adoration and worship, almost wholly wanting in
late Nonconformist hymnody, are here conspicuous.
In the last New Congregational and Baptist books,
where hymns of adoration are separated from the
rest, and classified by themselves, it will be found
that such as are not Primitive Roman or Anglican
are almost wholly taken from the school of Watts.

This school is the parent of the Congregational
and Baptist hymn-books—with an exception to be
presently noticed. Josiah Conder, the great Con-

gregational hymn-writer of the first half of this century, who wrote the Eucharistic hymn, "Bread of Heaven, on Thee we feed," compiled the present *Congregational Hymn-Book*, and did not depart from Watts's traditional theory; he only modified and softened it down. Modern Congregationalism, however, is rapidly dropping, under Broad Church influence, all that was left of Calvinism to Watts, and the revision of the *Congregational Hymn-Book* is a most curiously eclectic production. Almost any hymn which has become popular among us is welcomed, in the hope, of course, of rivalling the hymnodic movement among ourselves; and apparently all sense of incongruity of doctrine is lost, though hymns are freely mutilated when expressions too plain-spoken occur. Thus Faber's "Dear Angel, ever at my side," is altered to apply to our Blessed Lord, apparently without a notion of the wild heresy which is taught by such a use of it. Dr. Allen has even adopted St. Thomas Aquinas's *Penge lingua*, and that with scarcely any alteration, apparently without any conception of that which it was meant to set forth.

The new *Baptist Hymnal* has only just reached me. It is the production of the more Liberal Baptists, and though less wildly selected than the Congregational, it is, so far as I have had time to look into it, open to the same remarks.

The second great school in historical order—the first by far in importance—is the Wesleyan. Much depends on our understanding its history. John Wesley was all his life long very ready to take up new ideas, and his will largely influenced his convictions. The groundwork of his theology was the decent, formal, narrow Anglicanism of the Restoration; but he was never thoroughly trained in theology, though an eager devourer of theological books. Probably his mother's influence gave a strong prominence to the emotional in his religion, which was increased by his acquaintance, through Law, with seventeenth century Protestant mysticism. Then he fell very readily under Moravian influence, and gradually shaped for himself his especial theories of Conversion and Assurance. All this was reflected in his brother's hymnody—for Charles was led on by John to a great extent, until John finally threw off his family Anglicanism in a fit of self-will and despondency; but this Charles never approved, and showed on his death-bed his disapprobation.

Wesleyans of the present day are often disposed to depreciate the hymns which rebuke most strongly their departure from their founder's principles, by drawing a line at some imaginary point at which he changed his views. But every hymn in the Wesleyan book—I may say every hymn in the thirteen volumes of their works—was written subsequently to the two dates which John and Charles Wesley respectively claimed as those of their conversion; and the only important modification which they ever made in the theology of their hymns was in the striking out all reference to human perfectibility on earth; a theory which Wesley at one time had adopted, and which some of his followers, especially in America, have taken up, but which he afterwards emphatically repudiated and strongly condemned.

The famous little book of *Hymns on the Lord's Supper* is chiefly a recast in verse of portions of a treatise by Dr. Brevint, a French Protestant, but a man who held very strongly the theory of a Memorial Sacrifice, coupled with what has since been called the "Virtual" Presence; and thus it accords very well with the views in which doubtless the Wesleys had been trained from childhood. These views the brothers never repudiated, nor is there any sign of their having modified them. In the compilation from their hymns made by John Wesley, which till last year was the standard Wesleyan hymn-book in England, he inserted several of them, and doubtless would have inserted more, but that he was so strongly averse to his preachers assuming the priestly office; so that he leaves out most of those hymns which absolutely imply a present celebration.

I have not had an opportunity as yet of seeing the present Wesleyan book, just published; but it has not, I believe, parted with any of the Communion Hymns which Wesley himself inserted in the older book. Its existence is, however, a significant token that the Wesleyans, ever so conservative of their Founder's views, are, like all other Nonconformist bodies now, in a state of flux, and likely to undergo yet further changes.

The special feature of real Wesleyanism was that it was a "Revival." And it has been the type which has been again and again followed in subsequent attempts made by other religious bodies to influence large masses of men through their emotions by systematic and organized efforts.

A "Mission" in an English parish now, though its form is of course borrowed from Rome, has certain elements in it which are undoubtedly of Wesleyan origin; and it may almost be said that the Roman and the Wesleyan type prevail pretty much in proportion to the dogmatic standard of the parish priest, or of the Missioner whom he has invited to conduct the Mission. Outside of the English Church the Wesleyan type in England and America is still the normal one. A certain class of Wesleyan hymns have therefore of late been brought into very prominent use; and these have, so to speak, created a whole literature of Revival Hymns, which form a curious index to the theology of large masses of earnest and well-meaning people among us. With them conversion is everything—about what follows they have really nothing to say. Almost inevitably, therefore, their hymnody has a taint of Antinomian teaching; or perhaps I should say lends itself readily to Antinomian theories of Christian sanctification. This is the great danger before so much of that loose and inorganic religious sentiment which is perpetually being stirred up by revival preaching, and the so-called "Evangelistic" services, which are so universal and so popular now. Another danger, not less great and deadly, is visible in the fact that not merely does all Church teaching, all Sacramental teaching, absolutely disappear, but the Sacraments themselves pass out of sight; grace itself is utterly misunderstood, the nature of our union with our Lord, the whole work of God the Holy Ghost utterly misconceived; not only is the individual everything, but the consciousness of the individual is everything. No one can take up a modern revival hymn-book without seeing what I mean. I lately saw the MS. of a new one prepared by professing Church people for the use of a congregation gathered from heathenism under a Bishop of our own Church, and ministered to by an Archdeacon. In this book all Church services are entirely ignored—even Christmas and Easter, the Sacraments, are not once mentioned, the work of the Holy Spirit is reduced to making people certain that they are the objects of the love of Christ; even penitence is very slightly and almost apologetically dealt with. The only people who can gain by such teaching are of course the Plymouth Brethren and their congeners; and of course Revivalism is largely recruiting their ranks.

The one definite theological standing-ground left for English Dissent is the Calvinistic. The great Calvinist theory which saturated Puritan England and Scotland, which slept through three-fourths of a century, till it blazed out afresh in George Whitfield and the early Evangelicals of our Church, has now entirely died out of the Church of England, and from nearly all the existing Dissenting bodies save one. Among the Baptists Calvinism retains its hold mainly through the wonderful energy and ability of one man, Mr. Spurgeon. His hymn-book, *Our Hymn-Book*, is the confession of faith of a strong, clear, definite Calvinism; but a Calvinism adapted to modern controversies, and opposing a well-defined system of belief to the vague and gelatinous hesitancies of modern Protestant Nonconformity ; let me add, too, opposing to our system a system more logically complete in its very narrowness, and in many ways skilfully adapted to the hard, practical, self-asserting temper of the English middle class. How long will it survive him is a different question. But some form of Christian Stoicism will doubtless always be a factor in the theology of the northern and western nations.

I only draw one moral from these rough notes. It is this. The study of Nonconformist hymn-books does not encourage me in any hopes of what is sometimes called Home Reunion. A solid body may absorb a fluid, or may be dissolved in a fluid, but there is no other way of uniting them. Catholic theology is solid—Protestant theology in England at last is becoming more and more fluid, not to say gaseous. Organic union, if we thought it right, seems to me simply impossible. If Nonconformists unite with us, it can be but by one way—by individual absorption, by conversion to the full Catholic faith.

FAVOURITE HYMNS

AND

THEIR AUTHORS

THE following series of articles on modern Hymn-writers was written in the autumn of 1892, at the request of Canon Erskine Clarke for the *Parish Magazine*. They afterwards re-appeared in the *Church Monthly*, and it is by the kind permission of Canon Clarke and of Mr. Frederick Sherlock, the Editor of the latter periodical, that they are inserted here. For the experienced hymnologist they may have but little value, as they are entirely elementary and popular, being merely designed to interest the general reader in those sacred poets to whom we owe some of our most favourite hymns.

The portraits which were engraved for the above-named Magazines are also reproduced by the kind permission of the above-named Editors.

The references throughout have been verified, and in many places corrected, on the authority of Dr. Julian's *Dictionary of Hymnology*.

JOHN COSIN AND THOMAS KEN

It is not too much to say that almost all who are attached to the services and the work of our Church take interest in her hymns. Not that by this pronoun I mean to claim for the English Church more than is her due. Very many of our best-loved hymns have been adopted into our books from those of other denominations. Nonconformists were before Church people in hymn-singing, mainly because our forefathers stuck loyally for many a long year to the "Old Version" or "New Version" of the Psalms. These were "allowed" by Royal authority; and I am old enough to remember when it was scarcely thought "orthodox" to sing anything else in church. The fact is, Psalms in metre are a relic of the Reformation, and of that particular school of reformers of which John Calvin was the master spirit, and which largely coloured the thoughts of the English Protestants of the sixteenth century. Their very reverence for the letter of the Bible made them think it hardly excusable to use in worship what they regarded as uninspired forms. Men might *pray* extempore, but they must *sing* Holy Scripture. It was not till the eighteenth century that hymn-books and hymn-singing in worship began in England. It was not till within the memory of some now living that they became really general in the Church of England. And now, it has been calculated by Mr. Julian, the compiler of the great *Dictionary of English Hymnology*, which has been many years in preparation, that there were some years ago no fewer than *seventeen thousand* English hymns in use *somewhere*. Yet out of these the really good hymns will always be but few. Different experiments have been tried to discover which of our hymns are the best loved and the most frequently used. In giving a few sketches of the writers of our *best-known* hymns, I cannot of course restrict myself to writers of our own Church; yet I do not believe that there is one in my brief list whose hymns are not now loved and welcomed among all our congregations.

The first two names on my list, however, are the names of English Bishops, men who wrought and suffered in defence of the Church of their baptism against enemies from opposite quarters. The first hymn I shall mention is one of the four hymns other than Scriptural, *authorized* for use, as distinguished from being merely *permitted*, in the Book of Common Prayer. These are the *Te Deum*, the *Gloria in Excelsis*, the *Media vita* ('In the midst of life we are in death,' said or sung in the Burial Service), and the *Veni Creator*. The first three are what we should call prose hymns, or canticles; the *Veni Creator* is, in the Latin, in what we call "long metre," only not in rhyme. All four hymns are from the Latin, but the *Gloria in*

Excelsis and part of the *Te Deum* were originally in Greek.

If you look at the Ordination Service you will see there are two versions of the hymn called *Veni Creator*—one in common metre, another, much shorter, in long metre, 'Come, Holy Ghost, our souls inspire,' which is the one we know best, and use most frequently. This was put into our Prayer-book in the year 1662, and its writer, or rather translator, was John Cosin, at that time Bishop of Durham.

John Cosin was born in 1594[1] at Norwich, where his father was in business. He was brought up at Caius College, Cambridge, and distinguished himself by his learning. The higher clergy of the Church of England in the time of James I. and Charles I. were many of them great and ripe scholars, so much so that they were sometimes said to be "the wonder of the world" for learning. Among these John Cosin took a high place. When the Puritan controversy broke out he was Archdeacon of the East Riding; Charles I. made him Dean of Peterborough. In the year 1627 he compiled a very simple and beautiful book of prayers for his Yorkshire flock, with devotions for the hours of nine, twelve, and three—such as were in common use before the Reformation, and in a reformed shape reprinted by order of both Henry VIII. and Elizabeth. But this innocent book gave great offence to the Puritans, who were never tired of making grim jokes about *Cozen's Cozening Devotions*, as they called it. For this

[1] ? 1596 (H. H.).

book John Cosin translated the *Veni Creator*, not intending it to be sung in Church, but said privately every morning at nine o'clock, in commemoration of the hour when God the Holy Ghost came down upon the Church. Poor Cosin, however, suffered from his Puritan foes. When the monarchy was suppressed he lost all his preferments, and had to live abroad, acting as chaplain to the English members of Queen Henrietta Maria's household in Paris. At the Restoration he came back again, was made first Dean, and then Bishop of Durham, and died in 1672, at the age of seventy-eight. He was one of the revisers of the Prayer-book in 1661-2, and thus it came to pass that his version of the *Veni Creator* was inserted in the Ordination Service—a small compensation to the good old man for the cruel attacks to which he had been subject.

The *Veni Creator* itself dates back at least to the ninth century. By some it is ascribed to the Emperor Charlemagne, which is scarcely possible; by others to one of his sons. It has been used at ordinations all over Europe for nearly nine hundred years. Cosin's version, though the best known, is not the most accurate, and is slightly abridged. The older one, which dates back to Archbishop Cranmer's time, has the opposite fault of being unnecessarily lengthened. There is a good version in *Hymns A. & M.*, No. 347, and another by Bishop Bickersteth in the *Hymnal Companion* (1890), No. 252, besides various others. But none of these come near to Cosin's in majestic simplicity of devotion.

Far better known even than the *Veni Creator*,

known wherever the English tongue is spoken, are the Morning and Evening hymns of Thomas Ken—" *the* Morning and Evening hymns," as we love to call them. These are not translations, but of home growth; and they keep green the memory of one

Bishop Cosin.

of the holiest and truest sons of the Church of England. Thomas Ken was born about forty years later than Cosin—probably in 1637, but the date is uncertain—at Berkhampstead, in Hertfordshire; but his home was in London, where his father was an attorney. He lost his mother when four years old, and his father when he was fourteen. But his excellent eldest sister, Anne, was more than a mother to him, and his boyhood, after he lost his parents, was spent in her married home, under the care of herself and her good husband, Izaak Walton, well known for his *Compleat Angler*, and his volume of " Lives " of several of the great Churchmen of the time. " Meek Walton," as the *Christian Year* well calls him, fished in the Lea and sold hosiery in Fleet Street during the troubled years of the conflict between King and Parliament, and his shop became a kind of house of call for many of the good Churchmen of the day, whose acquaintance was useful in after life to the boy Ken. In due time Ken entered at Winchester, where his name is still shown, carved schoolboy-fashion in the stonework of the cloisters of the venerable College. From Winchester he passed to Oxford—first to Hart Hall (now Hertford College) and then to New College. Oxford was at that time under Puritan rule ; but though Ken always did justice to the religiousness of some of the devouter Puritans, he never fell in with their views. By the time of the Restoration he was already well known as a scholar, and yet more as a man of earnest piety. For two happy, peaceful years he lived as Rector of Little Easton, in Essex, and chaplain to Lord Maynard and his saintly wife. Then honours which he did not seek came upon him. He first became Chaplain to the Bishop of Winchester, Prebendary of the Cathedral, and Fellow of the College—his own old school. For love of that school he published, in 1674, his beautiful *Manual of Prayers* for the use of Winchester scholars. It is believed that he had already written the "Three Hymns," for Morning, Evening, Midnight, but they were not added to the *Manual* till 1695. They were altered (perhaps more than once) by Ken

Bishop Ken.

himself before his death; and this accounts for the different readings (such as "All praise" for "Glory") which appear in different books. For, audaciously as hymns are altered, Ken's have been generally respected, though of course much shortened. It need scarcely be said that they were not originally meant for singing in church, but to be learnt and repeated by the Winchester boys at their bedsides. Tallis's well-known tune, which we sing to 'Glory to Thee,' is much older than Ken's time. Thomas Tallis was organist to Elizabeth's Chapel Royal, and died in 1585.

There is no space to tell at any length the story of Ken's eventful life. It was his lot to "stand before kings," and to prove his faithfulness through evil report and good report. He was chaplain to Princess Mary at the Hague, and was never liked by her husband, afterwards William III., whose anger he incurred by plain speaking about the immorality of his Court. Charles II. he treated no less faithfully; and Charles did not resent his honesty, but made him Bishop of Bath and Wells in 1685. He did not long enjoy that perilous honour. He was one of the famous Seven Bishops who resisted James II.'s Romanizing schemes in 1688, and were sent to the Tower. But he could not take the oath to William after he had taken it to James, and in April, 1691, he was driven from his See. He was thenceforward homeless, but God raised up friends for him, and though often in great poverty, yet his needs were always supplied. He spent much of his time at Longleat, a splendid house in Wiltshire, the seat of Lord Weymouth; and here, after much suffering, he closed his holy life, March 19, 1711. His tomb, with its iron crosier, is still to be seen. He was laid to rest at sunrise on March 21, carried to his grave by "twelve poor men."

ISAAC WATTS AND PHILIP DODDRIDGE

IT is curious that the Puritan tradition of singing metrical psalms and nothing else in public worship should have been first broken through by one who was himself a descendant, both in blood and in spirit, of the Puritans. Various hymn-writers arose during the seventeenth century, some of whose hymns have been lately revived among us—as John Mason, Samuel Crossman, and, far greater than both, Richard Baxter. Others, once esteemed, are now forgotten. George Wither had even obtained James I.'s permission to have his hymns printed for fifty years at the end of the Prayer-book; but not more than one or two of his are now found in any hymn-books. The real pioneer of modern English hymn-singing was Isaac Watts. This good man's grandfather was a sturdy Independent of the Cromwellian age. Some say that he had been one of Oliver's troopers, but it is known that he sailed with Blake, and perished at sea. His son fell upon the times which followed the Restoration, when hard measure was dealt out to Nonconformists. "He suffered for Nonconformity"—that is, he was more than once imprisoned. In 1683 his son writes, "My father persecuted and imprisoned for Nonconformity six months. After that, forced to leave his family and live privately for two years."

Isaac was the eldest of nine children. The home of the family was Southampton, where the father, when not in prison, kept a private school. It is pleasant to know that young Isaac was taught by the Rector of All Saints', Southampton, a Mr. Pinhorne, and that this worthy clergyman took a great interest in the clever little fellow, and exerted himself to raise a sum of money for his maintenance at one of the Universities. But the Church just then was doubtless looked upon as a "hard stepdame" by the son of an often imprisoned Dissenter, and to none but Churchmen could Oxford or Cambridge open its portals. We may regret, but we can scarcely wonder, that at sixteen young Isaac "declared his resolution to cast in his lot with the Dissenters." He was sent to an academy kept by a Mr. Rowe—oddly enough, among his fellow-pupils was one who came to be an Irish archbishop—and he "joined Mr. Rowe's Church," *i.e.* became a communicant there, two years later. He was only three years at the academy—perhaps because his father could not keep him there—and then spent two years at home, 1694 to 1696. These were memorable years in the history of English hymn-singing. We do not know what was sung at the Southampton chapel—perhaps Sternhold's psalms. At any rate, young Watts complained of the sad doggerel which was in vogue. He was asked—or, it may be, challenged—by his father, who was one of the deacons, to attempt something better. His first attempt was a paraphrase of Rev. v., 'Behold the glories of the Lamb;' and it was indeed "something better" than that congregation had yet sung. So he went on, and

Isaac Watts.

hymn after hymn followed. In 1706 he published a small volume of sacred verse, called *Horæ Lyricæ*, and one year afterwards (July 1707) a volume of hymns.

Meanwhile, after being two years at Stoke Newington as a private tutor, he had been ordained as the Independent minister of a congregation in Berry Street in 1702. By this time toleration was established, and Dissenters were winning their way to wealth and honour. A certain Sir Thomas Abney, who was Lord Mayor in 1700, now occupied King James's old hunting lodge at Theobalds in Hertfordshire. He opened his house to Watts, who lived under the Abneys' hospitable roof for six-and-thirty years, in feeble health, but yet preaching and writing diligently, and gradually growing in fame and honour. His personal income never exceeded, it is said, 100*l.* a-year, notwithstanding the great popularity of his works, but a third of this was spent systematically in charity. His wants were doubtless well supplied by his good host, and after Sir Thomas's death by his widow and daughters. He lived to see his *Logic* adopted as a text-book in the very University from which his Nonconformity had once excluded him; to be honoured and loved by Churchmen like Bishop Wilson of Sodor and Man, and to receive the degree of D.D. from the Universities of Edinburgh and Aberdeen. His holy and useful life came to a peaceful close at Lady Abney's house at Stoke Newington at the age of seventy-four, on November 25, 1748. His last resting-place is in the memorable graveyard of Bunhill Fields, where lies John Bunyan.

Watts's hymns are of very varying merit. But it is not the volume of *Hymns* by which his influence on the Church is so marked, as that other which he published in 1719, *The Psalms of David imitated in the language of the New Testa-*

ment, and applied to the Christian State and Worship. The right of Christians to adapt the Psalter thus was fiercely contested in Watts's own day; and no doubt his "adaptations" were many of them forced and far-fetched; but the principle has been long established, and to it we owe many of our best hymns, notably those of Henry Lyte, Sir Robert Grant, and Sir H. W. Baker. Perhaps the finest of Watts's Psalms are 'Before Jehovah's awful throne' (slightly altered by John Wesley), 'O God, our help in ages past,' and 'Jesus shall reign where'er the sun.' Among the hymns, 'When I survey the wondrous Cross,' stands higher, I think, than any other of Watts's. Next to it comes the beautiful 'There is a land of pure delight' (said, strangely enough, to have been suggested by the view across Southampton Water). Watts is remarkable in another way, as the first writer of children's hymns. But his "Divine and Moral Songs" are now being fast forgotten. Their theology is harsh and narrow, and their versification dull and not attractive to children.

The popularity of Watts's hymns as a whole was not only maintained, but increased till nearly the middle of the present century; and even now, not the Congregational hymn-book alone, but countless other collections, are largely indebted to him. He has had many imitators—few of them who copied his excellences, many his defects. If the ancient hymnists may be called singers of the Incarnation, the Wesleyans of the spiritual life, and modern Church poets of the Kingdom of God, then Watts and his school may be classified as especially singers of the Atonement. 'The glories of the Lamb' are the theme not only of his earliest hymn, but of hundreds of those which follow. It is impossible to enumerate all the writers of this school, which in later times may be considered as

Philip Doddridge.

continued by James Montgomery, and Thomas Kelly, who has been called a "fervid Irish Watts."

Philip Doddridge, Watts's closest follower and personal friend, was born June 26, 1702. Like Watts, he was offered the means of education at either University, and, like Watts, he declined the offer on religious grounds. He became at first an Independent, but afterwards a Presbyterian minister, and after some vicissitudes of fortune he settled at Northampton, where he had both a chapel and also an academy for the training of Dissenting ministers. His hymns were chiefly written to be sung after his sermons. None of them were collected till after his death, on October 26, 1751. His best-known hymns are 'Hark, the glad sound! the Saviour comes,' 'High let us swell our tuneful notes,' and 'My God, and is Thy table spread?' It has been truly said that none of them are so good as Watts's best, and none so bad as Watts's worst. He had better taste upon the whole than Watts, and less fervour. His *Rise and Progress of Religion in the Soul* occupied in the estimation of the devout Evangelicals of the early part of the century very much the place which Goulburn's *Thoughts on Personal Religion* has done among devout Anglicans of our own time. But it was never in true harmony with Church doctrine, and the Dissenters as well as the Church have in great measure lost touch with it. His hold of fundamental doctrine was never very firm, and many of his pupils and followers drifted into Unitarianism.

THE WESLEYS AND TOPLADY

ON October 14, 1735, a little party embarked at Gravesend for the new colony of Georgia. The head and founder of the colony was Mr. (afterwards General) Oglethorpe, an excellent man and devout Churchman, who earnestly desired to supply the new colony from the first with Church privileges. The clergyman selected and sent out by S. P. G. was a Fellow of Lincoln College, Oxford, already known as the master-spirit of a new religious movement in his University, now known to all time as John Wesley. With him, acting as Mr. Oglethorpe's private secretary, was his younger brother, Charles, a Westminster student of Christ Church, Oxford, and an ardent sympathizer with his brother John. John was at this time thirty-two years old, having been born June 17, 1703. Charles was five years younger, and not yet in Holy Orders.

The voyage then begun is memorable, not only for its influence on the career of the great founder of Methodism, and so upon the whole subsequent history of religion in England and America, but in particular as a turning-point in the history of English hymnody, which is our present subject.

For on board the same vessel was a party of twenty-six Germans, members of the community called the "United Brethren," or Moravians, with whom the Wesleys and their two companions, Ingham and Delamotte, soon became friendly. John Wesley's impressible nature was especially touched by the bright faith and humble, cheerful piety of these good people, who sang their beloved Lutheran hymns day by day through the most tempestuous weather. It was the first time that Anglicans and Lutherans, singers of psalms and singers of hymns, had worshipped and travelled together in familiar intercourse; and one of the results of their fellowship undoubtedly was the large extent to which hymn-singing entered into the devotions of the future Methodist Societies.

Neither of the brothers stayed long in America. Charles returned to England in 1736, John two years later. Then it was that their great systematic Evangelistic work was brought into full action, and the "Societies" were rapidly formed all over the country. Simultaneously with this began the long series of their hymn-books. The earliest was a *Collection of Psalms and Hymns* by John Wesley, in 1738, largely taken from Watts and George Herbert, but also containing some translations of German hymns by Wesley himself. In 1739 appeared *Hymns and Sacred Poems*, which were enlarged in 1740 and 1742, and supplemented by two additional volumes in 1749. It was in this book that Charles Wesley's great powers as a hymn-writer first showed themselves. The 1739 edition contains his five great festival hymns, beginning with that for Christmas, 'Hark how all the welkin rings!' afterwards unadvisedly altered by some one else to 'Hark, the herald angels sing!' and followed by those for Epiphany, Easter, and Ascension, with a less-known and inferior one for Whit-sunday. The next year appeared 'Christ, Whose glory fills the skies;' 'Jesu, lover of my soul;' 'Depth of mercy;' with others less known but not less striking. For a time the two brothers published their verse jointly, and it is not always easy to distinguish their work; but all the translations of German hymns are believed to be by John; and those mentioned above, with many others, have the unmistakable character of Charles's acknowledged hymns. In 1745 appeared the remarkable volume of *Hymns on the Lord's Supper*, with the names of both brothers on the title-page; but the hymns are said by Mr. Miller to be all Charles's. The magnificent 'Ye servants of God, your Master proclaim' (unhappily excluded from *Hymns Ancient and Modern*), was written in 1774, among *Hymns for a time of trouble* during the savage persecution of the Methodists. The *Hymns of Intercession for all Mankind*, published in 1758, contains that which is perhaps the most widely known, though not the best of the Wesleyan hymns—'Lo! He comes, with clouds descending.' But this is a recast by Charles Wesley of one published by John Cennick, one of the early preachers, in a Dublin hymn-book, some years earlier. Cennick's hymn is poor stuff compared to that into which Wesley recast it, putting into it at once fire and tunefulness.

The separate hymn-books of the Wesleys are nearly forty in number, varying from four or five special hymns, to the *Hymns and Select Passages of Scripture*, which number 2145. Besides this, Charles Wesley left behind him a version of the Psalms, nearly complete, and many MS. hymns. The edition published by the Conference in 1869 comprises thirteen large volumes. No English hymn-writer approaches him in copiousness. Of course, in so vast a collection there must be many repetitions, and many pieces that we no longer remember or care for; but yet it is only doing justice to these famous men to say that the depth of spirituality, the reverent tone, and the clear grasp of truth which as a whole the hymns exhibit is truly marvellous.

As time went on, the hymn-writing passed almost entirely from the hands of John Wesley into those of the younger brother. In the selection which the brothers left behind them for use throughout the Wesleyan congregations, Mr. Kirk estimates that out of 771 hymns by various authors 626 are by Charles, and only 33 by John Wesley. The best of these last are his translations from the German, the two first being, 'Lo! God is here, let us adore,' and 'Thou hidden love of God,' both by the saintly mystic, Gerhard Tersteegen.

Charles Wesley, after his marriage in 1749, gave up, to a great extent, itinerant preaching, and ministered chiefly in Bristol and in London. The brothers were closely united in affection to the last; but as time went on, Charles shrunk from some of his brother's ecclesiastical irregularities, and clung more closely than ever to the Church of England. He died on March 29, 1788, and it is said that by his own request the pall was borne at his funeral, at St. Pancras Church, by six clergymen. John Wesley lived till 1791.

As might be expected, Wesleyan hymn-writing was by no means confined to the two brothers. Many fine hymns were written by their fellow-labourers and sympathizers. Thus, 'All hail the power of Jesus' Name,' is by Edward Perronet; 'The God of Abraham praise,' by Thomas Olivers; 'Hail, Thou once despisèd Jesus,' by Henry Bakewell; 'Children of the Heavenly King,' by John Cennick; 'Sweet the moments, rich in blessing,' is a recast from James Allen, by the Hon. Walter Shirley. Each of these was connected more or less with the Wesleys, though Allen was a follower of Ingham, who had seceded from them, and Shirley was the leading spirit of the Countess of Huntingdon's "Connection," which was opposed to Wesley.

Many of these good men, it must be owned, were bitter controversialists, and the Calvinist controversy, as time went on, divided those who in all essential matters were of one heart and one soul. But the hymn which of all English hymns is perhaps best known and loved, which is sung in all languages, which has been faltered by thousands of dying lips, which is for almost every one connected with some dear memory, came from a pen which was never weary of pouring contempt and scorn upon the Wesleys and all that they taught. That Bishop Bonner should have written the

Homily on Charity is scarcely more wonderful than that 'Rock of Ages' should have been the work of Augustus Montague Toplady.

Yet, happily, Toplady's libels on the Wesleys have been long forgotten, and we need only think of him as a self-denying, warm-hearted Christian and a zealous evangelist. He was the son of an officer who was killed while his child was a baby. From his Irish mother he inherited his warmth of temperament, and perhaps his pugnacity. Born in 1740, and first seriously impressed at fifteen, he became in his eighteenth year an earnest Christian, and an extreme, uncompromising Calvinist. In 1762 he was ordained, and after being for a short time at Blagdon, in the Mendips, the scene of Hannah More's religious work at a later date, he became in 1768 Vicar of Broad Hembury, near Exeter. But already the seeds of consumption were in his feeble frame, and he resigned his benefice and went to London to die. Yet he made a gallant fight against death, writing and preaching almost to the last. On his arrival in London he became editor of the *Gospel Magazine*, the only religious periodical in England, which, after a hundred and fifteen years, still survives under its old name. In that magazine for March, 1776, he inserted 'Rock of Ages, cleft for me,' with the title (itself a glance at Wesleyan notions of perfectibility), 'A Living and Dying Prayer for the Holiest Believer in the World.' This great hymn, by a strange irony of fate, has been attributed to Charles Wesley, just as Wesley's 'Christ, whose glory fills the skies,' has on the other hand been printed

x

among **Toplady's** works. Indeed, either hymn might have been written by either man. Toplady has written many other hymns, among others a beautiful evening hymn from which a selection, 'Inspirer and Hearer of prayer,' is dear to many who use **Bishop Bickersteth's** *Hymnal Companion.* Almost simultaneously with 'Rock of Ages,' he wrote and gave to Lady Huntingdon another which, barring one or two blemishes, I venture to think scarcely surpassed as a dying man's last utterance by 'Abide with me' itself—the wonderful and heavenly-minded 'When languor and disease invade.' The light of God must have been already upon the face of one who could thus write. He died in 1778. Charles Wesley and he both rest under the roar and dust of the London streets; but both are together now "where beyond these voices there is peace."

WILLIAM COWPER AND JOHN NEWTON

THE last quarter of the eighteenth century brought a new and powerful tributary to the ever-broadening stream of English hymnody—a tributary remarkable in several ways. It was the unaided work of two members of the Church of England, a clergyman and a layman, living in a small country town, unconnected with either the Wesleyan or the rival Calvinist organization; and it brought to the work of hymn-writing the cultivation and taste of an educated man of letters on the one hand, and the spiritual fervour on the other of a man whose religious history was very remarkable, and whose character was singularly powerful. Its great success, therefore, is not wonderful. There is no other book of hymns, the work of two men only, from which so large a *proportion* of material has passed into the Church's permanent store of sacred song. In the *Hundred Best Hymns* of the Religious Tract Society, the number selected from the 347 Olney Hymns is exactly the same as that from the thousands of hymns of the two Wesleys and the 750 psalms and hymns of Isaac Watts.

Each of the two writers, as I have hinted, brought his own special qualifications to his task. William Cowper's bright, pure, and genial life was overclouded by the heaviest of all trials. He was born November 26, 1731, at the now-demolished parsonage of Berkhamsted, where his father, a son of the famous judge, Spencer Cowper, was rector. At six years old he lost his mother. My readers are all familiar with his infinitely pathetic lines on her picture. He was educated at Westminster, which he left at eighteen to live with an uncle, and read for the bar. In 1748 he entered the Middle Temple, and was called six years later. Till 1763 he lived the usual life of a literary young Templar, not troubling himself much about briefs, but writing, like Pendennis, for the magazines, and making love to his beautiful cousin Theodora. But in that year came the crisis of his life. He had been promised a clerkship in the House of Lords, which would have placed him in easy circumstances for life. But the right of appointment was disputed, and Cowper was told he would have to contest it. The shock unnerved him, and brought on an attack of insanity. All hope of his marriage was over; he found himself poor for life, and in despair he attempted suicide. In December 1763 he was placed in a private asylum, kept by an excellent man, a Doctor Cotton, from whence he emerged temporarily restored to reason and with a heart subdued and surrendered to God. He became a boarder in the family of a Mr. Unwin, at Huntingdon, and on his death removed to Olney, in Buckinghamshire, to be tended and watched over for thirty years by his widow, Mary Unwin. At Olney he fell in with the singular man who held the curacy of the parish, John Newton, and the two became very intimate friends.

John Newton's early life might form the groundwork of a story by Defoe, but that it transcends all fiction. He was born in London in 1725. His mother was a pious Dissenter, his father a sea-captain, a stern, silent man, who had been educated in a Jesuit college in Spain. After only two years' schooling, the captain took his boy at eleven years of age on board his ship, and at eighteen John Newton was seized by a press-gang, and sent on board a man-of-war at the Nore. His father was able to make interest, and he was made a midshipman. But he had now become utterly reckless, attempted to desert, and was brought back, and once more sent before the mast. At Madeira he managed to get himself exchanged into a merchant vessel, landed at Sierra Leone, and took service with a planter, who treated him with savage cruelty. In 1747 he contrived to escape, and, after strange vicissitudes, became first the mate, and then the captain of a slave ship. Hitherto he had lived a life of profaneness and dissipation, he had lost all faith and all hope ; but one good influence only remained—his boy-love for his cousin, Mary Catlett. He had first met her in Kent when he was eighteen and she fourteen, and through all the terrible years which followed his heart was true to her, and in his worst outbursts of vice he was ever "faithful to his future wife." In 1748, on a voyage home from the Brazilian coast, he was awakened to a sense of sin by reading the *Imitation of Christ*, and his impressions were deepened by a providential deliverance from foundering at sea almost immediately afterwards. At last, in 1750, he was married to his early and only love. For six years longer he followed his profession, the long hours of the voyages giving him ample time to study the Bible and the classics, and he began to think seriously of giving up the sea and seeking ordination. But Georgian Bishops were—perhaps pardonably—shy of a man with such strange antecedents. From Archbishop Gilbert he received "the softest refusal imaginable." He was tempted to become a dissenting minister, but his Mary, always his good angel, kept him steadfast to the Church. At last Lord Dartmouth (Cowper's "one who wears a coronet and prays"), in whose gift was the living of Olney, made the absentee Rector keep a curate, and persuaded Bishop Green of Lincoln to ordain John Newton and license him to Olney. The strange pair, the rough and homely sailor and the gentle, heart-broken Templar, settled down together to work as clergyman and lay helper in the long-neglected town. They worked hard and earnestly—too hard, probably, for Cowper's brain and nerves ; and one fruit of their work was the hymns, which, from time to time, were written as occasion served. Thus Cowper wrote 'Jesus, where'er Thy people meet,' for the opening of what we should now call a Mission Room. Other hymns were written by Newton for his annual sermon to young people on New-year's Day. At last they determined to collect and print their hymns, arranging them in three books, the first on select passages of Holy Scripture, the second miscellaneous and occasional, the third on the spiritual life. The progress of the work was interrupted by a second attack of Cowper's insanity in 1773. The last hymn he wrote was the wonderful 'God moves in a mysterious way,' composed during a country walk just as he felt his brain giving way, and the "clouds" he "so much dreaded" returning over his spirit. For three years he kept silence, but he recovered his reason at length, and his charming poems were written and published at intervals during the rest of his life, which was cheered by the constant attentions of Mrs. Unwin, and by the pleasant society of friends he had made in the neighbourhood. His cousin, Lady Hesketh, Theodora's sister, sought him out, and though his lost love never wrote to him, yet the two combined in many ways to make his declining years easier. He never, however, wrote a hymn or any devotional verse again, and after a third attack of insanity in 1787, never spoke on religious subjects. He died April 25, 1800, still under the delusion, shadowed forth in his last poem, that he was a "Castaway."

The Olney Hymns were published in 1779. Those written by Cowper are marked by the initial C. They are, as might be expected, more tuneful and more tender than Newton's. 'Oh for a closer walk with God!' 'Hark, my soul! it is the Lord,' 'There is a fountain filled with Blood,' 'Heal us, Emmanuel,' 'God moves in a mysterious way,' are among the best known of his; and each one has its own spiritual beauty and power to waken the echoes of the heart. John Newton's have a strength and vitality of their own ; his most popular is perhaps the lovely 'How sweet the Name of Jesus sounds!' a reminiscence, but by no means, as it has been called, a version, of St. Bernard's famous rhythm. Next to this is the fine hymn founded on Psalm lxxxvii., 'Glorious things of thee are spoken.' Several others will occur to my readers, probably as being heard at home rather than sung in church.

Newton and Cowper saw little of one another after the hymns were printed. In 1779 John Thornton, the large-hearted philanthropist, father of a noble succession of generous, religious men, who had allowed John Newton 100*l.* a-year for charities during his tenure of the Olney curacy, presented him to a city living, St. Mary Woolnoth, the twin towers of which are so conspicuous at the entrance of Lombard Street. Here he preached and worked till the close of his life. He published many books, but was most of all employed as a spiritual director, and had a great influence in giving to the early Evangelical school its robust and practical piety. In 1790 his beloved " Mary " was taken from him ; but, broken-hearted though he was, he worked on cheerfully and bravely till he joined her in 1807, seven years after his former colleague had passed through the clouds for ever.

REGINALD HEBER AND HENRY HART MILMAN

THROUGHOUT the closing years of the last century, and for the first ten years of the nineteenth, the many hymns which were written, whether by Churchmen or Nonconformists, were entirely disconnected with the formularies of the Church of England. Even in the Olney hymns none of the great festivals—not even Christmas and Easter—were provided for; a few hymns by Wesley and Doddridge, with Nahum Tate's paraphrases, appended to the New Version of Psalms, were all that Churchmen could find to sing in connection with the most jubilant services of the Christian year. But in the month of October 1811 there appeared the first four of a series of hymns, intended to supply this defect, the first instalment of a small but very remarkable contribution to hymnody, based avowedly on the lines of the Book of Common Prayer. These hymns were sent to a magazine called the *Christian Observer*, at that time edited by Zachary Macaulay, the father of Lord Macaulay, which had been established, and flourished for many years, as the organ of the Evangelical School in the Church of

England, which it represented with great ability, moderation, and earnestness. The hymns, of which only six more were published at that time, bore the initials D. R., being the final letters of a name which ever will be memorable in the Church of England, the name of Reginald Heber.

Reginald Heber represents the highest Christian culture in England of the beginning of the century. He was of a good Yorkshire family, and his father, a former fellow and tutor of Brasenose, had inherited from his mother a good estate in Shropshire, including the Rectory of Hodnet. He held this with the Rectory of Malpas, in Cheshire, when his son Reginald was born, April 21, 1783. The room in which the future poet-bishop was born is still preserved in the beautiful old " Higher Rectory," and the font in which he was baptized is pointed out in St. Chad's Church, Shrewsbury, to which it was transferred from Malpas many years ago. The living of Malpas has the distinction of being held by two rectors, and of possessing an upper and lower house of residence. The former of these, Heber's home in childhood, is an ideal country rectory, with its beautiful " Parson's walk " overlooking the wide valley of the Dee and the picturesque range of the Vale of Clwyd mountains. Reginald was the eldest son of his father's second marriage. His half brother, Richard Heber, became noted as the greatest book collector in the world, and is said to have left behind him nearly 500,000 volumes, gathered in eight great collections in London, Paris, Rome, and various towns on the Continent.

Reginald, after being educated at the neighbouring Grammar School of Whitchurch, was sent in

Reginald Heber,
Bishop of Calcutta.

1800 to his father's College of Brasenose. It may almost be said that he took Oxford by storm. Never did a young man make distinguished friends more rapidly; and he never lost a friend save by death. All who knew him loved him. In 1803, in the second year of his undergraduateship, he won the prize for English verse (not the "Newdigate") by his famous poem of *Palestine*. Walter Scott sat in his rooms and criticized it; but Scott was a family friend, and had dedicated a canto of *Marmion* to Heber's brother. Southey, the two Hares, J. J. Blunt, Henry Milman, all were among his admirers. His prize poem was recited before an immense audience in the Theatre at the Duke of Wellington's installation as Chancellor. In 1805 he was elected Fellow of All Souls. After two years of continental travel with John Thornton he came back to England, was ordained, and instituted at once to the family living of Hodnet, on the edge of the great park at Hawkstone. The same year, 1807, saw his marriage to Amelia Shipley, daughter of the Dean of St. Asaph.

Of his happy life at Hodnet a most fascinating picture has been drawn in a well-known book of recent times, *Memorials of a Quiet Life*. Perhaps the only "bitter drop" in his cup arose from the eccentric religionism of his neighbour, the famous Rowland Hill, younger son of the great baronet of Hawkstone, a man full of loving earnestness, but born to set at defiance all rules and conventions of Church order and discipline. But Heber's heart was large enough to endure what his judgment disapproved.

It was while at Hodnet that Heber began hymn writing. Why he did not continue the course he began in 1811 we do not know; but the project of a Church hymn-book was never absent from his mind thenceforth to the end. His great diligence as a parish priest still left him time for various literary activities. He joined with Southey and J. J. Blunt in writing for the *Quarterly Review*; he edited the works of Jeremy Taylor, prefacing them with a delightful life; he was made Bampton Lecturer in 1815; and in 1822 Preacher of Lincoln's Inn. He had previously been made Prebendary of St. Asaph, of which his father-in-law was Dean. Staying with Dean Shipley at his vicarage at Wrexham, he wrote for Whit-sunday, 1819, the famous hymn, 'From Greenland's icy mountains,' to be sung before a sermon for S. P. G.

Heber's appointment as Preacher of Lincoln's Inn marked him out clearly as one who might one day be appointed to a bishopric. But the call which came to him at the close of that year 1822 was an unexpected one to himself and his friends. It was to succeed Bishop Middleton in the see of Calcutta. It was a tremendous charge; for at that time there was no other Bishop of the English Church in the eastern hemisphere. Not only all India with Ceylon, but even Australia, was supposed to be under his jurisdiction. To some of his friends it seemed like a call to martyrdom; all felt that it meant heroic sacrifice. He accepted it as what it was—God's will. Gradually his faith had been growing clearer, his saintliness deeper, though his bright wit and keen enjoyment of life were unchanged. From the hill above Hodnet he gazed upon the quaint, beloved tower with many tears, and then turned his back upon it for ever. He won all hearts in India as he had done in England. He completed a long and laborious visitation tour in 1825. Then in the spring of 1826 he began a second. He reached Trichinopoly on Saturday, April 1. On the Sunday and Monday his day was filled up with confirmations, preachings, and all the exhausting work which a colonial Bishop finds ready to his hands wherever he goes. At last on the Monday afternoon he was able to take some rest. It proved to be eternal rest. He was found dead in a warm bath that evening, having apparently fainted.

In 1827 his widow published all that was complete of the *Hymns adapted to the weekly Church Service of the Year*, containing various additions to the tentative volume which Heber himself had published in 1812. The hymns were evidently meant to be gathered from various sources—Jeremy Taylor, Drummond of Hawthornden, Dryden, Addison, Charles Wesley, Cowper, are all laid under contribution. But his principal coadjutor was Henry Hart Milman, the son of a London physician, whose career had in some respects been a curious parallel to Heber's own. He came up to Brasenose from Eton about ten years after Heber; like Heber, he rose into fame by a striking prize poem, the "Apollo Belvidere;" like him, he became Bampton Lecturer. But he soon developed into the eminent historian whom we all remember, and died, beloved and honoured, as Dean of St. Pauls, 1868.

Heber's finest hymn is undoubtedly that for

Trinity Sunday, 'Holy, holy, holy, Lord God Almighty.' As a hymn of direct adoration it

Henry Hart Milman,
Dean of St Pauls.

stands in the front rank of English hymns. One speaks with more hesitation of two others, 'The Son of God goes forth to war,' and ' Brightest and best of the sons of the morning,' both of them open to serious criticism, especially the latter, with its somewhat sentimental prettiness. But Heber is so tuneful, that we too often overlook his deficiencies. I cannot help owning that I think some of his less-known hymns among his best, such as his very first, 'Hosanna to the Living Lord,' 'Lord of mercy and of might,' 'Creator of the rolling flood,' the two very beautiful Holy Communion hymns, 'Forth from the dark and stormy sky,' and 'Bread of the world in mercy broken,' and the Miltonic hymn for Michaelmas, 'O Captain of God's host' (except for its curious confusion between our Lord and St. Michael).

Of Milman's hymns the most popular are 'Ride on, ride on in majesty,' and 'When our heads are bowed with woe,' the latter singularly beautiful. 'O help us, Lord, each hour of need' is an excellent hymn on the Syrophenician woman (the hymns were originally meant to explain the Gospel for the day), but the special verses referring to her are too often omitted.

JAMES MONTGOMERY

It was the fashion thirty or forty years ago to speak of James Montgomery as the Cowper of the nineteenth century. Each was a literary man; each published several volumes of poems; each had a vein of melancholy. But Montgomery's was only quiet and sentimental melancholy; his poems are nearly forgotten, and even in this day of reprints no one will resuscitate the "Wanderer in Switzerland," or the " Pelican Island." Comparisons of this kind do injustice to the weaker man. Good James Montgomery was not a genius; but he was a hard-working literary man, a devout and simple-minded Christian, a tasteful versifier, and a man who did very great services to English hymnody. He was our first *hymnologist ;* the first Englishman who collected and criticized hymns, and who made people that had lost all recollection of ancient models understand something of what a hymn meant, and what it ought to be.

His gentle, useful life ought not to be forgotten. His father was a Moravian minister in the little town of Irvine, in Ayrshire, known to us of the present day by its delightful poet-preacher, William Robertson. There James was born, November 4,

1771. While quite a child he was sent to school at Fulneck, the Moravian settlement, then recently founded in Yorkshire, on the high ground above the Aire valley, between Leeds and Bradford. Here, no doubt, he was trained in the "Children's House," under kindly and firm, but strict discipline. His father and mother, meanwhile, were sent by the Society as missionaries to the West Indies; there they both died, and little James never saw them again. When the time came for him to leave Fulneck, he felt no inclination for the Moravian ministry, for which he had been designed, but settled down as a small shopkeeper in the Calder Valley, at Mirfield, between Huddersfield and Dewsbury. In the intervals of business he "cultivated the muse," and, hardy Scotchman that he was, trudged up to town with a wallet full of verses, which, alas! the hard-hearted publishers refused.

From Mirfield he removed to Wath, near Sheffield, and in 1792 to Sheffield itself, his home till death. Two years after this the work of his life opened out for him. He was assistant in the shop of a Mr. Gales, printer, bookseller, and auctioneer. Mr. Gales was the editor and proprietor of a paper then called the *Sheffield Register*, an organ of very pronounced opposition politics, on which the Government of the day looked with small favour. Poor Mr. Gales was threatened with prosecution for some article a little too strong in its reflections on the Ministry; he went into hiding, and his assistant James, at the age of twenty-three, took his place in the editorial chair. His time was come. He changed the name of the paper from the *Sheffield Register* to the *Sheffield Iris* (not perhaps without thinking of the bow of hope which he saw in the clouded sky of his party), and made the paper a really powerful organ of Yorkshire liberalism in things political and ecclesiastical. He was

James Montgomery.

twice prosecuted (once for an ode on the Bastille in his "Poets' Corner"), and each time condemned to a short term of imprisonment. But his paper grew and throve and became a power. It was always honestly and well conducted, with a high tone of morality. And, hard-worked as he was,

Montgomery beguiled his time with many volumes of verse, which found at last not only publishers but readers, and kindly or unkindly reviewers. The Whigs of the *Edinburgh* condescended to laugh at him; so the Tory *Blackwood* cried him up, Dissenter and Liberal though he was. Professor Wilson praised the "Pelican Island" (which nobody would now guess to mean Australia), and even Byron called his "Missionary" "very pretty."

Up to the mature age of forty-three, Montgomery, though always a thoughtful and religiously disposed man, had not attached himself to any denomination. He was for years perplexed by doubts and difficulties in the way of believing. But at length the sky cleared for him. His father had been a disciple of Cennick, the friend of the Wesleys, and it is said that a volume of Cennick's sermons was made the means of a change in James's faith. He now became a member of the Wesleyan Society for a time, and began to take great interest in sacred poetry and hymns.

In 1817 there came to St. Paul's Church, Sheffield, an Evangelical clergyman from Staffordshire, the Rev. Thomas Cotterill, who brought with him a hymn-book which he had compiled for his former congregation, and which he proceeded to enlarge and adapt for his new charge. But orthodox Sheffield rose in arms, and dragged Mr. Cotterill and his book into the Consistory Court at York. Archbishop Vernon Harcourt undertook to mediate, and the Wesleyan editor of the *Iris* joined himself with Mr. Cotterill in the preparation of a hymnal which the Archbishop not only criticized and revised but actually supplemented with hymns of his own selecting; a curious contrast to his brother Primate's discouragement of Heber. Montgomery confessed that he and Mr. Cotterill "clipped, interlined, and remodelled hymns of all sorts." Meanwhile, hymns were beginning to flow freely from Montgomery's facile pen. In 1822 he printed a version of some fifty-six of the Psalms, called *Songs of Zion*, and in 1825 a far more important work, the *Christian Psalmist*. This was the first really critical selection of English hymns, and the introductory essay is a valuable and interesting historical notice of the work which our hymn-writers had by that time done. Montgomery showed a very clear notion of what our hymns should be, and of the leading defects and vices of existing hymns. He added to the volume a certain number of his own, written at various times. Among these was 'Angels from the realms of glory,' written for Cotterill's book, and the remarkable one, 'Prayer is the soul's sincere desire,' written for Mr. Bickersteth. The fine paraphrase of the 72nd Psalm, 'Hail to the Lord's Anointed,' was written a little earlier, at Christmas 1821, and is said to have been repeated by Montgomery at the close of a speech for the Wesleyan Missionary Society at Liverpool.

From that time forward, Montgomery's pen was very frequently employed upon hymns for special occasions, school anniversaries, charity sermons, stone-layings, and openings of various kinds. He wrote many fugitive pieces also, some of which were collected in the *Poet's Portfolio*, 1835, where there appeared a hymn which of late years has become remarkably popular, 'For ever with the Lord,' not, in my judgment, one of his best. In 1853 he collected all his own hymns, amounting to 355, in one volume.

For many years before his death Montgomery had become a communicant of the Church of England, worshipping regularly at St. George's Church, Sheffield, to the incumbent of which, Mr. Mercer, a zealous hymnologist and compiler, like himself, he was warmly attached. His house, the Mount, at Sheffield, was often visited by admiring strangers. He never married. He fell asleep at the age of eighty-two, April 30, 1854.

James Montgomery can scarcely perhaps be spoken of as the author of any famous hymn. Some have even denied him (very unjustly) the true hymnic power. His hymns often disappoint one, and perhaps no hymn-writer has suffered more from being over-praised. But on the other hand he is always reverent and sincere; his rhythm never jars upon the ear, and some of his more directly devotional hymns are really noble. Besides those already specified, I may mention as instances of true and elevating acts of worship, 'O Spirit of the Living God,' 'Pour down Thy Spirit from on high,' and 'Lord, teach us how to pray aright.' To have written but these three would be to have earned a true place among the singers of the Universal Church.

I cannot leave Montgomery without referring to his friend and contemporary, Josiah Conder, born eighteen years later, and dying a year after Montgomery. Conder was a bookseller's son in the city; like Montgomery, he edited for many years a Liberal and Dissenting newspaper; like him, outside of the political arena, he was a gentle and saintly man. He was among those deputed to compile the *New Congregational Hymn-book* when the Independents had outgrown Watts, and the lion's share of the work fell to him. He has written many good hymns, but to us Church people he will always be known by his lovely hymn for Holy Communion, 'Bread of Heaven, on Thee we feed,' a hymn which might have been written by Bonaventura; and a remarkable instance of the power which deep and true devotion and living faith have to lift a man above the level of his traditional or intellectual belief, and open to his inward eye the mysteries of the Kingdom of God.

HENRY FRANCIS LYTE

OF all the multitudinous hymns of the last fifty years, in which the Church of England has been so fruitful, I think it may be said without hesitation that the most widely diffused and most generally loved is 'Abide with me.' In Mr. King's *Anglican Hymnology* it stands fifth in the first rank of hymns, immediately next to 'Rock of Ages.' In the *Hundred Best Hymns* of the Religious Tract Society (the result of a large *plebiscite* of subscribers to the *Sunday at Home*) it actually stands second only to 'Rock of Ages.' Mr. King's classification is based on a comparison of hymn-books, a rough but somewhat misleading test. At any rate there can be no doubt that this great hymn has already taken its place among the choicest devotional treasures of the Christian Church.

The life of its author was a singularly quiet and uneventful one. Henry Francis Lyte, the son of an officer of a good Somersetshire family, was born on the Border, at or near Kelso, June 1, 1793. He lost his father while a mere child, and spent his youth in Ireland, first at school near Enniskillen, and then at Trinity College, Dublin, which he entered in 1809, winning a scholarship and three prize poems. His contemporary (matriculated in the same year) was the gifted Charles Wolfe, the author of the famous verses on "The Burial of Sir John Moore," and it would be interesting to know if two men so much alike in their tastes and sympathies ever became friends.

Lyte's friends wished him to adopt the medical profession, but he determined upon taking Holy Orders. He was appointed in 1815[1] to a curacy in the county of Wexford, but soon resigned it, and for a while took pupils. Then came the great spiritual change of his life. A clerical neighbour was taken ill, and sent for Henry Lyte to visit him. On his sick-bed he had been awakened to a deeper interest in things eternal, and a clearer view of the leading truths of the Gospel than before. The two friends read and prayed and communed much together, and Henry Lyte's own eyes were opened to the realization of the truths which were now the support and comfort of his dying friend. Soon Lyte was left with the care of the widow and family of his friend, and the arrangement of their concerns upon his hands. This trust involved him in long-continued anxiety, and probably contributed, with the mental and spiritual conflicts through which he had passed, to leave behind permanent delicacy of health. He was unable for a time to take any clerical work, but at length accepted a lectureship at Marazion, in Cornwall, where he was happily married to the

[1] If this is correct, and Dr. Julian corroborates it, he could only have been twenty-two when ordained Deacon.—H. H.

daughter of a clergyman who had some property in the north of Ireland.

He lived for a time at Lymington, in Hampshire, and afterwards at Dittisham, on the Dart; but finally settled down about the year 1823 to that which became the work of his life—the charge of a new church built specially for the fisher folk of Lower Brixham, under the red cliffs of Berry Head, the southern horn of Torbay. For more than twenty years he led the life of a faithful and diligent parish priest among his poor people, by whom he was greatly beloved. But he was always a student, gradually collecting an excellent library, both of Patristic and Anglican theology, never losing his hold on the deep Evangelical convictions of his early manhood, but growing yearly in the perception of those aspects of the truth which our great earlier divines set before it. His recreation was poetry. In 1826 he published a small volume of *Tales in Verse on the Lord's Prayer*, and in 1835 a collection of miscellaneous poems. But his great desire was to carry out more happily than Watts had done the adaptation of the ideas of the Psalter to the services of the Christian Church. His *Spirit of the Psalms* appeared in 1834. He did not know that this scheme and his very title had already, about five years previously, been anticipated by a lady, Miss Harriet Auber. Miss Auber's little book contains some good versions of psalms, but is known now only by her very beautiful hymn on the Holy Spirit, 'Our Blest Redeemer,' which she added with a few others to her Psalter. She was the daughter of the Rector of Tring, and died unmarried, advanced in years, but "full of good works," after a happy and useful life, at Broxbourne, in Hertfordshire, in 1862.

Lyte's *Spirit of the Psalms* is a better book on the whole than its earlier namesake. He is often very happy in seizing the leading idea of a psalm, and embodying it in a few verses, such as 'Far from my heavenly home' (137), 'Oh that the Lord's salvation' (14), and 'God of mercy, God of grace' (67). But his happiest versions are certainly those of the 84th Psalm, 'Pleasant are Thy courts above,' and the 103rd, 'Praise, my soul, the King of Heaven,' both which are glorious additions to our Church hymnology. The book, however, is full of interest. It is, unhappily, now very scarce. There are some good experiments in the emendation of Tate and Brady, and there is one curious attempt to turn Ps. xxi. into a sort of 'God save the King,' which is said to have been very popular with his fishermen, for whom he made the Accession an annual parish festival, perhaps mindful of the historic associations of Brixham Quay. Among other things he wrote for his people some popular sea-songs.

But Lyte's strength, never great, gave way gradually under his manifold exertions. The interference of the Plymouth Brethren in his parish caused him much uneasiness, and made him regret his neglect of more definite Church teaching among them. His schools, too (he had 800 children in his Sunday School), were a great tax upon him. He tried a winter in Rome and South Italy in 1844-5, but returned home no better. All through 1847 he was sinking lower. He was persuaded again to winter abroad, and prepared to leave home with the conviction that he should return no more. He had not preached for some time, but in his desire to leave with his people one last testimony to the faith in which he was to die, he preached once more, September 4, 1847, an earnest appeal to them on Holy Communion, which he then celebrated for the last time. That evening he put into the hands of a friend the MS. of 'Abide with me.' That week he left England and travelled by slow stages to Nice, where he died, November 20, 1847.

'Abide with me' was thus his dying song. It is often abridged in the hymn-books, but the whole hymn of eight verses is given in *Church Hymns* (S. P. C. K.) with the correct reading of the last verse, 'Hold *then* Thy cross.' It is often, with curious dulness of perception, printed among *evening* hymns, simply because of the words 'fast falls the eventide.' Some people feel it too intense and subjective for public worship; to many it is associated with the laying to rest of those dear to them—it was sung at the funeral of Frederick Maurice,—and doubtless Mr. Brown Borthwick is quite right in speaking of it as "not for congregational use, but for the quiet and meditative devotions of Christians of advanced spiritual experience." Nevertheless, especially as wedded to Dr. W. H. Monk's beautiful tune, 'Eventide,' it is so dear to our congregations that we can scarcely wish its public use ever to be discontinued.

And surely the *Nunc Dimittis* is a precedent for the public use of an act of private devotion which may well be applied to a hymn breathing so much of its spirit.

I may close this paper with a short notice of another "favourite hymn" and its author. Sir Robert Grant was the son of an East India Director. He was educated at Cambridge, but led a busy life as a barrister and Member of Parliament for many years, during which he and his brother Charles were well-known worshippers every Sunday among the congregation assembled in the once famous chapel of St. John's, Bedford Row, under Daniel Wilson and Baptist Noel. Each brother rose to eminence. Charles became Lord Glenelg and Colonial Secretary; Robert, a Privy Councillor in 1831, was appointed in 1834 Governor of Bombay. He died in India in 1838. Two of his hymns, 'When gathering clouds around I view,' and the better known Litany, 'Saviour, when in dust to Thee,' were published, like Heber's, in the *Christian Observer*. These, with a few more, were reprinted after his death by Lord Glenelg. Among them is the fine version of Psalm civ., 'O worship the King, all glorious above.' This, and the beautiful "Litany Hymn," are sure to keep their places. The latter, I think, will outlast most of the "Metrical Litanies" which have followed in its wake.

THE HYMNS OF THE OXFORD MOVEMENT. THE TRANSLATORS

IN dealing with English hymnody we have now arrived at a period which involved a wide and far-reaching change in its character—a change by no means confined to the Church of England, but showing itself in the worship of every denomination—I had almost said, of every English-speaking congregation—throughout the world. The Oxford movement has, indeed, brought as distinct a new departure in hymnody as the Wesleyan movement did. The number of English hymns has enormously increased; their character has been largely altered; their use has been extended to every congregation; and, what is best of all, there has arisen a spirit of Christian fellowship in hymn-singing which is a great help to Christian unity. In every denomination hymns from all sources—ancient and modern, Catholic and Protestant, Church and Dissenting—stand side by side in the hymn-book, and are sung with delight and heartiness by the congregation; and nothing has done so much as this to draw closer together the divided members of Christ's body, and to kindle fresh hopes of a future, if distant, unity.

This new development in hymnody is due, no doubt, to various causes, but it is mainly due to the general introduction of hymns into the services of the Church of England. Sixty years ago it was *orthodox* to sing the "new version" of Psalms: now there is probably not one church left in London, and few, if any, in all England, where this version is exclusively used. The great Latin and Greek hymns have been translated; clergy and congregations who would never have used the hymns of the Wesleys, Watts, and Cowper, first accepted these ancient hymns, and then by degrees discovered the beauty and fitness of English ones which they had formerly overlooked, and thus "things new and old" were brought out of the Church's treasury, and each found its appropriate value.

The earliest translations of ancient hymns (except the *Veni Creator*) were probably those of William Drummond, of Hawthornden, in the beginning of the seventeenth century, one of which Heber included in his collection. A few others appeared from time to time, such as Dryden's *Veni Creator;* and William Hammond, one of the early Calvinistic Methodists, translated a good many Breviary hymns. None of these, however, seem to have been used in churches; but in 1837 appeared two collections of "Ancient" hymns, which were as the first drops of a new shower. Richard Mant, Bishop of Down and Connor, a former Fellow of Oriel and Bampton Lecturer, an orthodox Churchman of the old school, and a rather voluminous versifier, published in that year his *Ancient Hymns from the Roman Breviary*, versions not very literal, and somewhat verbose and stilted, but yet the first introduction to many English readers of the work of St. Ambrose and St. Gregory. Some of his hymns keep their place still.

In that same year, 1837, there came forward a much more important volume, John Chandler's *Hymns of the Primitive Church*. Mr. Chandler had not long left Corpus—John Keble's college—and had entered upon his lifelong home in the beautiful parish of Witley, near Godalming. His preface is a very interesting revelation of the change going on in the minds of Churchmen. He was afraid of modern hymns as unchurchlike and unauthorized; yet he felt Tate and Brady insufficient for Christian worship. So he bought a Parisian Breviary and one or two Latin hymn-books, and set to work to translate, avowedly for congregational use. The "Parisian Breviary" hymns were written in France, but in the Latin language, in the seventeenth and early years of the eighteenth centuries. The excellence of his translations is shown by the number which still keep their place in *Hymns Ancient and Modern* and other Church books. They have been repeatedly revised and improved since his time, and, moreover, the seventeenth-century French hymns have lost their popularity to a great extent now that we have the really primitive and mediæval hymns translated; but Chandler's was a *pioneer* book, and it was conceived in a spirit of true and simple devotion.

Chandler's attention had been called to these

French hymns of the seventeenth century by some very scholarly translations of them which appeared from time to time in the *British Magazine*. These

Isaac Williams.

were collected in one volume, two years after his own, in 1839; they were the work of Isaac Williams, a man who impressed his friends and

z

companions with the mark of sanctity more than
any of his contemporaries, except John Keble.
He was the son of a London barrister, educated at
Harrow, and sent up to Trinity College, Oxford,
where he won a Fellowship in 1832. For a time
he was John Henry Newman's curate at St. Mary's.
He was associated with Newman, Pusey, and
Froude in the *Tracts for the Times*, and many of
his verses appear side by side with Newman's and
Keble's in the *Lyra Apostolica*. In 1842 he took
the living of Bisley, in Gloucestershire, but in-
creasing ill-health soon compelled him to resign it,
and for twenty years longer, till he was called to
rest in 1865, his gentle and holy life was passed in
almost constant suffering, though he was occasionally able to help his brother-in-law, in whose parish
—Stinchcombe—he lived. Isaac Williams wrote
many volumes of verse, dear to devout souls in
the generation now passing away. From one of
them, *The Baptistery*, is taken the solemn penitential hymn, 'Lord, in this Thy mercy's day.'
He translated, besides the Parisian hymns, those
of St. Ambrose and Synesius; but none of them
were intended for congregational use, and only
one or two are fitted to be sung in church. The
metres are often artificial, and Williams had not a
musical ear. One, indeed, stands out conspicuously
from the rest as a singularly happy inspiration, the
noble translation of Jean Baptiste Santeuil's hymn
for Apostles' Days—'Disposer Supreme and Judge
of the earth,' an instance in which the version
surpasses the original in dignity and beauty.

Translations of Latin hymns now became exceedingly common. Some will be mentioned later; but the rest of the present article must be devoted to a notice of the greatest of all translators, and one of the most remarkable of modern hymn-writers—John Mason Neale.

Dr. Neale was the son of a clergyman, Cornelius Neale, who had been Senior Wrangler. He was born in 1818, and early lost his father; but his mother, the daughter of an accomplished and literary physician, Dr. Mason Good, was able to direct his great abilities. He was sent to Trinity College, Cambridge, where he took his degree in 1840. He threw himself early in life into the Church controversies of the day, and he knew how to strike hard at an abuse, and to uphold with lightly-carried learning a truth which he thought had been overlooked. But he was far more than a brilliant pamphleteer and an enthusiastic ecclesiologist—his reading was simply enormous. One winter, when driven by ill-health to Madeira, he spent days in the library of the Cathedral at Funchal. His great work, the *History of the Eastern Church*, was left unfinished, but neither this, nor his commentaries and sermons, nor even perhaps the great Sisterhood which he founded at East Grinstead, will keep his memory green so long as his hymns.

He was appointed in 1846 Warden of Sackville College, East Grinstead, a small ancient almshouse, and this gave him leisure for study and work of many kinds. He ransacked all Europe for hymns; he wrote with equal facility in Latin or Greek as in English, and sometimes he amused himself by mystifying his College friends by "ancient" Church songs of his own production! His earliest important hymnic work was done for the Ecclesiological Society, for which he assisted in preparing the *Hymnal Noted*, a translation of Latin hymns, chiefly from the Sarum use. Of this work Neale did the lion's share, and he soon showed his extraordinary vigour and felicity as a translator. His early versions are indeed somewhat stiff and over-literal in places; but as time went on he wielded his weapon with far greater facility and power. Only once was he surpassed in this volume, by William Josiah Irons, the Vicar of Brompton, whose translation of the greatest of all mediæval hymns, 'Day of wrath, O day of mourning,' is a truly wonderful achievement, for he has solved a difficulty which has baffled almost every one who has attempted it.

In the first part of the *Hymnal Noted* appeared among others Neale's beautiful version of St. Bernard's hymn, 'Jesu, the very thought is sweet,' and the well-known 'All glory, laud, and honour.' In the second part, five years later, which was entirely the work of Neale and Mr. Benjamin Webb, appeared the lovely hymns, 'Oh, what the joy and the glory must be,' 'Of the Father's love begotten,' 'Light's abode, celestial Salem,' and others now well known. Meanwhile Neale had gathered his own translations into a little volume called *Mediæval Hymns and Sequences*, among which appeared in 1851 the translation of a portion of the rhythm of Bernard de Morlaix, from which were taken 'Brief life is here our portion,' 'For thee, O dear, dear country,' and 'Jerusalem the Golden.' In 1858 he translated and published the rest of the "Rhythm," excluding

John Mason Neale.

the satire with which it begins. But the translations from which the largest number of popular hymns have been selected are the *Hymns of the Eastern*

Church (1862 and 1866). Neale was the first to draw attention to the vast stores of Greek hymnody, from which he selected such specimens as 'The day is past and over,' 'Art thou weary,' 'The Day of Resurrection,' 'O, happy band of pilgrims!' and many others now familiar to us all. Some of these are nearly, if not quite, original hymns of his own, and contain, it is said, but little trace of their Greek parentage. Neale's own hymns were some of them very good, and he sang on to the last, publishing a little volume on his dying bed. His *Hymns for Children* have not the merit of his many tales and legends; for no one could tell a martyr story like him, and he wrote many children's books. His learning in hymnology was unrivalled, and he may be said almost to have created the science of Liturgiology. As life went on, his hymns, like his sermons, advanced in beauty and spirituality, and the old polemic, who had made many foes in his time, but had won much love and had done great work for the Church, departed on August 6, 1866, in childlike faith and humility.

JOHN KEBLE AND JOHN HENRY NEWMAN

A STORY is told of William Wilberforce that one day in his old age he and his four gifted sons were planning a holiday together. It was agreed that each of the five should bring to the meeting-place fixed upon some new book which might be read aloud to the rest of the party. When they met together it was found that each of the five had brought the same book. It was the *Christian Year*. This is a slight illustration of the deep impression which the book produced, almost at its first publication, upon the religious mind of England. It appeared in June 1827, having been for some years in preparation. It was rather a sleepy age for English religion. The first group of evangelical leaders had most of them passed away, or were rapidly passing; there was no great controversy pending. The separation, too, between Church and Dissent was growing wider, and the appreciation of the Prayer-book and of Church order was growing keen and strong among many clergy, who, had they lived earlier, would have made light of the irregularities of Wesleyan and Calvinistic Methodism. A book of lofty and beautiful verse, which glowed with love for the Church and her services, and which penetrated so deeply into the spiritual life and power of our Prayer-book, was, therefore, a gift from God which fell upon soil ready to receive it; and it is no wonder that its influence in the Church of England was vast and abiding. Ten years before the author's death more than a hundred thousand copies had been sold, and in the nine months after his death alone more than eleven thousand copies.

John Keble was born on St. Mark's Day, April 25, 1792, at Fairford, in Gloucestershire. His father, himself a John Keble, was Vicar of Coln St. Alwins, a small parish about three miles from Fairford; a devout old scholar, one of those who kept up the tradition, well-nigh lost at that time, of the Ken type of Churchmen. He had himself been Fellow of Corpus College, Oxford; he educated his two sons at home, never sending them to school, and took his eldest son, John, up to Oxford in his fifteenth year to try for a scholarship in his own old College. The home-bred youth carried all before him, took a double first in 1811 (which, it is said, no one but Sir Robert Peel had yet done), and that same year, while only eighteen, was elected Fellow of Oriel, at that moment the most distinguished College, intellectually, in Oxford. Next year he won both the University Essay Prizes, and while only just twenty-one was made one of the University Examiners. None of these honours, however, impaired the simplicity of his meek and humble piety. His humility and his sanctity deepened year by year.

His first curacy was in the parish which will ever be associated with his memory, Hursley, in Hants; but on the death of a beloved sister he moved to Fairford to cheer the declining years of his aged father, whose parish he served as Curate. In 1831 he was made Professor of Poetry in Oxford, and four years afterwards the death of his father set him free to accept the living of Hursley, which was now offered him for the second time. In 1835 he married, and settled there. He was already known half over the world as the Christian poet of his time. The holy and beautiful life which he and his wife lived together has been well drawn for us by loving hands in Sir J. T. Coleridge's memoir and in Miss Yonge's *Musings on the Christian Year*. My space will only suffice for the mention of his poetical work. In 1839 he published a metrical version of the Psalms, a book which has never been used for public worship, and which was very unduly depreciated on its appearance, for, as a guide to the true understanding of the Psalter, it is, as might be expected, of the greatest value. His contributions to the *Lyra Apostolica* will be noticed presently.

In 1846 appeared the exquisite *Lyra Innocentium*, a lovely study of child life from the pen of a childless man, coloured by the developed teaching of the movement of which he was so important a part, but now and again attaining to heights of spiritual insight even beyond those of the *Christian Year*. It need scarcely be said that neither of these books was ever designed for congregational use; but many of the *Christian Year* verses had found their way into our hymn-books by this time, and in 1856 Keble gave assistance to his friend Earl Nelson in the compilation of a hymnal for the Diocese of Salisbury, of which the first edition, called the *Salisbury Hymn-book*, appeared in 1857. The new and larger edition has the somewhat misleading title of the *Sarum Hymnal*. For this book Keble wrote four original hymns, of which the best-known is his marriage-hymn, 'The voice that breathed o'er Eden.' He also translated a considerable number of Latin hymns, and recast some older English ones. As a translator, however, he does not attain the vigour and spirit of Neale, though it need hardly be said that he is most accurate and scholarly. He also made his own selections from the "Morning" and "Evening" verses in the *Christian Year*, known to all the world as 'New every morning is the love,' and 'Sun of my soul, Thou Saviour dear.' But he selected for the former the verse, 'Oh, timely happy, timely wise,' and made the latter begin with 'When the soft dews of kindly sleep.' The beautiful Septuagesima poem, 'There is a book who runs may read,' was also inserted in the Salisbury book, as well as one or two others. At an earlier period he had written the little-known but charming *Hymns for Emigrants* (1854), and four hymns for the *Child's Christian Year*. Before his death he had corrected for the press the ninety-sixth edition of the *Christian Year*. He fell asleep at Bournemouth, early in the morning of March 29, 1866, followed in six weeks' time by the companion of all his joys and sorrows and labours.

In the days of controversy and reproach through which he passed, John Keble was ever loyal and faithful to the Church of his baptism. It was otherwise with that great man whose name will ever be associated with his and Dr. Pusey's in connection with the Oxford movement. But the loss

John Henry Newman.

to the world of Cardinal Newman is too recent for me to speak much of his life. My concern here is with John Henry Newman as a writer of hymns. As I have not dwelt on Keble's other literary and theological work, so I must be silent about Newman's.

John Henry Newman, the son of a London banker, was born in London, February 21, 1801. From school at Ealing he went up to Trinity College, Oxford. He has told us himself with what awe he looked at Keble when he was pointed out to him in the streets of Oxford shortly after his entrance. In 1822 he became Fellow of Oriel, and in 1828 Incumbent of St. Mary's, Oxford, which is in the gift of his College. There it was that he began those marvellous sermons which produced so profound an effect on the younger men of his University, as they have since on many others. After writing the *Arians of the Fourth Century* he took a voyage in the winter of 1832, accompanied by Richard Hurrell Froude, a pupil of Keble's. By this time the foundations of the "Movement of 1833," as it is sometimes called, had been laid. Its history has now come to us from various sources— from Newman's own pen, and last, though not least, from the interesting volume of him whom we have recently lost, Dean Church. I am only concerned here with its bearing on hymnody. All through his foreign tour Newman was writing verses, pouring out his thoughts upon the Church and its faith, and the "work" before him. He was becalmed off Sardinia for some days on his way home from Sicily in June, 1833, and many of his finest poems are the fruit of those days; among them, 'Lead, kindly Light,' written June 16, 1833. This was included with many others, beginning with 1829, in a volume called *Lyra Apostolica*. Most of them, if not all, appeared in the *British Magazine*, but they were collected in 1836. The writers were designated by letters of the Greek alphabet. They were John Bowden, Hurrell Froude, Keble, Newman, Robert Wilberforce, and Isaac Williams. Williams's are the most numerous, Keble's, and above all Newman's, the most important. It seems almost accidental that 'Lead, kindly Light,' beautiful and significant as it is, should have been the one which has found its way into all hymn-books. Two or three others of Newman's are, in my judgment, quite equal to it, especially 'Lord, in this dust Thy sovereign voice,' written in 1829. Only one of Keble's poems in the volume has reached our hymn-books, his fine translation of the old Alexandrian 'Candlelight hymn,' 'Hail, gladdening Light!' It is Keble's best translation. Newman in after years translated several ancient hymns, especially those for the Hours, some of which (with alterations) appear in *Hymns Ancient and Modern*. Newman was received into the Church of Rome in 1845. His wonderful poem on the Intermediate State, the "Dream of Gerontius," was written in January 1865. From it has been taken one of the choruses, 'Praise to the Holiest in the height,' a truly magnificent hymn on the Fall and Redemption of Man. The great Cardinal passed away August 11, 1889.

EDWARD CASWALL AND FREDERICK WILLIAM FABER

THE ten years which followed 1840 were especially the years of secession to the Church of Rome, on the part chiefly of the extreme wing of the Oxford movement. The seceders were mostly young and ardent men, some of them, like Ward and Oakeley, of brilliant attainments. But, with the exception of John Henry Newman (and one living name, which will occur to all, but which belongs to a secession of somewhat later date), it can scarcely be said that they contributed much to the strength of the Church of their adoption. On the other hand, those who remained faithful to the Church of their baptism have lived to see her all the stronger and richer for the loss of some who were not in true harmony with her. Still, it is undeniable that those who joined the Church of Rome brought with them an energy of service and a fervour of devotion which showed itself in art and letters as well as in theology. It was to be expected, then, that the innovators would influence, among other things, hymnology. Following the precedents set in France, Italy, and Germany, they broke through the circle of Latin Breviary hymns, and appealed boldly to popular taste in a new Anglo-Roman hymnody. The characteristic names of this movement were Edward Caswall, and, above all, Frederick William Faber.

Edward Caswall was one of the younger sons of

Edward Caswall.

a Hampshire vicar. He was born at his father's parsonage, at Yateley, Hants, in July 1814. He went up to Brasenose in 1832, and took his degree in 1836. He held for a time a small incumbency near Salisbury, married, resigned his living in 1846, and was received into the Church of Rome in 1850.

He had lost his wife the previous year, and now (1850) he became an Oratorian at Birmingham, under Dr. Newman, with whom he remained in close alliance and friendship till his death in 1878.

The best of Caswall's hymns are his translations; and these were chiefly made just before his secession. Most of them appeared in his *Lyra Catholica* in 1849. They are less careful and accurate than Neale's, but there is great spirit and facility in many of them, and they go well to modern tunes. Thus his translation of St. Bernard's famous hymn, 'Jesu, the very thought of Thee,' though really inferior to Neale's (who, however, only translated a few verses), is sung five or six times as often. 'The sun is sinking fast' and 'Glory be to Jesus' are later translations. The best known probably of his original hymns, 'Days and moments quickly flying,' has, I think, become popular mainly through Dr. Dykes' fine tune. The strange Calvinist refrain, 'As the tree falls,' added from another hymn of Caswall's, has in the later edition of *Hymns Ancient and Modern* been wisely superseded. His translation of St. Francis Xavier's hymn, 'My God, I love Thee,' does not do justice to the original; but as the only form in which this most striking hymn is known to most English readers, it has gained a wide popularity.

Henry Collins, whose faith failed him during the troubles which marked the early days of his work in Charles Lowder's mission to the East End, has left behind him two striking hymns, 'Jesus, meek and lowly,' and 'Jesu, my Lord, my God, my all.'

To Frederick Oakeley we owe the popular version of *Adeste fideles*, 'O come, all ye faithful,' inserted in *Hymns Ancient and Modern*.

But the most interesting figure, and the most influential as a hymn-writer of all the converts to Rome, is undoubtedly Frederick William Faber. He was born at Calverley Vicarage, in the Aire Valley, between Leeds and Bradford, being the grandson of the vicar. In his infancy his family removed to Bishop Auckland, on his father, a layman, being made secretary to Bishop Barrington, of Durham. His first school was at Auckland; he was afterwards sent successively to Kirkby Stephen, Shrewsbury, and Harrow. From Harrow he went up to Balliol, matriculating in 1832. He soon made his mark, being made scholar of University College in 1834, and winning the Newdigate in 1836 for a poem on the "Knights of St. John." In 1837 he was chosen fellow of his college, and won the Johnson Theological Scholarship. The long vacation of that year was memorable to him. He spent it with pupils at Ambleside, and there made the acquaintance of Wordsworth. The exquisite poem, "To a Lake Party," was his farewell to his pupils when term time came. In the August of this year he was ordained deacon at Ripon, and came back to help the Vicar of Ambleside. He was much there during the next two years, living as private tutor at Green Bank, Ambleside, taking long walks with Wordsworth, writing much poetry, and preaching occasionally sermons which deeply impressed those who heard them, and copies of which are still tenderly cherished by the few who possess them.

In 1839 Wordsworth came up to Oxford to receive an honorary degree at Commemoration, and was the guest of Faber, who introduced him to John Keble. Keble's Latin oration in the theatre contained a noble eulogy of the great poet, who was deeply gratified by his reception.

In 1841 Faber was for some months in France and Italy, and published the following year his *Sights and Thoughts in Foreign Countries*, a sufficiently startling book in its undisguised sympathy with the Church of Rome. He soon left Ambleside, and accepted in 1843 the Rectory of Elton, in Huntingdonshire; and three years afterwards, November 16, 1845, he was received into the Church of Rome. He had previously written a life of St. Wilfrid of York, for Newman's series of *Lives of the English Saints*, and, on his change of religion, he at first attempted to found a new community of "Brothers of the will of God," of which St. Wilfrid was supposed to be the Patron Saint. But in 1848 he joined the Oratorians at Oscott under Newman, and the next year removed to the London branch of the community, with whom he continued, at the now well-known "Brompton Oratory," till his death on September 26, 1863.

Faber published many devotional works after his secession, with which we are not here concerned. But they have the same characteristics as his hymns. They are full of noble passages, and often show deep insight into the secrets of the human heart; but they are curiously wanting in the sense of proportion, their emotionalism is at times all but hysterical. The extravagances of popular Continental Romanism, which are generally kept in the background by sober English Roman Catholics, are just what Faber delights to display and to insist upon. Those who know Faber's hymns only through a carefully prepared selection, and have

Frederick William Faber.

learned to admire and delight in the series on prayer, those on the Holy Trinity, and the Spiritual Life, and a few more, had better not desire to see the complete collection. His first hymns were a few written for the Oratory in 1848, added to in 1849 and 1852 with the title, "Jesus and Mary," followed by the *Oratory Hymn-book* in 1854. They were avowedly written to compete with Dissenting and other Protestant hymns; and many of them (such as 'O Paradise' and 'Hark, hark, my soul') introduced the "refrain" which modern Revivalist hymnody has since made popular. In 1862 he published a complete collection of his hymns divided into seven parts. He limited their number to 150, as being the number of the Psalms.

Roman as they are, nearly all English-speaking congregations have accepted Faber's hymns, of course with prudent omissions and alterations. Grave critics have rebelled against them, but all in vain. It is useless to say that 'O Paradise' contains weak and effeminate lines; the people assent and sing on, and after all one is glad that some of them learn for the first time that there is such a place as Paradise. We inquire in vain into the meaning of the 'Pilgrims of the Night;' congregations are carried away by the rhythm and the musical ring of the lines. Happily there are better things than these in Faber. 'I was wandering and weary;' 'O come to the merciful Saviour;' 'Souls of men;' 'We came to Thee, sweet Saviour;' and others, are most telling in mission services. 'Sweet Saviour, bless us ere we go' (duly altered) ranks among our favourite evening hymns; while as to the spiritual value of some of the more chastened and sober hymns on God the Father and the Spiritual Life, the 'Gifts of God,' the 'Eternal Years,' the 'Shore of Eternity,' the series on prayer, and most of those on Death, these are treasures of Christian thought and spiritual comfort which can never die.

In reading them one can **understand the attraction** which the warm-hearted, **lofty-minded, emotional** young poet **must** have **had for** his mighty **master** at Rydal ; **and** one can but regret all the more deeply the alloy of foolishness and superstition which in after time mingled with the gold of his devout and elevated thoughts.

CHRISTOPHER WORDSWORTH AND HORATIUS BONAR

As these papers draw to a close, the press of names worthy of note in modern English hymnody becomes embarrassing. I feel almost sure that at every turn some reader will think me strangely blind to the merits of some favourite hymn or author, simply because I am obliged here to select representative names. I ought not to pass unnoticed such men as John Samuel Monsell, whose warm and loving devoutness so often is counter-balanced by his incorrectness; Henry Alford, Dean of Canterbury, whose harvest hymn, 'Come, ye thankful people, come,' is the best of our "In-gathering" songs; or one yet more recently lost, but whom English hymn-singers will never forget —Henry Williams Baker. But I must confine myself to two names, one from the heart of our English Church, one from among our Presbyterian brothers across the Tweed.

Christopher Wordsworth, Bishop of Lincoln, is one of whom we certainly do not first think as a writer of hymns, but as a great scholar, a diligent and careful expositor, an accurate theologian and controversialist, a great and wise ruler in the

Church, and a most holy, humble, loving, self-denying man. And the man is reflected in his verse. To read one of his best hymns is like

Christopher Wordsworth.

looking into a plain face, without one striking feature, but with an irresistible charm of honesty, intelligence, and affection. Take, for instance, his Offertory Hymn, 'O Lord of heaven, and earth, and sea.' It is not in the least poetical; it is full of halting verses and prosaic lines. And yet it is such true praise, so genuine, so comprehensive, so heartfelt, that we forget its homeliness.

The good Bishop was the son of another Christopher Wordsworth, Master of Trinity College, Cambridge, and brother of the great poet. He was born October 30, 1807, was trained at Winchester, took a brilliant degree at Cambridge in 1830, and was made Fellow of Trinity almost immediately. From 1836 to 1844 he was Head Master of Harrow. In that year he was appointed Canon of Westminster, and while holding that office he began to write his *Holy Year*, which was published as a collection for Church use in Lent, 1862. Of its 200 hymns the first 117 were his own. He prefaced it with a really remarkable critical essay on hymns, full of learning and wisdom, but with scarcely one single note of sympathy with existing English hymnody. He added a few more hymns subsequently, but, having laid down his canons and made his protest, he left the book to become a literary curiosity. He was cheered, however, by the warmth with which the few tuneful hymns it contained soon began to be received; and these few have been stored up in the permanent treasury of the Church of England. Dr. Wordsworth was appointed to the see of Lincoln in November 1868, and administered it in a way which won the reverence and love of all good men till he entered into rest in 1885. We pass into a very different atmosphere.

Horatius Bonar was one of a group of men who

were called in God's Providence to carry out a remarkable revival of spiritual life in the heart of Scottish Presbyterianism. His father, James

Horatius Bonar.

Bonar, was an Edinburgh solicitor, and a great philologist. A "holy ancestry" and "godly parentage" were among the gifts for which he blessed

God in his memorial hymn. He was "a child of the city," born in Edinburgh December 19, 1808. His father was a strict religious man, but "it was at their mother's knee that he and his brothers learnt their first and perhaps most abiding lessons in the faith." He was educated at the University óf Edinburgh, and in due time licensed as a preacher. He and his friends early began mission work in the courts and alleys of Edinburgh and Leith. Leith was the special scene of "Horace's" work. He preached in a mission hall there, and began writing hymns for those whom he gathered in. His first was, 'I was a wandering sheep;' his second, 'I lay my sins on Jesus;' his third, 'A few more years shall roll.'

In November 1837 he was called to be minister of the "North Parish," in the beautiful old border-town of Kelso, and there, by the swift-rushing Tweed, and amidst the green woods of Floors, he poured out his gift of song from a full heart, while for nearly thirty years he worked and prayed with loving energy. He and his two brothers organized a kind of order of "Border Evangelists" to carry on mission work among the dales. He was in touch with all that was most living and earnest in the Church of his fathers. He took a keen interest in the controversies which ended in 1843 in the memorable Disruption. He and his brothers, and most of their personal friends, followed Chalmers and Candlish in the great exodus from St. Andrew's Church, which Jeffrey watched with amazement. They became the founders of the "Free Church of Scotland." Most of them had to give up home and parish. Horatius Bonar, however, was enabled to retain possession of his church in Kelso, where, as he himself said, he had found "plenty of work, plenty of workmen, and plenty of sympathy." At length, in 1866, he returned to his native Edinburgh to become the minister of a new church, built as a memorial to Dr. Chalmers, in Grange, one of the suburbs of the city. He often visited London, taking part in the annual conference at Mildmay Park. He died July 31, 1889, at the good old age of eighty-one.

His own favourites among his hymns were the beautiful one for the dedication of a church, 'When the weary seeking rest;' and that pearl of hymns, 'I heard the voice of Jesus say,' which Bishop Fraser of Manchester ranked above every other in the language. But Bonar's seven volumes contain many a less known gem of Christian "faith and hope," and there is no more striking testimony to his power as a "sweet singer," than the very remarkable change which, during his lifetime, passed over the whole of Scotland in the matter of hymnody. Forty years ago, every Presbyterian congregation, of whatever denomination, clung to the old Scottish national Psalms and Paraphrases with a tenacity which seemed as if it could never be shaken. The Psalms were endeared to high and low, rich and poor, throughout the land. No doubt they are still sung in all their quaintness and force in many a country congregation; but from the towns they have almost wholly disappeared. Each of the great Presbyterian bodies, the Established Church, the

Free, the United Presbyterians, and the English Presbyterians, has its own authorized hymn-book, compiled by its own members; and the use of hymns in congregations has become practically universal. Many regret the old; some, like the gifted Robertson of Irvine, thought the new comparatively weak and poor, though he himself largely contributed to swell the tide of change, but there can be no doubt that Scottish devotion has gained much in breadth, colour, and heartiness; and it is scarcely too much to say that this great change is, in large measure, due to the silent leavening of the taste of religious Scotland by the hymns of Horatius Bonar. I do not know, indeed, whether he took any part at all in compiling any of the new hymn-books; I do not know whether he personally approved of the beautiful and spiritual volume which his own denomination has compiled; but I do say that the " new wine " of the *Hymns of Faith and Hope* has enriched the blood of all religious Scotland, and made it impossible for her to rest content with the merely veiled and indirect praise of her Risen and Ascended Lord which was all that her old Psalmody allowed her. Her heart grew hot within her, and at last she spake with her tongue, in new and freer accents of praise. The change is significant of much which is beyond the province of these articles; much which may need anxious watching and prayer. But may it not be significant, too, of a growing unity among some hearts long saddened? may it not be one of the faint and far " preludings " of that " burst of song " which shall usher in the day for which we wait and hope?

CHARLOTTE ELLIOTT AND FRANCES RIDLEY HAVERGAL

WE must not close these notices of our hymn writers without a reference to the share of Christian women in the work of supplying the materials for sacred song.

We need not dwell upon the hymns written by Christian women in the last century and the earlier years of this. But Anne Steele, Anna Barbauld, Sarah Adams, and Alice Flowerdew (surely predestined by her very name to write a harvest hymn!) are still represented in our best collections. Of Harriet Auber we have already spoken. Anne and Jane Taylor of Ongar will always rank among the pioneers of children's hymnody. Their hymns have been too much overlooked of late years. Jemima Luke will be remembered by the 'Sweet Story of Old.' Anne Mozley, the gifted sister of Cardinal Newman, has left us a lovely children's litany, ' By Thy birth, O Lord of all.'

But of all the "daughters of the *Magnificat*," those who have made the most profound impression on our own time are the two whose names appear at the head of this article.

Charlotte Elliott was the sister of two well-known

clergymen, Henry Venn Elliott, of St. Mary's, Brighton, and Edward B. Elliott, whose book on the Revelation, *Horæ Apocalypticæ*, was once exceedingly popular, though, like many commentaries which looked into futurity, it has been in great measure obliterated now by the stern logic of events. Charlotte was born in 1789. A severe illness in 1821 left her a confirmed invalid. The following year she formed a friendship which was to leave a permanent influence both on her writings and her life; she was introduced to César Malan, of Geneva, one of the leaders of what was then the new Evangelical movement among the Reformed Churches of France and Switzerland, and one of the most prolific of modern French hymn-writers.

This excellent man had many English friends and much sympathy with our Church; he translated into French more than one of our best-known hymns. A small volume was printed privately in 1834 (afterwards published), called the *Invalid's Hymn-book*. To this Miss Elliott contributed an appendix containing twenty-three hymns of her own, among them the first draft of one by which she has since become known to hundreds of thousands, 'My God, my Father, while I stray.' This hymn she recast two or three times, altering among other lines the first. Two years later, 1836, she published *Hours of Sorrow Cheered and Comforted*, containing the greatest of all her hymns, 'Just as I am.' This hymn is said to have been translated into more languages than any other; it is perhaps even more popular on the Continent of Europe than with ourselves; but it certainly takes rank with 'Rock of Ages' and 'Abide with me,' as among the hymns which have left the deepest impression upon the English religious mind, in its earnest and true expression, without any qualifying

Charlotte Elliott.

or compromising phrases, of entire consecration to our Lord, and absolute trust in Him. Another admirable hymn of Miss Elliott's, 'Christian, seek not yet repose,' appears as the Wednesday morning hymn in a beautiful little volume of hers,

Hymns for a Week. To have written three such hymns as these entitles her indeed to take a front rank among the Christian singers of the world. Miss Elliott died at Brighton, September 22, 1871. The gift of sacred song, it may be mentioned, has not departed from a younger generation of the family to which she belonged.

Frances Ridley Havergal virtually belongs to our own generation, for she was only forty-two when she was called home in 1879. She was, as it were, born in an atmosphere of hymns. She was the daughter of one hymn-writer, William Henry Havergal, and was baptized by another, John Cawood, of Bewdley. Her father held a country rectory in Worcestershire, and removed thence in 1845 to the city of Worcester, where he became incumbent of St. Nicholas, and became known both as a composer of hymn-tunes and as a critic with a special knowledge of the history of our Metrical Psalmody. Frances was his youngest child; her second name, Ridley, was derived from her saintly godfather, W. H. Ridley, vicar of Hambleden, Berks, whose well-known little books on Confirmation and Holy Communion are probably the very best ever written on these subjects for the country poor. The record of Frances Havergal's holy life has been compiled, largely from her own reminiscences and letters, by her sister Maria, who has since followed her. There are, so to speak, no events in it. She lost her mother in childhood. She published two volumes of verse—*Under the Surface*, and *The Ministry of Song*—and many other booklets and leaflets. She was constantly writing hymns. She was joint editor of a collection called *Songs of Grace and Glory*, but it took no permanent hold on the Church. But her real life was a life of personal, spiritual influence upon others. She lived habitually in an atmosphere of

Frances Ridley Havergal.

perfect love and entire consecration to God, of which one reads with awe; but her high ideal was consistent with the warmest human affection for a large circle of friends, and with the most perfect, unaffected, child-like simplicity and sincerity. It is too soon to estimate which of her numerous hymns will live on to another generation, yet there are some which we are sure must be remembered. Many of them cover the same ground; consecration of the life to God is their most frequent subject, as in the most solemn 'Take my life.' Another, of peculiar power and reality written as a motto beneath a German print of the Crucifixion, begins in its original form, 'I gave My life for thee.' So little did she esteem it that she threw it into the fire in turning out an old desk. She consented, however, to recast it for the S. P. C. K., and in its present form, 'Thy life was given for me,' it has already become dear to thousands who know perhaps little of her other hymns. Her hymns for workers, too, such as, 'Lord, speak to me that I may speak,' and 'Jesus, Master, Whom I serve,' are the reflection of a life which to the last was spent in "service." Her beautiful Ascension hymn for children, 'Golden harps are sounding,' written for one of her father's tunes, embodies the leading thought which dominated her life. Christ was her King, she loved to call Him so; loving, loyal service for Him in every way was the law of her life.

HORATIUS BONAR AND HIS HYMNS

CHRISTIAN congregations, wherever the English tongue is spoken, felt, on receiving the announcement that Horatius Bonar had entered into rest, at the ripe age of eighty-one, that the Church militant had been bereaved of one of her sweetest singers. With how many of the most sacred times of our lives have his words been associated! As I write, a scene in a village churchyard many years ago rises before my eyes. It was the funeral of a poor lad, one of my own flock, who had been drowned while bathing on his way to work on an autumn morning. His remains had been reverently and lovingly tended by the members of a little community whose house was on the bank of the river half-a-mile off. He was laid to rest just at sunset, with, of course, a large gathering of his mates and neighbours. And as the words of the Burial Office died away, and the last gleam of parting day tinged with pale gold the line of low wooded hills behind the church tower, the brothers and their choir began the hymn, 'A few more years shall roll.' How the words came home to every heart in their solemn reality—

> "A few more suns shall set
> O'er these dark hills of time,
> And we shall be where suns are not—
> A far serener clime."

How often since has that solemn hymn closed our services on New Year's Eve, each time with a fresh impression of its deep reality! And this is the quality of all Bonar's verse. It is sometimes trite and commonplace. It is sometimes unpoetical. He often repeats himself. His range of vision is limited. His views are those of a plain Scotch Calvinistic Evangelical and a Millenarian. But he is a believer. He speaks of that which he knows; of Him whom he loves, and whom, God be praised, he now sees at last, for whose coming he looked and waited. And, therefore, his hymns have in them the power which belongs to one to whom to live was Christ. They are, indeed, what he called them, 'Hymns of Faith and Hope.'

Bonar was one of a remarkable group of young Scotchmen to whom it was given fifty years ago to rekindle the dying fire of spiritual life in the respectable but dull and lifeless Established Church. Foremost among them was the saintly and eloquent Robert Murray McCheyne, also a hymn-writer, whose words I have found this week, as I have often done before, to give peace and comfort by a sick bed; the two brothers Burns, Andrew and Islay, the former a mission-preacher to be compared in power only to Whitefield himself; the latter, the scholar of the group, McCheyne's successor, afterwards for many years Professor of Ecclesiastical History at Glasgow, a man of rare learning, deep piety, and most large-hearted charity; John Milne of Perth, and "Horace's" brother, Andrew Bonar of Collace, whose commentary on Leviticus is still a most valuable and interesting exposition of the symbolism of the Mosaic ritual, and whose *Life of McCheyne* has inspired the zeal of many a young minister to tread in his steps. Every one of these was a remarkable man. Every one had to endure the ridicule, opposition, and misinterpretation which is the lot of all reformers, and which doubtless, like all reformers, they did something to provoke. Every one, except McCheyne (who did not live to see it), "went out" from St. Andrew's Church with Chalmers and Candlish on the memorable "Disruption Day" in 1843; and every one, I believe, took part in the formation of the Free Church of Scotland. Horatius Bonar, who had been minister of what is oddly called in Scotland a "quoad sacra" Church (that is, an ecclesiastical district) in Kelso, soon found himself the minister of a new church there, formed doubtless in great measure of the members of his old congregation. There, amid the green braes and haughs, by the side of the swift-rushing Tweed, or in the woods of Floors, or under the shadow of the grey Abbey tower, many of his most touching verses were written, and many of his happiest years passed. But, as he said of himself, in one of his most striking poems, he knew and loved and clung to the City. And his latter years were spent in Edinburgh. Nor was he unknown in London, where his venerable form might often be seen—sometimes presiding at the meetings of the "Mildmay Conference" in June, especially when some subject connected with prophecy or eschatology was discussed.

I have always thought his first volume of hymns contained the choicest—the first crush of the grape. The very earliest, 'Divine Order,'—John Keble's great favourite—is perhaps his most perfect poem. But among others in this volume are the great Advent hymns, 'Come, Lord, and tarry not,' 'A few more years shall roll,' 'The Church has waited long,' and 'Far down the ages now.' It contains also—'I was a wandering sheep,' 'I lay my sins on Jesus,' 'Calm me, my God, and keep me calm,' 'Thy way, not mine, O Lord,' 'Go, labour on,' and, loveliest of all, 'I heard the voice of Jesus say.' The second series contains that very noble, but less known hymn, 'O love of God, how strong and true,' also 'O Everlasting Light,' and the rapturous 'Heaven at last,' often attributed to Faber. The third contains the lovely hymn for the dedication of a church, 'When the weary, seeking rest,' which Sir John Stainer has recently wedded to music not unworthy of it.

These titles alone will show both the range and the limitations of Bonar's gift of song. As he grew in years, he drew more inspiration from the Church songs of the past, some of which he has successfully translated ; and yet more from his knowledge of Bible lands, their scenery and their associations. But from first to last there is a unity about his work. He never imitated, never affected to be what he was not. He is always the Presbyterian, Bible loving, uncompromising, unmistakable in his principles, his views, his very prejudices. But he is, more and more, the holy singer, inspired by the Spirit of Christ, steeped in love to Christ, at one with all, of all Churches, who love and own the same Lord, "both theirs and ours." Let us bless God for one more departed in His faith and fear.

SOME FAMOUS HYMNS

SOME FAMOUS EASTER HYMNS

As the greatest and oldest of Christian festivals, Easter has, as might have been expected, wakened the voice of Christian song in many lands and in every age of the Church. Hence it is that there have been an unusual number of Easter hymns which from time to time have acquired popularity, and that although some of these are now forgotten, there are not a few which, in the hymnals compiled of late years in England (such as *Hymns Ancient and Modern*, *Church Hymns*, and the *Hymnal Companion* of Bishop Bickersteth), have recovered their ancient place in the affections of Church people, and bid fair to be welcomed for generations to come. It may interest my readers to hear of a few of these more famous Easter hymns of the Church.

The vast collections of hymns of the Greek-speaking Churches, of which all but a few are unknown to English readers, have yielded two Easter hymns to our modern collections, viz. 'The Day of Resurrection' (*H. A. M.; C. H.; H. C.*), and 'Come, ye faithful, raise the strain' (*H. A. M.;*

C. II.). Both these are translated by Dr. Neale (in his *Hymns of the Eastern Church*), and both are by the same author, St. John of Damascus, a Christian poet and philosopher of the eighth century, who ended his days in the monastery of Mar Saba, near the Dead Sea ; and who is, as all have agreed, the greatest of Greek hymn-writers. Of St. John's two hymns it is especially the first which may claim notice as one of the famous hymns of the world, the series (for Easter morning) to which it belongs being called the "Golden Canon," and sung throughout the Greek Churches as the opening hymn for Easter-day. A "Canon" in the Greek service-books is the name applied to a series of hymns, sung in a certain invariable order, and governed by fixed rules, during Matins on certain days. The second of our Greek hymns, also by St. John of Damascus, is part of a "Canon" for Low Sunday, or, as the Greeks call it, St. Thomas's Sunday.

It need hardly be said that these Greek hymns were quite unknown to our own fathers ; nor is it likely that more than a few versions, turned into metre, or fragments from among them, will find their way into our hymn-books. We are far more at home in the West with the hymns of the Latin-speaking Churches, the true progenitors of our own, as the Latin services are (on the whole) of our Book of Common Prayer. The old English rule for some centuries was that no hymns were sung in the Offices for the Hours on Easter-day itself. But the great service for the day opened (after the singing of 'Christ being raised from the dead,' etc.) with the splendid processional of Fortunatus, 'Salve Festa dies,' probably for many centuries the most popular Easter hymn in the world. It was translated by Cranmer, and his design was to print it after the Litany, as a special hymn for Easter; but his translation is now lost. It has become known in late years through more than one translation, 'Welcome, happy morning' (*H. A. M., C. H.*, and *H. C.*), and has recently acquired new popularity, in London especially, through Mr. Baden Powell's fine tune to a version (I believe by Mr. Chambers[1]), 'Hail, festal day, for evermore adored.' The original is probably the finest processional hymn in the world. There are in the York Processional imitations of it for Ascension, and for a Church Dedication. Each day in Easter week had its own "sequence" hymn in the Sarum Missal; the best known of these is the 'Victimæ Paschali,' of which a free version is in *H. A. M.* 131. This was long sung by the Lutherans, and in some German hymn-books is still printed in the original Latin. Of the other Latin Easter hymns, the most famous were the following :—'Ad cœnam Agni,' of which *H. A. M.* has two versions, 127 and 128; the former a fine one, by Mr. Campbell, also in *C. H.*, translated from the modern Roman version of this hymn; the latter reproducing *nearly* all its original quaintness. It was originally a hymn to be sung by the newly baptized in their white dresses, on the first Sunday after Easter. 'Aurora lucis rutilat,' a very fine hymn in three parts, is in *H. A. M.* 126,

[1] Signed "W. A." in *Lyra Eucharistica* (Julian).

and a version of the first part, by Dr. Hort, in *C. H.* 130. Both these hymns are, at latest, of the sixth century; they are sometimes called St. Ambrose's, and, at any rate, belong to his school. The hymn for the eves of Sundays in Easter, 'Ye choirs of new Jerusalem' (*H. A. M.* 125), is attributed to a French bishop, St. Fulbert of Chartres, of the eleventh century. 'The strife is o'er' ('Finita jam sunt prælia') is referred by Dr. Neale to the thirteenth century. It is in *H. A. M., C. H.,* and *H. C.*

The Reformation, as every one knows, divided the Reformed Communions into psalm-singing and hymn-singing bodies. Till early in the present century no hymns were sung in our churches, and at Easter it was the fashion to use the very tame and prosaic paraphrases of the Easter Anthems, which had found their way to the end of the New Version of Psalms. There was, however, one singular and important exception, the familiar 'Jesus Christ is risen to-day—Alleluia!' Its origin was for a long time unknown; and it is still impossible to discover under what circumstances it attained its unique position. The original is an Easter carol of the fourteenth century still existing at Munich, apparently written in imitation of the famous Christmas carol 'Puer natus in Bethlehem.'[1] A translation of a portion of this in three verses appeared in English in a book of sacred melodies called *Lyra Davidica*, in 1708. From this translation our present first verse is

[1] See, however, *Dict. of Hymnology*, p. 596 ii., where the original is given as *Surrexit Christus hodie.*—H. H.

taken. The second and third verses, however, were replaced in 1749 (in *Arnold's Compleat Psalmodist*) by the two with which we are all familiar, which, though in no sense a translation of the old carol, breathe the same spirit, and have made the whole into a good hymn. The tune, commonly attributed to Dr. Worgan (but published before his birth), was thought by Sir John Goss to be by the celebrated Henry Carey; possibly he also translated the words.

Germany, the land of vernacular hymns, produced many Easter hymns. The grandest of all these was Luther's own, far less known in England than it deserves; it was the first German hymn ever translated into English (by Myles Coverdale, the reforming Bishop of Exeter, under Henry VIII.). About thirty years ago a fine version by the late Mr. Massie was inserted in Mercer's Hymn-book, with the chorale to which it is usually sung; an abbreviated version of the hymn ('Christ Jesus lay in death's strong bonds') is in *Church Hymns*, 129. There is a still earlier hymn, a recast of an old Bohemian hymn ('Christus ist erstanden'), which, through Miss Winkworth's version, 'Christ the Lord is risen again' (*H. A. M.* and *C. H.*) is happily now well known and loved. One other German Easter hymn may be mentioned, the lovely 'Jesus lives' (*H. A. M.; C. H.; H. C.*), of Christian Gellert, the saintly old Professor at Leipsic (d. 1769), the teacher of Lessing and Goethe.

The most famous Easter hymn of purely English origin is probably Charles Wesley's 'Christ the

Lord is risen to-day' (*C. H.* and *H. C.* 210), one of the same set with his better-known Christmas and Ascension hymns. It is a pity it has not found a place beside these in *Hymns Ancient and Modern*, as well as the little-known but very striking Epiphany hymn in the same series. They appeared in 1739. It is too soon to say whether any later hymns will grow to be famous. But there are one or two, such as Bishop Wordsworth's florid but stately 'Alleluia! Alleluia! hearts to heaven and voices raise' (*H. A. M.* and *C. H.*), and Mr. Chatterton Dix's 'Alleluia! sing to Jesus' (*H. A. M.* and *C. H.*), which bid fair to take root among us; to which I feel strongly disposed to add one by Mrs. Cousin in a Scotch book, 'To Thee, and to Thy Christ, O God,' Mr. Baring Gould's touching 'On the Resurrection morning' (*H. A. M.* and *C. H.*), and 'O Voice of the Beloved' (for Easter Monday), by the late Vicar of Settle, Mr. Jackson Mason, a "sweet singer" too early lost to the Church, all of them likely to become better known and loved ere long.

The list ought not to close without the mention of one hymn, which though not formally an Easter hymn, is so full of Easter teaching and spirit as to form a noble close to the services of the "Day of Days," namely, 'Jerusalem luminosa,' 'Light's abode, celestial Salem' (*H. A. M.* 232), a selection by Dr. Neale from a long hymn for the dedication or restoration of a church. It is of the fifteenth century, and is found in a hymn-book at Carlsrühe. How wonderfully these unknown singers of the past live on in their inspiring strains!

SOME FAMOUS ADVENT HYMNS

ADVENT is not one of the earliest of the Church Seasons. Although in many Churches, especially those in France, a penitential season, of length variously prescribed, was observed as a preparation for Christmas early in the sixth century, it was not until the close of that century, that the four Sundays in Advent became, with their due collects and gospels, a part of the recognized order of the Roman Church under St. Gregory the Great; nor did their use become general for nearly a century and a half longer. But hymns on the subject of our Lord's Advent are found earlier than the formal observance of the season; though, as might be expected, they are mainly hymns of preparation for Christmas, and celebrate the first coming of our Lord.

The typical primitive Advent Hymn is St. Ambrose's 'Veni Redemptor gentium,' one of the most stately and solemn of his hymns. A fine translation of it, by the late Mr. Morgan, was inserted in the enlarged edition of *H. A. M.*, where it is No. 55.[1] The allusions to the manger show that it was intended for use on Christmas Eve or Day, and it was doubtless originally a

[1] 'O come, Redeemer of mankind, appear.'

hymn for vespers at Christmas; but it is essentially an Advent hymn, and was thus used more commonly in the middle ages, celebrating our Lord's two-fold coming and the Church's expectation of both. This hymn was very widely used; it was translated by Luther, and a version of it in German, by Franke, has become popular in the Lutheran Churches. Franke's is a fine translation, and as its language is better adapted for modern use than the plain-spoken phraseology of the Latin, it was made the basis of Professor Hort's admirable version of the hymn in *C. H.* 70. A little later, probably, comes another hymn from Milan, 'Conditor alme siderum' (*H. A. M.* 45, *C. H.* 65). This, too, was universally employed through the middle ages, and has found its way through more than one translation into German books. Its popularity in England has been, unfortunately I think, overshadowed by that of another hymn of the same date, 'Vox clara ecce intonat,' known to us chiefly through Mr. Caswall's very spirited and melodious version of it, 'Hark! a thrilling voice is sounding' (*H. A. M.* 47, *C. H.* 67). A third hymn, equally popular in the middle ages, 'Verbum Supernum prodiens,' also of the Ambrosian school, is less known to us, but it appears as No. 46 in *H. A. M.* It was the Morning Hymn for every day in Advent. All three hymns were revised (and as usual nearly spoiled) by the compilers of the Roman breviary in the sixteenth century. The seventeenth and eighteenth centuries brought a large crop of Latin Advent hymns, of the same type, into the various French breviaries, from which thirty or forty years ago several passed into our English hymn-books. The best of them is Charles Coffin's 'On Jordan's bank' (*H. A. M.* 50, *C. H.* 71), both translations being revisions of Mr. Chandler's. Of our English hymns on the First Advent, the one to which I would give the palm is undoubtedly Doddridge's noble 'Hark, the glad sound! the Saviour comes,' written December 28, 1735, probably (as was his custom) to be sung after a sermon on St. Luke iv. 17-19. This is in nearly all English hymn-books. The Bishop of Exeter has rescued from oblivion, for the *Hymnal Companion,* another good hymn of a similar type, by Dr. Watts: 'Joy to the world! the Lord is come'; but it is, in my judgment, inferior to Doddridge's.

Bishop Jeremy Taylor's *Golden Grove* (written about 1654) contained a series of irregular odes, which he called "Festival Hymns." They were meant for private use. From one of these, for Advent, 'Lord, come away,' Earl Nelson constructed a really fine hymn for the *Salisbury Hymn Book*, which was inserted in *C. H.* 66. It has, however, failed to attain the popularity which I think it deserves. Bishop Heber had previously failed in another attempt at adapting the same hymn. It is on the Gospel for the First Sunday in Advent. Lord Nelson's hymn begins, 'Draw nigh to Thy Jerusalem, O Lord.'

I must not leave this part of my subject without a reference to an interesting early usage in Advent, which has left its mark on our hymns, I mean the practice of singing a special short anthem or antiphon at Evensong on each of the eight days before Christmas Eve, beginning with December 16. The words in the calendar against that day, "O Sapientia," may have puzzled some readers. They are meant to indicate the use of the first of these short hymns, "O Wisdom that camest forth out of the mouth of the Most High, mightily and sweetly ordering all things, come and teach us the way of understanding." It is founded on a passage (viii. 1) in the apocryphal Book of Wisdom. The other six antiphons are all of them invocations to our Lord under some one of His Old Testament names, attributes, or symbols, and were supposed to represent the longing of the faithful in old days for His appearing. In the twelfth century (according to Dr. Neale) they were collected into a metrical hymn: 'Veni, veni, Emmanuel'; and five of them now form an admirable hymn for the last fortnight of Advent (*H. A. M.* 49), and all seven in *C. H.* 74, so arranged that one verse may, if desired, be sung on each of the appropriate days. But the *H. A. M.* form, with its lovely mediæval melody, is the most popular.

In the middle ages, especially in the sorrows and troubles of Europe in the eleventh century, the thought of our Lord's second coming to judgment came more and more prominently before the minds of believers. A notion had sprung up that the end of the thousandth year of the Christian era would witness the consummation of all things; and the awe and terror of coming judgment lasted on for a long time afterwards. Peter Damiani's awful hymn, 'Gravi me terrore pulsas,' which its translator, Dr. Neale, calls the "Dies Iræ of the individual life" (Neale, *Med. H.*, p. 52), was a symptom of the feeling of his day (1002-72). A century later we have the 'Hora novissima' of Bernard of Cluny ('The world is very evil,' *H. A. M.* 226), though the later stanzas, 'Jerusalem the Golden,' have taken a far greater hold upon our own less serious century. And then, standing out in unparalleled grandeur above every other "Judgment" hymn, old and new, there appears before us the unapproachable 'Dies Iræ,' probably written by Thomas of Celano, the friend and biographer of St. Francis of Assisi, about the middle of the thirteenth century. There is no need to quote here the judgment of critics, who all agree in doing homage to the majesty of the 'Dies Iræ.' The best proof of its power lies in the fact that it has more or less influenced almost everything that has since been written on the subject of the last judgment. The hymn has been many times translated into various European languages. Of late years Dean Alford and Archbishop Trench have been among its translators into English; but the best version for singing is the very remarkable one by the late Dr. Irons, which appears in *H. A. M.*, in *C. H.*, and in the *Hymnal Companion*, and which Dr. Dykes's noble setting has made still more impressive. The fine paraphrase of a part of the hymn by Sir Walter Scott, in the *Lay of the Last Minstrel*,—'That day of wrath, that dreadful day,'—is also to be found in *H. A. M.* and in Bishop Bickersteth's book.

Numberless have been the hymns either suggested by the 'Dies Iræ,' or at least influenced by its train of thought. Among the best known is 'Great God, what do I see and hear?' a hymn universally, but quite erroneously, known as Luther's, since he had nothing to do with either the words or the music. The tune was a chorale by Klug, written after Luther's death. The hymn, all but the first verse, is by the late Dr. Collyer, a Congregationalist minister. It may be fairly said that the hymn is one which has been popularized by its tune, and I own I should much like to see it some day superseded by Mrs. Leeson's far more hopeful and beautiful hymn in the same metre, 'Stand we prepared to see and hear' (*C. H.* 505), which strikes the true keynote of preparation for the coming of the Lord. But I fear I shall not carry my readers with me.

The Wesleyan hymnody, as might be expected, dealt largely with the expectations of the Second Advent, and to it we owe the most famous of English "Judgment" hymns—that which most readers would recognize as *the* Advent hymn if none other were named; I mean, of course, 'Lo! He comes.' This hymn, as we know it, is a curious refutation of the popular theory that a hymn ought always to appear exactly as its author wrote it. The original writer, John Cennick, one of Wesley's best preachers (though he afterwards left the Wesleyans), is well known as the author of 'Children of the heavenly King.' Cennick's Judgment hymn appeared in 1752, and six years afterwards it was recast by a man of genius, Charles Wesley, and became what it is now. My readers may like to see what they would have had to sing if Charles Wesley had left the hymn as its author wrote it. Happily he saw its capabilities—

> "Lo! He cometh, countless trumpets
>   Bow before the bloody sign;
> Midst the thousand saints and angels
>   See the glorifièd shine!
>   Hallelujah!
>   Welcome, welcome, bleeding Lamb!
>
> Now His merit, by the harpers
>   Through the eternal deep resounds;
> Now resplendent shines [sic] His nail-prints,
>   Every eye shall see His wounds;
>   They who pierced Him
>   Shall at His appearance wail."

There are four more stanzas, which it is needless to give; one of them, 'Now redemption, long expected,' is still found in some versions of the hymn. But it is to Wesley, not to Cennick, that we really owe the words which touch so many hearts in the dusk of the solemn Advent afternoon.

We must not forget, among English Advent hymns, Wesley's striking "Watch-night" hymn, 'Thou Judge of quick and dead,' nor Doddridge's 'Ye servants of the Lord'; John Newton's 'Day of Judgment' seems to me only a weaker 'Lo! He comes.' These three are all in the *Hymnal Companion*, and the first two in *H. A. M.*

The "Second Advent" hymns hitherto mentioned all bring into prominence the 'Dies Iræ' side of the Last Day, and, except Mrs. Leeson's, scarcely touch upon that aspect of it presented by our Master's exhortation to His faithful disciples:

"Look up, and lift up your heads, for your redemption draweth nigh." Of late years, however, this element of believing and hopeful expectation has been largely awakened in the Christian Church, and has found its expression already in her songs. Such hymns as Mr. Hensley's 'Thy kingdom come,' Mr. Tuttiett's noble 'O quickly come,' and Miss Havergal's beautiful and jubilant 'Thou art coming, O my Saviour' (all in *H. A. M.*), are indeed treasures for which we must be thankful to the Divine Spirit who is breathing new life into the waiting Church. But the great singer of Advent expectations is he who so recently has passed within the veil, Horatius Bonar. Such hymns as 'Come, Lord, and tarry not,' 'The Church has waited long,' 'Far down the ages now' (all in *C. H.*, and the last also in the new appendix to *H. A. M.*), may well help to rekindle in many hearts that "looking for the blessed hope and glorious appearing of our Lord and Saviour Jesus Christ," which was the especial characteristic of the Church of the first days, and for lack of which she has been, till of late, shorn of so much of her strength, and chilled in the energy of her love.

CHILDREN'S HYMNS BY MRS. ALEXANDER

THE present century has done much for the religious life of children within the Church. In nothing is this more manifest than in the provision made for their devotions. Hymns for children as children were all but unknown before the Reformation. The famous "Shepherd" hymn of Clement of Alexandria is not really a hymn at all, nor is it fitted or intended for use by a child. The yet more famous 'All glory, laud, and honour' (attributed, on doubtful authority, to Theodulf of Orleans) was written, no doubt, to be sung by chorister boys, but merely as an adjunct to the Palm Sunday Offices; and the hymns which Savonarola taught the boys at Florence were the product of a noble but merely local and temporary revival. A "children's hymn-book" in the middle ages meant a collection of the usual Office Hymns and Sequences, with notes and helps to construing —a school-book for the choristers' schools. One such is preserved in a Cheshire church, with a grim frontispiece representing three little boys seated on a low bench before a stern ecclesiastic, who wields a formidable birch-rod;—a curious illustration of the method then accepted of "teaching a child to be good." The Reformation brought at least the possibility of a change, though it was long before the change came. There is, indeed, no manual of Christian teaching in any country to be compared to our Church Catechism; but how much "accommodation" and exposition it needs to make it a child's book! Luther, indeed, understood children's religion, as his Christmas hymn for his boy Hans shows us; and we have occasional glimpses, from time to time, of light upon children's spiritual needs; Herrick's lovely 'Grace' is one such; but still there was wanting a real sympathy with the beginnings of child-like religion. Ken's 'Good Philotheus' is no child, but a sixth-form boy.

We come to Isaac Watts as the pioneer in the attempt to provide children with hymns and prayers of their own. Watts, though a valetudinarian old bachelor, was a kindly little man, really fond of children, and his *Divine and Moral Songs* were a labour of love. There is much to commend in his work. With all the quaintness, there is in his *Moral Songs* a "sanctified commonsense" which is excellent; and he now and then rises into real poetry, as in the 'Cradle Hymn,' which Tennyson has singled out for praise. In the *Divine Songs* there are fine thoughts here and there—thoughts of a devout and God-fearing mind. But Watts never rose beyond the theology of his environment; and that theology was singularly ill-adapted to call out the elements of a child's religion. He never, to begin with, grasped the idea of a child's covenant relation with its Father in heaven. His children were not even prodigal sons; they had never yet been in the Father's House at all. He writes a hymn for believers who practise infant baptism, and gives those who don't a hint to leave out certain verses. For Infant Baptism was to him a devout and graceful, but purely optional form—just as one might prepare a book for "believers who practise" chanting the Psalms. He is, of course, like all his school, happily inconsistent; he loves children so much that he believes in his Master's love for them; but he does not believe that a Christian child belongs to Christ in any special sense at all. Contrast St. Matthew xviii. 10, with such words as—

> "Can such a wretch as I
> Escape this cursèd end?
> * * * *
> Then will I read and pray,
> * * * *
> Lest I should be cut off to-day,
> And sent to eternal death."

Or consider the difference of the conception of the character of God as revealed by Christ in the words, "It is not the will of your Father which is in heaven that one of these little ones should perish," with that embodied in the monstrous lines—

> "What if the Lord grow wroth, and swear,
> While I refuse to read and pray,
> That He'll refuse to lend an ear
> To all my groans another day?

> What if His dreadful anger burn
> While I refuse His offered grace,
> And all His love to anger turn,
> And strike me dead upon the place?
> 'Tis dangerous to provoke a God!
> His power and vengeance none can tell:
> One stroke of His Almighty rod
> Shall send young sinners quick to hell"——

and so forth. The contrast between this and the 'Cradle Song' shows the difference between a good man writing from his own heart and from the necessity of being consistent with the traditional theology of his school.

Charles Wesley, who thought that Watts had "succeeded admirably well" in letting himself down to children, himself wrote, he tells us, on the other plan of lifting them up to us. But except the fine 'Captain of our Salvation,' for the Kingswood pupils, there is nothing worth noting in the first part of his hymns for children, certainly nothing so good as Watts's best. His *Hymns for the Youngest* contain, however, some really beautiful little hymns, the first being 'Gentle Jesus, meek and mild.' It is true he sometimes "lets himself down" so much, that some of his lines are absolutely silly; and sometimes, in trying to lift up the children, loses hold of the little hands. Nor does his theology, on the whole, differ much from Watts's. The repentance, faith, hopes, and terrors of the little ones are still cast in the mould of their elders. The foundation text of a child's religion is still read backwards—"Except the little children be converted, and become like you."

The establishment of Sunday Schools doubtless

brought a new demand for children's hymns; and soon a far truer note was struck by the Taylors of Ongar. The authoresses of the *Hymns for Infant Minds* and *Hymns for Sunday Schools* found out at last how to put into really childlike words the root-truths of every child's faith. Dissenters though they were, and (I believe) Baptists, the groundwork of all true Church teaching is in such hymns as 'Great God, and wilt Thou condescend,' 'Lord, I would own Thy tender care,' 'Lo, at noon 'tis sudden night' (a really sublime hymn on the Passion), 'Jesus Christ, my Lord and Saviour.' 'Jesus, Who dwelt above the sky,' though the most popular of all, has grave defects of taste and doctrine. And more might be enumerated. But now "all can grow the flower" from the seed which the Taylors sowed; and the luxuriance of Nonconformist child-hymnody is such that it would be invidious to select names. But it is to be noted that the best of these are those that have shaken themselves most free from the dominant theology of Watts's day, and dwell mainly upon the Fatherhood of God, the love of the Good Shepherd, and the personal relation of the child to Him. Such are those of Mr. Midlane ('There's a Friend for little children'), Mrs. Luke ('I think when I read that sweet story of old'), and Mrs. Duncan ('Jesus, tender Shepherd, hear me').

And now as the spirit of hymnody began to awake within the English Church, and one singer after another arose to translate the words of the past, or to add new treasures to the ever-growing store of Church hymns, there arose a new demand for definite Church teaching in the songs put into the lips of our little ones, and the Church of England began to produce children's hymns of her own, conceived in the spirit of her Prayer Book and Catechism. Isaac Williams's *Hymns on the Catechism*, though rather hard and formal, were a step in the right direction; then came the successive parts of Neale's *Hymns for Children*, many of them devout and instructive, but not inspired; Mrs. Leeson's *Hymns and Scenes of Childhood*; and a most excellent and useful, though rather unchildlike book, *The Child's Christian Year*, to which Keble contributed, and in which appeared many of Anstice's hymns, and some by Cardinal Newman's sister, Mrs. Mozley. But none of these were all we wanted for our little ones. At last, in 1848, amidst the storms of political revolution and social agitation, when a new tide of thought was flowing full and strong into English religious life, in the year which saw Tennyson's splendid maturity in the 'Princess,' and Charles Kingsley's brilliant dawning in the 'Saint's Tragedy,' there came quietly and unnoticed into the Church, from the far north of Ireland, a little book signed by no name but the three modest initials, "C. F. H."; a book which will live upon the lips of generations of children yet unborn, even of many who will perhaps never care to read the two other great poems; and will put into the mouth of thousands of "babes and sucklings" the first notes of that praise which God will perfect on high.

Miss Humphreys, as she then was, had already published one or two graceful volumes of verse for young people, and two years before had brought out, with a Preface by Dr. Hook, a little book of *Verses for Holy Seasons*, dedicated to John Keble. These are arranged according to the Sundays and Holy Days of the Christian Year. They scarcely give promise of what was to come; but there is much beauty in them here and there. One specially lovely poem on the healing of the deaf stammerer has, I believe, been reprinted in her *Moral Songs*. But the "Verses" were not hymns.

It is superfluous to praise the *Hymns for Little Children*, which must have sold by the million. Its true praise is in the thousands of little lips which daily utter such strains as, 'Now the dreary night is done,' 'All things bright and beautiful,' 'Once in royal David's city,' 'Do no sinful action,' 'There is a green hill far away,' and many another. It was an excellent plan to make the hymns follow the order of the Church Catechism, upon which they are so good a commentary.

The *Hymns for Little Children* were followed by the scarcely less beautiful, but less known *Narrative Hymns on the Gospels*; and these again by the *Verses on Subjects in the Old Testament*, containing, among others, the noble poem on the 'Burial of Moses,' which the late Lord Houghton —no mean critic—pronounced to be the finest sacred lyric in the language. Before these were given to the world, Miss Humphreys had married Mr. Alexander, one of the two Irish deans who took the Church of England by storm at the York Church Congress, and who have now been long recognized as the two most eloquent preachers on the bench of Bishops.[1] Mrs. Alexander's hymns, however, as is well known, are by no means all written for the little ones. Some of these best known and loved first appeared in the S.P.C.K. *Psalms and Hymns*, 1850, edited by the late Mr. Fosbery of Reading. Among these were 'Jesus calls us; o'er the tumult,' 'The roseate hues of early dawn,' 'The golden gates are lifted up.' The beautiful 'When wounded sore the stricken soul' is a little later. This hymn is understood to be her husband's favourite.

Mrs. Alexander edited for Messrs. Macmillan a charming little *Sunday Book of Poetry for the Young*, one of the "Golden Treasury" series; less known than it deserves. She is frequently asked to write hymns for special occasions. Some of the Hymns for Saints' Days in *Hymns Ancient and Modern* are hers, including a beautiful one for St. Peter's Day, 'Forsaken once, and thrice denied.' Some of these, however, are less adapted for singing than her earlier hymns. She has also written a pretty collection of *Moral Songs*, and one or two allegories and tales; among them a rendering into verse of the lovely legend of Saint Francesca of Rome, called 'The Legend of the Golden Prayers.'

Many years ago two ladies in a country house were watching all night in terrible anxiety by the bedside of the child of one of them, who had been struck down by a dread accident. As night slowly passed into dawn hope seemed to die out of their

---

[1] She died after this paper was written.

hearts. Suddenly from the adjoining nursery rose the clear, fresh voice of the sufferer's little brother, saying, as he sat up in bed—

> "Now the dreary night is done,
> Comes again the glorious sun."

The tones came like a message of hope to the two weary watchers; and the hope new kindled found fulfilment ere long.

GENERAL INDEX

ADAMS, Sarah, 381
Advent, and Advent Hymns, 397
Alexander, Mrs., 410
Alford, Dean, 374
Allen, James, 320
American Hymn-Book, 169, 222, 231, 286
Attwell, Professor, 102, 117, 167
Auber, Harriet, 346, 381
Augustine's definition of a Hymn, 161, 225
Authorized Hymnal, 206, 260, 284

Baker, Sir Henry W., 47, 280, 374
'Baldur, death of,' 25
Barbauld, Anna, 381
Barnes, 66
Baxter, Richard, 309
Bickersteth, Bishop E. H., 70, 123, 139, 399
Bird, F. M., letter from, 171
Blunt, Rev. Gerald, 23, 69
Bonar, Horatius, 376, 387
Bonar, Andrew, 388
'Bondage of Creeds,' 40
'Book of Praise,' 238
Brock, Mrs. Carey, 87
'Burial of Moses,' 411
Burns, the brothers, 388

'Canon' in Greek service books, 392
Caswall, Rev. Edward, 367
Cennick, John, 318, 340, 402
Centuries, 16th, 17th, poor in hymnody, 199

Chandler, Rev. John, 352
Child's Christian Year, The, 410
'Children's Almanac,' 156
Children's Hymns, 405
'Children's Hymn-Book,' The, 64, 87, 95, 98
'Children's Hymns and School Prayers,' 64
Chillon, 100
Choral Associations, value of, 256
'Christian Observer,' The, 329
'Christian Year,' The, 240, 359
'Church of England Hymn-Book,' The, 92
Church of England Temperance Hymn-Book, 70
'Church Hymns,' 72, 95, 98
Collins, Henry, 368
Compton, Rev. Berdmore, 74, 82
Conder, Josiah, 342
Copyright of hymns, 123
Cosin, Bishop, 303
Cotterill, Rev. Thomas, 340
Coverdale's collection of hymns, 195
Cowper, William, 237, 324
Cradle Hymn, Watts's, 406
Cranmer, Archbishop, 187
Creeds are hymns, 232
Crewe Green, 36
Critical estimate of Canon Ellerton's hymns, 161
Crossman, Samuel, 309

Denmark, hymns of, 78
'Dictionary of Hymnology,' 156

Doddridge, Philip, 200, 314
'Dream of Gerontius,' 365
Drummond, William, 351

Elizabeth, Injunction of, 196
Ellerton, John, birth and baptism, 16; his descent and parents, 16; at Norham-on-Tweed, 18; death of his father and mother, 18; early boyhood in London, 18; unfulfilled prophecy, 19; at Ulverston, 20; goes to King William's College, 20; at Brathay, 21; matriculates at Trinity College, Cambridge, 21; Cambridge Society, Henry Bradshaw, Dr. Hort, 21; influence of Maurice's works on his mind, 21; tone of his Churchmanship, 22; College life, Rev. G. Blunt's recollections of him, 23; competes for the Chancellor's medal, 24; ordained Deacon, 24; curate life at Easebourne, 32; ordained Priest, and appointed Senior Curate of Brighton, and evening Lecturer at St. Peter's, 33; Frederick Robertson, 34; appointed Vicar of Crewe Green, 36; marries, 36; activity as a Parish Priest, 37; 'Bondage of Creeds,' 40; the Endless Alleluia, explanation of the term "endless" by Sir H. Baker, 46; hymns written at Crewe Green, 46—60; appointed Diocesan Inspector, 63; presented to the Rectory of Barnes, 65; disabled by illness, 98; resigns Barnes, 98; retires to Switzerland, 98; Chaplain at Pegli, 102; appointed Rector of White Roding, 115; publishes 'Hymns Original and Translated,' 127; stricken with paralysis, 156; withdraws to Torquay, 157; resigns White Roding, 157; nominated Canon of St. Albans, 157; death, 158; funeral, 158
Elliott, Charlotte, 381

English hymnody, recent growth of, 192; begins in 18th century, 199; its subjective character, 202; past history of, 185

Faber, Rev. F. W., 369
Faioum fragment, The, 119
Florence, 112
Flowerdew, Alice, 381
Free Church of Scotland, its founders, 378, 389

Gales, Mr., 338
German hymns, the older, 78, 278; the later, 204
Grant, Charles Lord Glenelg, 349
Grant, Sir Robert, 349
Greek hymns, 392

Hammond, William, 351
Havergal, Frances Ridley, 276, 384
Heber, Bishop Reginald, 230, 330
Heber, Richard, 330
Henry VIII. Primer, 193
Hinstock, 61
'Holy Year,' The, 376
Hort, Dr., 119
How, Bishop Walsham, 64, 70, 82, 87, 116
Hymn, Augustine's definition of a, 161, 225
Hymn, original form of, not necessarily the best, 208
'Hymnal Companion,' 98, 124, 270
Hymn-book, principles on which it should be constructed, 223; how to use, 245
'Hymnologia Christiana,' Dr. Kennedy's, 72, 94, 198
'Hymns and Scenes of Childhood,' 410
'Hymns Ancient and Modern,' 74, 98, 130, 224, 280
'Hymns of Faith and Hope,' 380
'Hymns for Children,' Dr. Neale's, 358, 410
'Hymns for Little Children,' 411
'Hymns for Schools and Bible Classes,' 34, 72
'Hymns on the Catechism,' 410

'Hymns Original and Translated,' 127
'Hymns,' Art. in 'Dict. of Christian Antiquities,' 62
Hymns for Saints' Days, **229** *n.*; care in selecting for singing, 251; giving out in church, 285; 'Jerusalem,' 235; 'Judgment,' 402; limits to length of, 242; modern compared with ancient, 204; of the Oxford Movement, 350; private use of, 257; sentimental and sensuous, 238, 239 *n.*, 264; speed in singing, 255; when unfitted for congregational use, 204
Hymn-singing of former days, 73

'Indwelling, The Great,' 121
Irons, Dr. W. J., 356
Irvine, Edward, 19

Jackson, Bishop, 105
Jewel, Bishop, letter to Peter Martyr, 196

Keble, Rev. John, 360
Kemble, Rev. Charles, 231
Ken, Bishop, 305
Kennedy, Dr., 72, 198

Leeds, singing in the parish church, 249
Litanies, metrical, 95
'London Mission Hymn-Book,' 70
Luke, Jemima, 381
'Lyra Catholica,' 368
'Lyra Eucharistica,' 96
Lyte, Rev. H. F., 344

Macaulay, Zachary, 329
McCheyne, Rev. R. M., 388
Malan, César, 382
Mant, Bishop, 351
'Manual of Parochial Work,' 68
Martin, St., 143 *n.*
Mason, Jackson, 396
Mason, John, 309
Matthewson, Rev. Thomas, letter from, 174
'Mediæval Hymns and Sequences,' 356

'Memorials of a Quiet Life,' 332
Mercer, Rev. W., 342
Milman, Dean, 334
Monsell, Rev. J. S., 374
Montgomery, James, 337
Moorson, W. M., 37
Mozarabic Liturgy, 51
Mozley, Anne, 381

'Narrative Hymns on the Gospels,' 411
Neale, Dr. J. M., 355
Nelson, Earl, 362, 399
Newman, Cardinal, 363
Newton, John, 201, 325
'Notes and Illustrations to Church Hymns,' 62, 68, 81
Novalis, 89

Oakeley, Frederick, 369
Olney Hymns, 323, 327, 329
Ouseley, Rev. Sir Frederick, 190
Oxenden, Bishop, 88

Parisian Breviary, 352
'Poor-House, an Italian,' 109
Pope's Ode, 231
'Prayers for School-masters and Teachers,' 34
Psalms, Book of, 226; Metrical, a mistake, 80

Rhys Prichard, Welsh Hymns, 279
Robertson, Rev. F. W., 34
Robertson of Irvine, 380

S. P. C. K., 67, 77
Salisbury Hymn-book, 362
Sedgwick, Daniel, 211, 276
Shirley, Hon. W., 320
Steele, Anne, 381
Sternhold, Thomas, his Version of the Psalms, 196
Stubbs, Thomas, funeral of, 52
Synesius, Bishop, 278

Taine, M., 190
Tate and Brady, 197
Taylor, Bishop Jeremy, 'Golden Grove,' 399
Taylor, the Sisters, 381, 409

Thomas of Celano, 401
Thornton, Archdeacon, 67
Thring, Prebendary Godfrey, 92
Toplady, Augustus M., 202, 321
Tracts for S. P. C. K., 68
'Twilight of Life,' 121

'Verses for Holy Seasons,' 411
'Verses on Subjects in the Old Testament,' 411
Veytaux, 99

Walton, Izaak, 306

Watts, Dr., 200, 234, 309, 406
Webb, Benjamin, 356
'Welshman's Candle,' The, 279
Wesleys, The, 201, 316
White Roding, 116
Wilberforce, W., anecdote of, 359
Williams, Rev. Isaac, 353
Williams, William, 279
Winkworth, Miss Catherine, 278
Wordsworth, Bishop Christopher, 56, 230 *n.*, 231, 374; on the doctrinal teaching of hymns, 232

LIST OF CANON ELLERTON'S HYMNS, TRANSLATIONS, AND POEMS

	PAGE
A CHILD is born in Bethlehem	148
Again the morn of gladness	64
Again Thou meetest in Thy way	129
All my heart to Thee I give	65
Another day begun	55
Ascended Lord, Thy Church's Head	138, 140
Before the day draws near its ending	69
Behold us, Lord, a little space	54, 83
Break Thou to us, O Lord	69, 125
Bride of Christ, whose glorious warfare	84, 134
Church of Christ, &c. *See* Bride of Christ, &c.	
Come forth, O Christian brothers	53
Day by day we magnify Thee	34
Down the lane at evening time	121
English children, lift your voices	128
Father, in Thy glorious dwelling	48, 166
Father! Name of love and fear!	55
"Follow Me!" the Master spake	140, 145
From east to west, from shore to shore	85, 134
Giver of the perfect gift!	58, 85
Glory in the highest! let our Church bells ring (*dated* 1884)	
God, Creator and Preserver!	54
God of the living, in Whose eyes	35
God the Almighty, in wisdom ordaining	53
Hail to the Lord Who comes	69
Here in this peaceful time and place of rest	107

	PAGE
In gladness to Thy House, O Lord	153
I would not linger idly by the strand	121
In the Name which earth and Heaven	57, 83
In the Name which holy angels	68
It was early in the morning	146
Jesu most pitiful	49
Jesu, Who alone defendest	51
Joy! because the circling year	85
King Messiah, long expected	55, 83
King of Saints, to Whom the number	56, 83
Lift the strain of high thanksgiving	51
Lo, the angel squadrons muster; lo, the armies of the sky	148
Mary at the Master's feet	56, 83
Morn of morns, the best and first	85
Now the labourer's task is o'er	56
Now returns the awful morning	35, 83
O Father, all creating	63
O Father, bless the children	128
O friends, from under skies of ashen grey	122
Oh come, all ye faithful, joyful and triumphant	57, 86
Oh how fair that morning broke	69
O Holy Spirit, Whom our Master sent	139, 144
O Jerusalem the blissful, Home of gladness yet untold	128, 134
O Lord of life and death, we come	55, 84
O Meat for travellers on their road	149
Once more Thy Cross before our view	63
On this the day when days began	48, 86
Onward, brothers, onward! march with one accord	71
O Sacred Head, beneath Thy veil of shame	150
O shining city of our God	52
O Son of God, our Captain of salvation	55, 84
O Strength and Stay, upholding all creation	85, 160
O Thou in Whom Thy saints repose	53
O Thou Who givest food to all	70
O Thou Whose bounty fills the earth	69
Our day of praise is done	48
Praise our God for all the wonders	33, 70
Praise our God, Whose open Hand	69
Praise to our God, Whose bounteous Hand	57
Praise to the Heavenly Wisdom	128
Saviour, again to Thy dear Name we raise	47, 159
Say, watchman, what of the night?	140, 147
Shine Thou upon us, Lord. (*See* Break Thou to us, O Lord)	125 *n.*

HYMNS, TRANSLATIONS, AND POEMS

	PAGE
Sing Alleluia forth in duteous praise	46
Sing, ye faithful, sing with gladness	54
Speak Thou to me, O Lord	63
Spirit of God, Whose glory	129
Take, dearest, this, thy Lenten thoughts to guide	122
The day Thou gavest, Lord, is ended	53
The hours of school are over	34
The Lord be with us as we bend	53
The years pass on. We name them good or bad	151
This day the Lord's disciples met	68
This is the day of Light	48
This is the hour when in full brightness glowing	129
Thou in Whose Name the two or three	84
Thou Who once for us uplifted	62
Thou Who sentest Thine Apostles	63
Thou Who, wearied by the well	70
Thrice Holy, Thrice Almighty Lord	128
Throned upon the awful Tree	63
Thy Voice it is that calls us, bounteous Lord	68
'Tis come, the day of exultation	139, 142
To-day we sing to Christ our King	139, 143
To the Name that speaks salvation	59, 86
"Welcome, happy morning!" age to age shall say	49
We sing of Christ's eternal gifts	59
We sing the glorious conquest	55, 84
What were Thy Forty Days?	139, 141
When the day of toil is done	52
When to the far-off country	155
Within Thy Temple, Lord, of old	70

OTHER HYMNS MENTIONED

	PAGE
ABIDE with me	65 *n*., 89, 348
Ad cœnam Agni	191, 393
Adeste fideles	231, 369
Adoro Te devote	79, 188 *n*., 278
Æterna Christi munera	230 *n*.
A few more years	378, 390
Alleluia dulce carmen	96
Alleluia ! fairest morning	94
Alleluia ! hearts to heaven	396
Alleluia ! sing to Jesus	396
All glory, laud, and honour	356, 405
All hail the power of Jesus' Name	320
All people that on earth do dwell	227
All things bright and beautiful	411
Angels, from the realms of glory	341
Art thou weary	358
As for Thy gifts	198
At the Lamb's High Feast	96, 191
Aurora lucis	191
Awake, my soul	252
Before Jehovah's awful throne	313
Bread of heaven, on Thee we feed	343
Bread of the world, in mercy broken	336
Brief life is here our portion	356
Brightest and best	335
By Thy birth, O Lord of all	381
Calm me, my God	390
Captain of our salvation	408
Children of the Heavenly King	320, 402
Christ lag in Todesbanden (*Christ Jesus lay*)	96, 191, 395
Christ the Lord is risen again	395
Christ the Lord is risen to-day	191, 395
Christ, Whose glory fills the skies	203, 318

OTHER HYMNS MENTIONED 423

	PAGE
Christus ist erstanden	191, 395
Christian! seek not yet repose	383
Come, Lord, and tarry not	390, 404
Come, see the place where Jesus lay	191
Come, ye faithful, raise the strain	391
Come, ye thankful people, come	374
Conditor alme siderum	398
Creator of the rolling flood	336
Day of Judgment	403
Days and moments quickly flying	368
Depth of Mercy	318
Dies Iræ	240, 356, 401
Disposer Supreme	354
Draw nigh to Thy Jerusalem	399
Ein feste Burg	228, 240
Exultet orbis gaudiis	230 *n.*
Far down the ages now	390, 404
Far from my heavenly home	347
Far from the world, O Lord, I flee	236
Finita jam sunt prælia	394
For ever with the Lord	342
Forsaken once, and thrice denied	412
For thee, O dear, dear country	357
Forth from the dark and stormy sky	336
Forth in Thy Name	93
From Greenland's icy mountains	333
Gentle Jesus	408
Gird thee at the martyr's shrine	95
Glorious things of Thee are spoken	328
Glory be to Jesus	368
Glory to Thee, my God, this night	307
God of mercy, God of grace	347
God moves in a mysterious way	327
Go, labour on	390
Golden harps are sounding	386
Gravi me terrore pulsas	400
Great God, and wilt Thou condescend	409
Great God, what do I see and hear	402
Guide me, O Thou Great Jehovah	279
Hail, festal day	393
Hail, gladdening Light	365
Hail, Thou once despisèd Jesus	320
Hail to the Lord's Anointed	341
Hark! a thrilling (*vox clara ecce intonat*)	398
Hark! hark, my soul	372

… 424 OTHER HYMNS MENTIONED

	PAGE
Hark, my soul ! it is the Lord	327
Hark, the glad sound	315, 399
Hark ! the herald-angels sing	190, 318
Heal us, Emmanuel	327
Heaven at last	390
High let us swell our tuneful notes	315
Holy, Holy, Holy	236, 335
Hora novissima	401
Hosanna to the Living Lord	336
Hosanna to the Prince of Light	191
How sweet the Name of Jesus sounds	328
I heard the voice of Jesus say	379, 390
I lay my sins on Jesus	378, 390
I think when I read	409
I was a wandering sheep	378, 390
I was wandering and weary	372
Inspirer and Hearer of prayer	322
Jam lucis	203
Jerusalem, my happy home	235
Jerusalem the golden	235 n., 357, 401
Jesu, Lover of my soul	236, 318
Jesu, meek and lowly	224, 368
Jesu, my Lord	368
Jesu, the very thought of Thee	368
Jesu, the very thought is sweet	356
Jesus calls us	412
Jesus Christ is risen to-day	191, 241, 394
Jesus Christ, my Lord and Saviour	409
Jesus lives (*Jesus lebt*)	395
Jesus, Master, Whom I serve	386
Jesus, tender Shepherd	409
Jesus shall reign	313
Jesus, Who dwelt above the sky	409
Joy to the world	399
Lead, kindly Light	89, 364
Light's abode, celestial Salem	356, 396
Lo, at noon 'tis sudden night	409
Lo ! God is here	319
Lo ! He comes	240, 318, 402
Lord, come away	399
Lord, I would own Thy tender care	409
Lord, in this dust Thy sovereign voice	365
Lord, in this Thy mercy's day	354
Lord Jesus, think on me	278
Lord of mercy and of might	336
Lord of our life	89
Lord, speak to me that I may speak	386

OTHER HYMNS MENTIONED

	PAGE
Lord, teach us how to pray aright	342
Media vita in morte sumus	302
Mistaken souls! that dream of heaven	232
My God, and is Thy table spread	190, 315
My God, how endless is Thy love	203
My God, I love Thee	368
My God, my Father, while I stray	382
Nearer, my God, to Thee	224
New every morning is the love	362
Now the dreary night is done	411, 413
O Beata Hierusalem	134
O Captain of God's host	336
O come, all ye faithful (*Adeste fideles*)	231, 369
O come, Redeemer (*Veni Redemptor gentium*)	397
O come to the merciful Saviour	372
O Everlasting Light	390
O God, I love Thee	126 *n.*
O God of our salvation, Lord	233
O God, our help in ages past	313
O happy band of pilgrims	358
O help us, Lord, each hour of need	336
O Lord of heaven, and earth, and sea	375
O love of God, how strong and true	390
O Paradise	372
O quanta qualia (*Oh, what the joy*)	126, 235, 241, 356
O quickly come	404
O Sapientia	400
O Spirit of the Living God	342
O voice of the Beloved	396
O worship the King	349
Oh, come and mourn with me awhile	224
Oh for a closer walk with God	79, 237, 327
Once in royal David's city	411
On Jordan's bank	399
On the Resurrection morning	396
Pange lingua	76, 83
Peace, perfect peace	126
Pilgrims of the night	372
Pleasant are Thy courts above	347
Pour down Thy Spirit from on high	342
Praise, my soul, the King of heaven	347
Praise to the Holiest in the height	365
Prayer is the soul's sincere desire	341
Preserve us, Lord, by Thy dear Word	197
Ride on, ride on in majesty	336

OTHER HYMNS MENTIONED

PAGE

Rock of ages 79, 209, 237, 240, 273, 281, 321, 344

	PAGE
Salve festa dies	49, 187 n., 393
Saviour, when in dust to Thee	349
Soldiers of Christ, arise	242
Songs of praise the angels sang	191
Souls of men	372
Sous ton voile d'ignominie	127
Stabat mater	240
Stand we prepared	402
Sun of my soul	79, 281, 362
Sweet Saviour, bless us	372
Sweet the moments	320
Take my life	386
Te Deum	240, 273
That day of wrath	401
The Church has waited long	390, 404
The day is past and over	358
The day of Resurrection	358, 391
The God of Abraham praise	320
The golden gates are lifted up	412
The roseate hues of early dawn	412
The Son of God goes forth to war	335
The strife is o'er (*Finita jam*)	394
The sun is sinking fast	368
The voice that breathed o'er Eden	362
There is a book who runs may read	362
There is a fountain filled with Blood	327
There's a Friend for little children	409
There is a green hill far away	411
There is a land of pure delight	313
Thou art coming, O my Saviour	404
Thou Judge of quick and dead	403
Thou hidden love of God	319
Thy kingdom come	404
Thy way, not mine, O Lord	390
To Thee, and to Thy Christ, O God	396
Through the night of doubt and sorrow	78 n.
Thy life was given for me	386
'Tis the day of Resurrection	191
Towards the eve	94
Veni Creator	194, 304, 351
Veni Redemptor gentium	397
Veni, veni, Emmanuel	400
Verbum Supernum prodiens	398
Vexilla Regis prodeunt	76, 188 n., 210
Victimæ Paschali	191, 393
Vox clara ecce intonat	398

OTHER HYMNS MENTIONED

	PAGE
We came to Thee, sweet Saviour	372
Welcome, happy morning	393
What had I been if Thou wert not	89
When gathering clouds	349
When I survey the wondrous Cross	313
When languor and disease invade	322
When our heads are bowed with woe	336
When the weary, seeking rest	379
When wounded sore the stricken soul	412
Ye choirs of new Jerusalem	394
Ye servants of God	318
Ye servants of the Lord	**403**

RICHARD CLAY & SONS, LIMITED,
LONDON & BUNGAY.

PUBLICATIONS
OF THE
Society for Promoting Christian Knowledge.

Church History Cartoons.

From Pictures drawn by W. J. MORGAN. Each picture illustrates an important event in the History of the Church of England. The Cartoons are bold and effectively coloured. Size, 45 in. by 35 in.

No. 1. Gregory and the English Slaves, A.D. 589.
 2. St. Augustine and King Ethelbert, A.D. 597.
 3. Manumission of Slaves by an English Bishop.
 4. The Martyrdom of St. Alban.
 5. St. Columba at Oronsay, A.D. 563.
 6. St. Aidan preaching to the Northumbrians.
 7. The Venerable Bede translating St. John's Gospel, A.D. 735.
 8. Stonehenge.
 9. Iona at the Present Day. Founded A.D. 565.
 10. Murder of Monks by the Danes, Crowland Abbey, about 870 A.D.
 11. The Martyrdom of St. Edmund, A.D. 870.
 12. St. Dunstan reproving King Edwy, A.D. 955.
 13. Norman Thanksgiving after the Battle of Hastings, A.D. 1066.
 14. The Murder of Thomas A'Beckett, A.D. 1170.
 15. The Crusaders starting for the East.
 16. Archbishop Langton producing before the Barons the Charter of Henry I., A.D. 1213.
 17. Preaching at St. Paul's Cross, A.D. 1547.
 18. The Seven Bishops sent to the Tower, A.D. 1688
 19. The Consecration of Matthew Parker as Archbishop of Canterbury, Dec. 17th, 1559.

1s. 4d. each on thick paper. | 3s. mounted and varnished.
2s. mounted on canvas. | 4s. ditto   ditto, on roller

WORKS ON CHURCH HISTORY, &c.

A Handy Book of the Church of England. By the Rev. E. L. CUTTS. New Edition. Crown 8vo. Cloth boards. 5s. [A work which aims at meeting inquiries upon the main points of the Church's History and present position. It covers a large area, and ought to be in the hands of all Church Workers as well as in those of General Readers.]

Ancient British Church, A Popular Account of the. With special reference to the Church in Wales. By the Rev. E. J. NEWELL, M.A. With Map. Fcap. 8vo. Cloth boards. 2s. 6d. [A lucid book on a department of history hitherto much neglected.]

A Story of the Church of England. By Mrs. C. D. FRANCIS. Post 8vo. Illustrated. Cloth boards. 1s. 6d. [A very simple narrative history of the English Church.]

By-Paths of English Church History. Home Missions in the Early Mediæval Period. By the Rev. CHARLES HOLE, B.A. Post 8vo. Cloth boards. 1s. 6d. [Gives a clear view of some of the roots of English Christianity.]

Celtic Church in Scotland, The. Being an Introduction to the History of the Christian Church in Scotland down to the death of St. Margaret. By the Right Rev. JOHN DOWDEN, D.D., Bishop of Edinburgh. Fcap. 8vo. Buckram boards. 3s. 6d. [The writer brings a wide knowledge to bear upon his subject, and deals with it in a bright and interesting manner: for General Readers.]

Church in England and its Endowments, A Brief Sketch of the History of the. With a List of the Archbishops, tracing their succession from the present time up to the Apostles, and through them to Christ. By the Rev. GEORGE MILLER. Post 8vo. Paper cover. 4d. [A clear and simple statement of the history of Church endowments. For General Readers.]

Church History in England. By the Rev. A. MARTINEAU. From the Earliest Times to the Period of the Reformation. 12mo. Cloth boards. 3s. [For reference and general use.]

Church History (A Chapter of English): being the Minutes of the S.P.C.K. for the years 1698-1703, together with Abstracts of Correspondents' Letters during part of the same period. Edited by the Rev. EDMUND MCCLURE, M.A. Demy 8vo. Cloth boards. 5s.

WORKS ON CHURCH HISTORY, &c.—*Continued.*

Church History, Illustrated Notes on English. By the Rev. C. A. LANE. Vol. I.—From the Earliest Times to the Dawn of the Reformation. Vol. II.—Its Reformation and Modern Work. Crown 8vo. Cloth. 1s. each. [Deals with the chief events during the period. The illustrations, amounting to over 100 in each Volume, add to its popular character.]

Church History, Sketches of. From the First Century to the Reformation. By the late Rev. Canon ROBERTSON, M.A. Post 8vo. Cloth boards. 2s. [A simple and attractive account of the leading events in Church History, from A.D. 33 to the Reformation: for general readers; suitable also for use in Sunday and day schools.]

Church History in Scotland, Sketches of. By the late Rev. JULIUS LLOYD. Post 8vo. Cloth boards. 1s. 6d. [An account of Church affairs in Scotland from St. Columba's Mission to Iona until the present time.]

Church History, Turning Points of English. By the Rev. E. L. CUTTS, D.D. A new and revised edition. Crown 8vo. Cloth boards. 3s. 6d. [The leading events in the Church of England from the earliest period of British history to the present day, showing the Church questions that have arisen, and yet remain as our inheritance; for Churchmen in general.]

Church History, Turning Points of General. By the Rev. E. L. CUTTS, D.D. Crown 8vo. Cloth boards. 4s. [The leading events in General Church History from the time of the Apostles to the present day; useful for a text-book in schools, &c., and for general readers.]

Churchman's Life of Wesley (The). By R. DENNY URLIN, Esq. Crown 8vo. Cloth boards. 3s. 6d.

Dictionary (A), of the Church of England. By the Rev. E. L. CUTTS, D.D. With Numerous Woodcuts. Crown 8vo. Cloth boards. 5s. [A manual for the use of clergymen and schools.]

Great English Churchmen; or, Famous Names in English Church History and Literature. By the late W. H. DAVENPORT ADAMS. Crown 8vo. Cloth boards. 3s. 6d.

WORKS ON CHURCH HISTORY, &c.—Continued.

Grosseteste, Robert, Bishop of Lincoln, The Life and Times of. By the Rev. G. G. PERRY. Post 8vo. Cloth boards. 2s. 6d. ["Grosseteste chiefly as a reformer in a corrupt period of the Church, and his quarrel with the Pope ": for general reading.]

History of the English Church, in Short Biographical Sketches. By the late Rev. JULIUS LLOYD. Post 8vo. Cloth boards. 1s. 6d. [Leads the reader, by a series of selected lives, to a general idea of the Church History of England.]

John Wicliff, His Life, Times, and Teaching. By the Rev. A. R. PENNINGTON, M.A. Fcap. 8vo. Cloth boards. 3s. [This work embraces the result of recent researches: for general reading.]

Lectures on the Historical and Dogmatical Position of the Church of England. By the Rev. W. BAKER, D.D. Post 8vo. Cloth boards. 1s. 6d. [Supplies in short compass a clear account of the historical position of the Church of England: for General Readers.]

Lessons from Early English Church History. By the Right Rev. G. F. BROWNE, B.D. Post 8vo. Cloth boards. 1s. 6d. [These lectures are true lessons, and have much to teach the ordinary Churchman.]

The Christian Church in these Islands before the Coming of Augustine. By the Right Rev. G. F. BROWNE, B.D. Post 8vo. Cloth boards. 1s. 6d. [A lucid and scholarly account of this obscure period of English Church History: for General Readers.]

The Church of England: its Planting, its Settlement, its Reformation, and its Renewed Life. Four addresses by the late Rev. E. VENABLES, M.A. Post 8vo. Cloth boards. 1s. [A useful summary.]

The Story in Outline of the Church of England. By the Rev. Canon GARNIER, M.A. Sm. post 8vo. Paper covers. 3d. [Gives a short and simple historical account of the Church of England.]

The Title Deeds of the Church of England: an Historic Vindication of her Position and Claims. By the Rev. Canon GARNIER. Post 8vo. Cloth boards. 3s. 6d. [The sub-title explains the aim of this book, which is written in a lucid and interesting manner.]

STORIES FOUNDED ON CHURCH HISTORY.

Attila and his Conquerors. A Story of the Days of St. Patrick and St. Leo the Great. By the late Mrs. RUNDLE CHARLES. Crown 8vo. Cloth boards. 3s. 6d.

Champions of the Right. By the Rev. E. GILLIAT, M.A. Crown 8vo. Cloth boards. 2s.

[A series of selected Biographies, illustrating English History.]

Conquering and to Conquer. A Story of Rome in the Days of St. Jerome. By the late Mrs. RUNDLE CHARLES, author of "The Schönberg-Cotta Family." Crown 8vo. Cloth boards. 2s. 6d.

[Presents a fair Picture of Society in Jerome's time: for General Readers.]

Gaudentius. A Story of the Colosseum. By the Rev. G. S. DAVIES. Crown 8vo. Cloth boards. 2s. 6d.

[A Picture of Roman Morals yielding to the Pressure of Christianity: for Educated Readers.]

Jack Dane's Inheritance. A Tale of Church Defence. By FRANCES BEAUMONT MILNE. With one page Woodcut. Post 8vo. Limp cloth. 6d.

[A story upon the rights and liberties of the Church of England.]

Lapsed, not Lost. A Story of Roman Carthage. By the late Mrs. RUNDLE CHARLES. Crown 8vo. Cloth boards. 2s. 6d.

[A Story of the time of St. Cyprian: for General Readers.]

Mitslav: or, The Conversion of Pomerania. By the late Right Rev. R. MILMAN, D.D. Crown 8vo. With Map. Cloth boards. 3s. 6d.

Narcissus. A Tale of Early Christian times. By the Right Rev. W. BOYD CARPENTER. Crown 8vo. Cloth boards. 3s. 6d.

Stories for the Saints' Days. By S. W., author of "Stories for every Sunday in the Christian Year." Fcap. 8vo. Cloth boards. 1s. 6d.

[An Epitome of the Lives of certain Saints and Fathers: for Ordinary Readers.]

The Church in the Valley. By ELIZABETH HARCOURT MITCHELL. With four page Woodcuts. Crown 8vo. Cloth. 2s. 6d.

[A story which introduces much Church History, and is well calculated to spread useful information upon the Disestablishment question.]

The Villa of Claudius. A Tale of the Roman-British Church. By the Rev. E. L. CUTTS, D.D. New Edition. With four page illustrations. Crown 8vo. Cloth boards. 1s. 6d.

DIOCESAN HISTORIES.

Bath and Wells. By the Rev. W. HUNT. With Map. Fcap. 8vo. Cloth boards. 2s. 6d.

Canterbury. By the Rev. R. C. JENKINS. With Map. Fcap. 8vo. Cloth boards. 3s. 6d.

Carlisle. By RICHARD S. FERGUSON, Esq. With Map. Fcap. 8vo. Cloth boards. 2s. 6d.

Chester. By the Rev. RUPERT H. MORRIS, D.D. With Map. Fcap. 8vo. Cloth boards. 3s.

Chichester. By the Rev. W. R. W. STEPHENS. With Map and Plan of the Cathedral. Fcap. 8vo. Cloth boards. 2s. 6d.

Durham. By the Rev. J. L. LOW. With Map and Plan. Fcap. 8vo. Cloth boards. 2s. 6d.

Hereford. By the Rev. Canon PHILLOTT. With Map. Fcap. 8vo. Cloth boards. 3s.

Lichfield. By the Rev. W. BERESFORD. With Map. Fcap. 8vo. Cloth boards. 2s. 6d.

Norwich. By the Rev. A. JESSOPP, D.D. With Map. Fcap. 8vo. Cloth boards. 2s. 6d.

Oxford. By the Rev. E. MARSHALL, M.A. With Map. Fcap. 8vo. Cloth boards. 2s. 6d.

Peterborough. By the Rev. G. A. POOLE, M.A. With Map. Fcap. 8vo. Cloth boards. 2s. 6d.

Salisbury. By the Rev. W. H. JONES. With Map and Plan. Fcap. 8vo. Cloth boards. 2s. 6d.

Sodor and Man. By A. W. MOORE, M.A. With Map. Fcap. 8vo. Cloth boards. 3s.

St. Asaph. By the Venerable Archdeacon THOMAS. With Map. Fcap. 8vo. Cloth boards. 2s.

St. David's. By the Rev. Canon BEVAN. With Map. Fcap. 8vo. Cloth boards. 2s. 6d.

Winchester. By the Rev. W. BENHAM, B.D. With Map. Fcap. 8vo. Cloth boards. 3s.

Worcester. By the Rev. I. GREGORY SMITH, and the Rev. PHIPPS ONSLOW. With Map. Fcap. 8vo. Cloth boards. 3s. 6d.

York. By the Rev. Canon ORNSBY, M.A. With Map. Fcap. 8vo. Cloth boards. 3s. 6d.

NON-CHRISTIAN RELIGIOUS SYSTEMS.

Fcap. 8vo. Cloth boards. 2s. 6d. each.

Buddhism. Being a Sketch of the Life and Teachings of Gautama, the Buddha. By T. W. RHYS DAVIDS. With Map.
Buddhism in China. By the Rev. S. BEAL. With Map.
Christianity and Buddhism: a Comparison and a Contrast. By the Rev. T. STERLING BERRY, D.D.
Confucianism and Taouism. By Professor R. K. DOUGLAS.
Hinduism. By Sir M. MONIER WILLIAMS. With Map.
Islam as a Missionary Religion. By CHARLES R. HAINES. 2s.
Islam and its Founder. By J. W. H. STOBART. With Map.
The Corân: its Composition and Teaching and the Testimony it bears to the Holy Scriptures. By Sir W. MUIR, K.C.S.I.
The Religion of the Crescent or Islam; its Strength, its Weakness, its Origin, its Influence. By the Rev. W. ST. CLAIR-TISDALL, M.A. 4s.

THE FATHERS FOR ENGLISH READERS.

Fcap. 8vo. Cloth boards. 2s. each.

Leo the Great. By the Rev. Canon GORE, M.A.
Gregory the Great. By the Rev. J. BARMBY, B.D.
Saint Ambrose: his Life, Times, and Teaching. By the Ven. Archdeacon THORNTON, D.D.
Saint Athanasius: his Life and Times. By the Rev. R. WHELER BUSH. 2s. 6d.
Saint Augustine. By the Rev. EDWARD L. CUTTS, D.D.
Saint Basil the Great. By the Rev. R. T. SMITH, B.D.
Saint Bernard, Abbot of Clairvaux, A.D. 1091—1153. By the Rev. S. J. EALES, M.A., D.C.L. 2s. 6d.
Saint Hilary of Poitiers and Saint Martin of Tours. By the Rev. J. GIBSON CAZENOVE, D.D.
Saint Jerome. By the Rev. EDWARD L. CUTTS, D.D.
Saint John of Damascus. By the Rev. J. H. LUPTON, M.A.
Saint Patrick; his Life and Teaching. By the Rev. E. J. NEWELL, M.A. 2s. 6d.
Synesius of Cyrene, Philosopher and Bishop. By ALICE GARDNER.
The Apostolic Fathers. By the Rev. Canon SCOTT HOLLAND.
The Defenders of the Faith; or, the Christian Apologists of the SECOND AND THIRD CENTURIES. By the Rev. F. WATSON.
The Venerable Bede. By the Right Rev. G. F. BROWNE, B.D.

Publications of the Society for

THE HOME LIBRARY.

Crown 8vo. Cloth boards. 3s. 6d. each.

Black and White. Mission Stories. By H. A. FORDE.

Charlemagne. By the Rev. E. L. CUTTS, D.D. With Map.

Constantine the Great. The Union of the Church and State. By the Rev. E. L. CUTTS, D.D.

Great English Churchmen; or, Famous Names in ENGLISH CHURCH HISTORY AND LITERATURE. By the late W. H. D. ADAMS.

John Hus. The Commencement of the Resistance to Papal Authority on the Part of the Inferior Clergy. By the Rev. A. H. WRATISLAW.

Judæa and her Rulers, from Nebuchadnezzar to Vespasian. By M. BRAMSTON. With Map.

Mazarin. By the late GUSTAVE MASSON.

Military Religious Orders of the Middle Ages: the Hospitallers, the Templars, the Teutonic Knights, and others. By the Rev. F. C. WOODHOUSE, M.A.

Mitslav; or, the Conversion of Pomerania. By the late Right Rev. R. MILMAN, D.D. With Map.

Narcissus: a Tale of Early Christian Times. By the Right Rev. W. BOYD CARPENTER, Bishop of Ripon.

Richelieu. By the late GUSTAVE MASSON.

Sketches of the Women of Christendom. Dedicated to the Women of India. By the late MRS. RUNDLE CHARLES, author of "The Chronicles of the Schönberg-Cotta Family."

The Church in Roman Gaul. By the Rev. R. TRAVERS SMITH. With Map.

The Churchman's Life of Wesley. By R. DENNY URLIN, Esq., F.S.S.

The House of God the Home of Man. By the Rev. Canon JELF.

The Inner Life, as Revealed in the Correspondence of Celebrated Christians. Edited by the late Rev. T. ERSKINE.

The Life of the Soul in the World: its Nature, Needs, Dangers, Sorrows, Aids, and Joys. By the Rev. F. C. WOODHOUSE, M.A.

The North-African Church. By the late Rev. JULIUS LLOYD, M.A. With Map.

Thoughts and Characters; being Selections from the Writings of the late Mrs. RUNDLE CHARLES.

CHURCH HYMNS.

Nos. 1 to 7, in Various Sizes and Bindings, ranging in price from 1d. to 4s. 8d.

Church Hymns, with Tunes. Edited by Sir ARTHUR SULLIVAN. Crown 8vo., Fcap. 4to., and Folio (Organ copy), in various Bindings, from 2s. to £1. 1s.

Common Prayer Book and Church Hymns. Bound in One Volume, and in Two Volumes in Cases. Can be had in various Sizes and Bindings, from 6d. to 4s.

Common Prayer Book and Church Hymns, with Tunes. Brevier, 8vo., Limp paste grain roan, red edges, 6s.

COMMENTARY ON THE BIBLE.

Old Testament. Vol. I., containing the Pentateuch. By Various Authors. With Maps and Plans. Crown 8vo. Cloth boards, red edges, 4s.; half calf, 10s.; whole calf, 12s.; half morocco, 12s.

Old Testament. Vol. II., containing the Historical Books. Joshua to Esther. By Various Authors. With Maps and Plans. Crown 8vo. Cloth boards, red edges, 4s.; half calf, 10s.; whole calf, 12s.; half morocco, 12s.

Old Testament. Vol. III., containing the Poetical Books, Job to Song of Solomon. By Various Authors. Crown 8vo. Cloth boards, red edges, 4s.; half calf, 10s.; whole calf, 12s.; half morocco, 12s.

Old Testament. Vol. IV., containing the Prophetical Books, Isaiah to Malachi. By Various Authors. With two Maps. Cloth boards, red edges, 4s.; half calf, 10s.; whole calf, 12s.; half morocco, 12s.

Old Testament. Vol. V., containing the Apocryphal Books. By Various Authors. Cloth boards, red edges, 4s.; half calf, 10s.; whole calf, 12s.; half morocco, 12s.

New Testament. Vol. I., containing the Four Gospels. By the Right Rev. W. WALSHAM HOW, Bishop of Wakefield. With Maps and Plans. Crown 8vo. Cloth boards, red edges, 4s.; half calf, 10s.; whole calf, 12s.; half morocco, 12s.

New Testament. Vol. II., containing the Acts, Epistles, and Revelation. By Various Authors. With Map. Crown 8vo. Cloth boards, red edges, 4s.; half calf, 10s.; whole calf, 12s.; half morocco, 12s.

THE HEATHEN WORLD AND ST. PAUL.

This Series is intended to throw light upon the writings and labours of the Apostle of the Gentiles.

Fcap 8vo. Cloth boards. 2s. each.

Saint Paul in Greece. By the Rev. G. S. DAVIES, M.A., Charterhouse, Godalming. With Map.

Saint Paul in Damascus and Arabia. By the Rev. GEORGE RAWLINSON, M.A., Canon of Canterbury. With Map.

Saint Paul in Asia Minor and at the Syrian Antioch. By the late Rev. E. H. PLUMPTRE, D.D. With Map.

Saint Paul at Rome. By the late Very Rev. Charles MERIVALE, D.D., D.C.L. With Map.

ANCIENT HISTORY FROM THE MONUMENTS.

This Series of Books is chiefly intended to illustrate the Sacred Scriptures by the results of recent Monumental Researches in the East.

Fcap. 8vo. Cloth boards. 2s. each.

Sinai, from the Fourth Egyptian Dynasty to the Present Day. By the late HENRY S. PALMER. With Map. A New Edition, revised throughout by the Rev. Professor SAYCE.

Babylonia (the History of). By the late GEORGE SMITH. Edited and brought up to date by the Rev. Professor SAYCE.

Assyria, from the Earliest Times to the Fall of Nineveh. By the late GEORGE SMITH.

Persia, from the Earliest Period to the Arab Conquest. By the late W. S. W. VAUX, M.A., F.R.S. A New and Revised Edition, by the Rev. Professor SAYCE.

NATURAL HISTORY RAMBLES.

Intended to cover the Natural History of the British Isles in a manner suited to the requirements of visitors to the regions named.

Fcap. 8vo. with numerous Woodcuts. Cloth Boards. 2s. 6d. each.

In Search of Minerals. By the late D. T. ANSTED, M.A.

Lakes and Rivers. By C. O. GROOM NAPIER, F.G.S.

Lane and Field. By the late Rev. J. G. WOOD, M.A.

Mountain and Moor. By J. E. TAYLOR, Esq., F.L.S.

Ponds and Ditches. By M. C. COOKE, M.A., LL.D.

Sea-Shore (The). By Professor P. MARTIN DUNCAN.

Underground. By J. E. TAYLOR, Esq., F.L.S.

Woodlands (The). By M. C. COOKE, M.A., LL.D.

MANUALS OF ELEMENTARY SCIENCE.

A Set of Elementary Manuals on the principal Branches of Science.

Fcap. 8vo. Limp cloth. 1s. each.

Electricity. By the late FLEEMING JENKIN, F.R.S.

Physiology. By A. MACALISTER, LL.D., M.D., F.R.S.

Geology. By the Rev. T. G. BONNEY, M.A., F.G.S.

Crystallography. By HENRY PALIN GURNEY, M.A.

Astronomy. By W. H. M. CHRISTIE, M.A., F.R.S.

Botany. By the late Professor BENTLEY.

Zoology. By ALFRED NEWTON, M.A., F.R.S. A New Edition.

Matter and Motion. By the late J. CLERK MAXWELL, M.A.

Spectroscope and its Work (The). By the late RICHARD A. PROCTOR.

Publications of the Society.

THE PEOPLE'S LIBRARY.

Crown 8vo.   Cloth boards.   1s. each.

A Chapter of Science; or, What is a Law of Nature? Six Lectures to Working Men. By Professor J. STUART, M.P. With Diagrams.

A Six Months' Friend. By HELEN SHIPTON, author of "Christopher." With several Illustrations.

British Citizen (The): his Rights and Privileges. A short History by the late J. THOROLD ROGERS, M.P.

Factors in Life. Three Lectures on Health—Food—Education. By the late Professor SEELEY, F.R.S.

Guild of Good Life (The). A Narrative of Domestic Health and Economy. By Sir B. W. RICHARDSON, M.D., F.R.S.

Household Health. A Sequel to "The Guild of Good Life." By Sir. B. W. RICHARDSON, M.D., F.R.S.

Hops and Hop-Pickers. By the Rev. J. Y. STRATTON. With several Illustrations.

Life and Work among the Navvies. By the Rev. D. W. BARRETT, M.A. With several Illustrations.

The Cottage Next Door. By HELEN SHIPTON. With several Illustrations.

Thrift and Independence. A Word for Working Men. By the Rev. W. LEWERY BLACKLEY, M.A.

SOCIETY FOR PROMOTING CHRISTIAN KNOWLEDGE.
LONDON: NORTHUMBERLAND AVENUE, W.C.;
43, QUEEN VICTORIA STREET, E.C.

www.ingramcontent.com/pod-product-compliance
Lightning Source LLC
Chambersburg PA
CBHW020534300426
44111CB00008B/665